Richard Sanders is a writer  maker. His films include Ka America, the multi-award-w murder of Colombian footb 1994 World Cup, and *Maradona: Kicking the Habit*, in which he took on El Diego at his own game. He is also the author of *If a Pirate I Must Be . . . The True Story of Bartholomew Roberts, King of the Caribbean.*

BEASTLY FURY

The Strange Birth of British Football

Richard Sanders

BANTAM BOOKS

LONDON • TORONTO • SYDNEY • AUCKLAND • JOHANNESBURG

TRANSWORLD PUBLISHERS
61-63 Uxbridge Road, London W5 5SA
A Random House Group Company
www.randomhouse.co.uk

BEASTLY FURY
A BANTAM BOOK: 9780553819359

First published in Great Britain
in 2009 by Bantam Press
an imprint of Transworld Publishers
Bantam edition published 2010

Typeset in Minion by Falcon Oast Graphic Art Ltd.

6 8 10 9 7 5

Penguin Random House is committed to a sustainable future for
our business, our readers and our planet. This book is made from
Forest Stewardship Council® certified paper.

Printed and bound in Great Britain by Clays Ltd, St Ives plc

For my wife, Mary

Contents

Contents

Acknowledgements

First of all I would like to thank my wife Mary for her endless support and encouragement, for reading and rereading countless drafts and for indulging my passion for Tottenham Hotspur over the last seventeen years. It gets better, I promise.

I'd also like to thank my agent, Julian Alexander, my editor at Transworld, Giles Elliott, and copy-editor Daniel Balado for their advice and comments, as well as my father, my brother Philip and my friend Chris Bunyan who read through early drafts. Needless to say, any errors are entirely my own. Jim MacCartney and Angus Graham-Campbell gave me lunch and were my guides for a fascinating afternoon watching the Field Game at Eton. And Richard McBrearty of the Scottish Football Museum gave me an equally fascinating tour of the historic sites of Scottish football in Glasgow. My thanks to them. I'm grateful to David Barber at the Football Association for opening the library to me and allowing me to read the FA's first minute book, and to Graham Curry for his help in identifying some of the early photographs. And I'd like to thank Arsenal Football Club for granting me access to the James Catton Archives. Finally I'd like to thank the ever polite and helpful staff at the British Library at St Pancras, the Newspaper Library in Colindale and the National Library of Scotland.

Preface

ON 9 JULY 2006 A TOTAL OF 715 MILLION PEOPLE IN 214 COUNTRIES watched the World Cup Final between France and Italy. It brought overall viewing figures for the tournament to 26.29 billion and total revenues for FIFA to well over £1 billion. Today, football is a sport like no other. It has conquered every corner of the globe and its merchandising potential spirals each year.

Foreigners sometimes like to tease us for our belief that we gave football to the world, surely part of that national delusion of grandeur which also elevates the 1966 World Cup – regarded abroad as one of the dullest and dirtiest in history, marred by dodgy refereeing and won by a goal that patently didn't cross the line – to a seminal moment in the annals of sport. That competition aside, not one of the home nations has ever even reached a major final. If we invented football, how come we are so bad at it?

Numerous alternative points of origin have been dredged up. In the third century BC the Chinese played *cuju* – 'kick-ball' – a game popular in the royal household which involved two teams trying to propel a stuffed ball through a hole in a silk sheet. Games using rubber balls were popular throughout Central America for hundreds of years before the arrival of Columbus. And aristocrats in Florence played a civilized, courtly ball game called *calcio* between the sixteenth and eighteenth centuries. The list goes on and on. The urge to kick, hit or throw a round object seems to be universal. But none of these games was football. When the Chinese, the Mexicans and the Italians began to kick inflated leather balls around in the twentieth century they were not playing their own ancient games, or even distant descendants of them. They were playing a game they had imported from Britain, and they knew it.

This game was one that had evolved in Britain in the middle of the nineteenth century and the story of it's emergence as Britain's national sport is a strange and convoluted one. It's a tale of testosterone-filled public schoolboys, eccentric mill-owners and bolshy miners; of their conflicts, their mutual antagonisms and ultimately their compromises.

It begins with traditional street football, rough and ready, but perhaps not quite as artless as historians have always thought. It progresses through the extraordinary world of the English public schools, which gave their own very special twist to the game, and from there to upper-class clubs such as Wanderers and the Crusaders that emerged in London in the 1860s. From there it is a story of the democratization of the game, of how it spread, first to the middle class and then to the workers, and of how, in the hands of the common people, it was transformed into the game we play today.

It is also the story of football's mortal struggle with rugby. Women, too, play a part. Above all it is a story of a magical alchemy, of how a set of factors came together to forge a game that was quite unique in its popular appeal – cheap, easy to play, yet beautiful and limitless in its potential for drama and excitement.

This is the story of how football was born.

*If Englishmen called this playing, it would be
impossible to say what they would call fighting.*

French visitor to Derby, early nineteenth century

1

O Ye Gods, What a Riot!

All Saints' v. St Peter's, Derby, Shrove Tuesday 1846

WILLIAM EATON MOUSLEY WOKE UP ON THE MORNING OF
24 February 1846 in high spirits. Elected Mayor of Derby the
year before, he was facing the greatest challenge of his political
career: to suppress the town's annual Shrove Tuesday riot,
masquerading as a game of football. And things were going
well. He'd sworn in several hundred special constables from
among Derby's more respectable citizens (vital, since the local
police force numbered fewer than twenty men), and two troops
of the 5th Dragoon Guards had trotted in from Nottingham
just a couple of days earlier. More importantly for Mousley – a
man who always preferred to avoid conflict – a delegation of
the town's leading footballers had knocked on his door, caps in

hand, the previous evening at the Town Hall. They'd pledged to obey the ban on football, issued the week before, and had said they would try to persuade others to do the same. At the end of the meeting they had solemnly handed over their ball.

If he could persuade the working men of Derby to give up the annual ritual it would be a major coup. Shrove Tuesday, an apprentices' holiday, was set aside for huge, tumultuous games of football not just in Derby but throughout Britain. These were widely believed to be of ancient origin – the birthright of every sturdy Brit. The people of Kingston in Surrey claimed football had first been played with the heads of vanquished Danes, and the men of Derby believed their game commemorated a victory over the Romans in AD 217. In fact the Derby game, like most others, dated from the seventeenth or early eighteenth century. But it made no difference. 'The inhabitants of Derby are born foot-ball players,' wrote a visitor in 1835. 'They have imbibed it with their first food and it animates them through their lives. Enthusiasm is but a cold word for their attachment to it.'

The match pitted the parish of St Peter's, in the south of the town, against the parish of All Saints' in the north. Each year the respectable classes watched anxiously from their windows as bodies of rough country folk trooped in from the surrounding villages to bolster the numbers of whichever parish lay closest to their home. The two teams gathered at separate pubs in the town centre and shortly before two o'clock began making their way towards the market place, stripped down to shirts and 'tightly strapped' trousers, their arms bare despite the freezing February weather. Church bells were rung and crowds of spectators cheered them on.

Women waved handkerchiefs from the upper windows of the houses.

At two o'clock silence fell, with the two sides – hundreds, sometimes thousands strong – facing each other across the central square. Originally the game had begun with the Mayor throwing the ball, made from horse leather and stuffed with cork shavings rather than inflated, from the Town Hall window. But as official disapproval had grown the custom had changed and by the 1840s it was the scorer of the winning goal in the previous year's game who 'threw the ball up'. A forest of arms was raised towards it. Then all hell broke loose.

'O ye Gods, what a riot!' wrote an observer in 1830. 'What pulling, hauling, tearing, bawling! The ball is instantly surrounded by the "dogs of war", who shortly form one solid and impenetrable mass of living clay . . . arms erect, eyes starting from their sockets, and mouths extended gasping for breath – just like so many madmen escaped from the asylum, and fighting for the recovery of their senses.' Clothes were torn, noses bloodied. For the spectators, the only clue to the whereabouts of the ball was the cloud of steam rising from the heaving throng, which was thickest at that point.

Like most early forms of football the Derby game was a soccer/rugby hybrid, allowing use of both hands and feet, and just about anything else for that matter. But as the town had become built up kicking had become less important – possibly to avoid smashing windows – and by the nineteenth century the term 'hug ball' was often used to describe it. The focus of the crowd in the market place was not so much the ball as the man holding it, whom both sides tried to propel towards their goal in a type of gigantic scrum. 'If

Englishmen called this playing,' said a French visitor watching the game, 'it would be impossible to say what they would call fighting.'

The All Saints' goal was a mill wheel in Markeaton Brook, just to the west of the town, while St Peter's was a garden gate just to the south. Unlike modern football, the aim was to score in your own goal. The struggle in the market place could last as long as an hour. Women threw oranges down from the windows to refresh the players trapped in the crush. When one side or the other finally broke free the ball often became wedged in another alley or yard and the scrum would start all over again. At other times the game ranged freely through the streets of the town, the players leaping fences and trampling gardens. Subterfuge could play a part. This was a game virtually without rules and it was not unknown for one side or the other to slash the ball, take out the cork shavings, and then smuggle it towards their opponent's goal beneath the petticoats of a woman. Sometimes the ball was taken underground, the players crawling on their hands and knees through narrow, rat-infested sewers.

The two goals were only about a mile from the market place but it was rare that either side was strong enough to force the ball directly towards them. Normally it ended up in the River Derwent and the players would strip off and leap into the freezing waters. 'The St Peter's players are considered to be equal to the best water-spaniels, and it is certainly curious to see two or three hundred men up to their chins in the Derwent continually ducking each other,' wrote a local historian in 1829. Once the ball was in the water St Peter's attempted to carry it south, downstream, towards their goal while All Saints' tried to get it to the far bank. From there they would begin a long, circuitous cross-country route around the town and back towards their own goal. Crowds of onlookers lined the banks, cheering the two sides.

'Thus the combat would go on hour after hour,' wrote the *Derby Mercury*, 'fresh men taking the places of those who were exhausted, women rushing about in a state of frantic excitement, urging on their husbands and brothers, bringing them stimulants and refreshments, lending them petticoats to cover their naked limbs, and binding up their wounds.' The game was notorious as an opportunity to settle scores and from time to time play would be punctuated by fierce fist fights.

The mayhem usually continued until late in the evening. The first side to score won. The bells of the victorious parish church were rung and the goalscorer chaired around the town by his team-mates. Supporters threw gifts of money and both winners and losers retired to the local taverns to nurse their wounds and swap tales of their heroics.

It's not hard to see why the more genteel inhabitants of Derby had become a little weary of this tradition. Attempts had been made to ban the football as early as 1731 when the town's jailer was locked up in his own jail as punishment for playing. Perhaps predictably, he used his inside knowledge to escape. Subsequent attempts at suppression in 1747 and 1797, the latter following the drowning of a man in the Derwent the previous year, were no more successful.

The footballers, mainly working class, were helped by the fact that a section of the town's upper class were sympathetic. Many of the well-to-do could be seen hovering on the fringes of the crowd in the market place, dressed in their finery, cheering on the players. Some, overcome with excitement, would even plunge into the heart of the fray, emerging bloodied but smiling, 'without a hat and with half a coat'. One gentleman was forced to advertise in the *Derby Mercury* in 1762 after losing 'a plain silver watch' in the mêlée, offering a guinea for its return.

This upper-class involvement was partly young bucks letting off steam. The toffs also loved to bet on the outcome and would sometimes pay star players to participate – all part of that earthy English tradition where patrician and plebeian culture rubbed together, also visible at the cock-pit, the prize ring and the racecourse. But it wasn't hard to see that the anarchy served a useful social function.

In Catholic countries Shrove Tuesday is Mardi Gras, carnival time, when conventions are suspended for twenty-four hours and the people indulge in wild excesses before the long austerity of Lent. In the same way, Shrove Tuesday football was a safety valve for social tensions. The social order was turned on its head for a day, the streets were surrendered to the mob, and the 'lords of misrule' were let loose. In the hours leading up to the game the footballers knocked on doors, demanding money to fund their drinking. Groups of youths roamed the streets throwing dirt at anyone who was well dressed. 'I was met by a band of ruffians who appeared to consider themselves outlaws,' wrote one correspondent to the *Derby Mercury* in 1844. 'Each was prepared with a bag filled with soot or charcoal dust, and on meeting any person who appeared respectable they threw the bag and its contents in his face, or upon that part of his dress that suited their purpose best.' It was a fantasy of revolution that the upper classes were prepared to tolerate, on the strict understanding that everything returned to normal the following morning.

But by the early nineteenth century this tolerance was becoming strained. Attitudes were changing. This was the age of progress. The industrial revolution was gathering pace, spawning a new, self-confident, increasingly religious urban middle class, fervently committed to a 'refinement of manners'. They recoiled from all that they saw as brutish and backward. The Shrove Tuesday game, declared one petition demanding its abolition, was 'disgraceful to humanity and civilization, subversive of good order and Government and destructive of morals, property and the very lives of our inhabitants'.

In the new industrial Britain some of the working class also saw it as degrading. Derby was a hotbed of militant trade unionism. In 1834 it was shaken by a long strike of textile workers, and union leaders denounced the football as 'barbarous recklessness and supreme folly'. They found the toffs egging the players on from the sidelines particularly repellent. 'Your "Betters" have been foremost in this fête,' they told the workers, 'hallooing you like brute dogs to the strife.' On Shrove Tuesday 1834, as an alternative to the football, the unions organized an orderly procession through the town, their members marching three and four abreast beneath banners proclaiming 'Liberty and Unity' and 'Let Prudence be our Guide'. But the strike was crushed, and by the 1840s it was the middle class leading opposition to the annual Shrovetide game, petitioning for an end to the 'barbarous and disgusting play of football'.

Derby was not alone. There were campaigns against

Shrove Tuesday football in towns and villages throughout the country, part of a broader offensive against a multitude of traditional working-class customs and pastimes which middle-class reformers felt had no place in the new, refined society of the nineteenth century. Often, they had a point. Who today would want to see the return of bull-baiting and cock-fighting, or the extraordinary sport of 'cock-throwing', which simply involved tying a cock to a stake and throwing things at it until it was dead? And what about 'riding the goose', which involved smearing a goose in grease and then competing to see who could be the first to rip its head off? There was much about the eighteenth century best consigned to history.

But there was a strong element of self-interest in the middle-class morality. The chaotic rhythms of rural life – the frequent holidays and irregular work patterns – did not suit the new industrial society. If you'd invested in a factory and machinery you couldn't afford to have it standing idle just because your work force had decamped en masse to a local village fair, justifying their absence through 'time honoured custom'. 'Real Christians,' wrote one reformer, 'who diligently discharge the duties of their stations . . . will find but little opportunity or occasion for amusement.'

This po-faced sanctimoniousness irritated many, and not just among the working class. A sympathetic observer of the Derby game in 1815 was repelled by the sour expressions on the faces of some of the onlookers. 'I perceived . . . among the spectators a few who seemed to eye the day's diversion not approvingly,' he wrote. 'They exclaimed; "What low work!" "What a contemptible object!" ' He felt these people exaggerated the degree of violence. 'I did not see a blow given, nor hear an oath uttered,' he said, which sounds a little unlikely, although the man drowned in the Derwent in 1796 was the only fatality ever recorded in connection with the game.

It was not just the Shrove Tuesday games that were under threat. It's often assumed they were the ancestors of modern football. This is a misconception. Because of their scale, and the disruption they caused, they caught the eye both of contemporaries and modern historians, but then, as now, the vast bulk of football played in Britain was small-scale and informal, groups of lads kicking a ball around on a patch of wasteland. Upper-class observers drew little distinction between the large, set-piece confrontations that occurred on traditional holidays and the more everyday form of the sport. 'Football . . . is nothing but beastly fury and extreme violence,' Thomas Elyot had written as early as 1531 in a book of advice for King Henry VIII, tarring both with the same brush. But for those who watched carefully they were very different.

The great holiday games were heavily ritualistic, mock-combats rather than sport. They were *meant* to be anarchic; that was their whole point. There were no boundaries. Indeed there was no 'pitch' in that sense, and the numbers on each side were unlimited. It would no more have occurred to anyone to fix equal sides and set clear parameters for football than for a battle. But in smaller games we find references to both from an early date. There were 'boundaries' in a game at Cauton in Nottinghamshire in 1500. In County Durham in 1683 'seven butchers' took on 'seven glovers'. There is even a reference to a six-a-side women's game (1747). By the time the folklorist Joseph Strutt was describing football in 1801 he was quite clear that the two sides contained 'an equal number of competitors' and that the pitch was more or less the same size as a modern pitch.

The method of scoring in these smaller games, which took place from at least 1314, varied. Sometimes the aim was to force the ball between two stakes driven into the ground, similar to modern football (there is even a reference to players throwing down their jackets for goalposts, in East Anglia in 1823). In other places players had to take the ball over a byline extending across the entire pitch, as in modern rugby. The degree of handling varied. Where it was dominant a small, hard ball was often used; where kicking predominated the ball tended to be larger, and inflated. Some forms were more violent than others. In Ireland and north-east England it was a mixture of football and wrestling. And Strutt's 1801 description stressed that foot-ballers would frequently 'kick each other's shins without the least ceremony'. But by the time matches between local teams began to be described in the sporting press in the 1840s, the sport, although rough and ready, was much closer to modern rugby and football than the Derby Shrove Tuesday game, with clear rules, equal numbers (often eleven-a-side) and, in some cases, officials to resolve disputes.

The Lord and Lady of the Manor, stumbling across a bunch of labourers hoofing a pig's bladder around, were probably blind to whatever subtleties this more everyday version of the sport may have possessed. But it was far less riotous and tumultuous than the great ritualistic holiday games, and probably contained rather more art than upper-class observers gave it credit for. It was from these smaller games rather than the Shrove Tuesday confrontations that the modern sport descended.

But by the 1840s the smaller games were also under threat. Leisure time was shrinking. The pre-industrial practice of taking Mondays off was dying out and had not yet been replaced by the Saturday half-holiday. With respect for the Sabbath ever more rigidly enforced it was becoming increasingly difficult to squeeze football into the working week.

The physical environment was also changing. In the countryside the old open fields of medieval England were being divided up and hedged in by the enclosure movement, which created the patchwork quilt of the modern countryside, and more and more communal land was falling into private hands. This not only restricted the great holiday games, which often ranged for miles over open countryside, it also meant there were fewer and fewer closes and patches of wasteland available for lads to play on. 'The labourers seem to be without innocent and manly amusements,' lamented the rector of Hitcham in Suffolk in 1844. 'They have no village green, or common, for active sports. Some thirty years ago, I am told, they had a right to a playground in a particular field ... and were then celebrated for their football; but somehow or other this right has been lost to them, and the field is now under the plough.'

An Act of Parliament in 1835 specifically banned football on the highways, and in the mushrooming towns no one saw it as their responsibility to provide open spaces for the working class. When, in 1844, it was suggested that five or six acres in Derby be set aside where the poor could play games the proposal was opposed by the town council on the grounds that it might be 'an encouragement to too much levity'.

The lives of working people were being slowly hemmed in, by fences and hedges, by walls and factory gates, by the harsh morality and pitiless work ethic of the rising middle class and the insatiable demands of the new industrial economy. There was little space for football. By the middle of the nineteenth century the glowing lights of the pub were often the only place of welcome left to the poor once the factory whistle sounded. And as the quality of life deteriorated, discontent grew.

Britain probably came closer to working-class revolution in the 1830s and 1840s than at any other time in its history. In 1842 large areas of the North and Midlands were paralysed by a general strike, and in Derby the carnivalesque, 'world turned upside down' element of the Shrovetide game was starting to feel a little uncomfortable. Revolution was no longer a game.

An attempt had been made to suppress the football the year before in 1845, but it ended in failure. The authorities were conciliatory. Keen 'to promote the rational enjoyment of the people', they organized a day of alternative sports, to be held just outside the town, on Shrove Tuesday. These included such traditional rural pastimes as climbing a greased pole for the prize of a hat, and grinning through a horse collar (also known as 'gurning' – the funniest, or most grotesque, grin won). Some of the footballers sneered at these 'low' entertainments. They were probably no more excited by the Derby Temperance Society's offer of a 'public tea festival' the following day, Ash Wednesday. But several thousand people turned up for the

Shrove Tuesday games and the day was going well until some rebels threw up a ball in the town centre and a half-hearted game began. Donations for the alternative sports had been raised on the strict understanding that there would be no football, and the entertainments were immediately cancelled. 'It is all disappointment; no sports, and no football. This is the way they always treat poor folks,' one man was heard to mutter as the crowds dispersed.

In 1845 the footballers had been offered the carrot. In 1846 they would get the stick. But the authorities made one last concession. The town's annual horse races had been suppressed the previous decade by the evangelical faction on the local council, who objected to the drinking and gambling associated with them. The races were now used as a bargaining chip: they would be resumed on the understanding that they replaced the football. It was this that lay behind the surrender of the ball to Mayor Mousley by leading footballers on the eve of Shrove Tuesday.

Mousley was a pragmatist. A hale and hearty Conservative, he had been involved in local politics for thirty-four years and was deeply immersed in the life of the town. He had little time for the joyless evangelicals. A wealthy solicitor himself, he was nevertheless aware, he said, 'of the weary life of toil and care that the majority of our working population are compelled to drag through' and he knew the workers needed their diversions. But he knew too there was now a firm middle-class consensus against the football and he was determined not to back down.

As he toured the streets towards lunchtime his mood darkened. Large numbers of people were gathering and there was defiance in the air. Mousley toyed with the idea of dispersing the crowds, but decided against it. Instead, the police and special constables were deployed and all streets into the market place were closed off. Two o'clock, the traditional starting time, came and went without incident. But then a cry went up. A ball had been released on Cock Pit Hill, just a few streets from the market place, and crowds quickly converged.

The ring-leader was a young tearaway called Henry Allen, well known in the town. It was he who had 'thrown the ball up' and it quickly found its way into a stream. Allen and the other players dived in after it, hotly pursued by the police, and for several minutes they splashed and wrestled with one another in the murky water. Then a PC Benjamin Fearn emerged triumphant, the ball in his hands. He handed it to his boss, Police Superintendent Thompson, who produced a knife, cut it to pieces and handed the shredded leather back to PC Fearn as a souvenir (he was still proudly displaying it forty years later).

Allen and the rest of the footballers escaped and Superintendent Thompson withdrew his forces to the Town Hall to calm tensions. But then word came that a second ball had been thrown into the Derwent. Thompson immediately set off for the town's new railway bridge to intercept it at the head of a force of police and special constables. But this time the resistance was more serious. When Mayor Mousley and other magistrates appeared a hail of missiles greeted them. Mousley was struck on the shoulder by a brick. When his attacker was arrested the mob overwhelmed the police and freed him. Faced with a full-scale riot, Mousley had no alternative. He read the

Riot Act and called out the two troops of Dragoon Guards. The players fled with the ball into open countryside, where the game continued, the Guards in hot pursuit.

By now both sides were rather enjoying themselves. 'The Dragoons, notwithstanding their heavy accoutrements, took the hedges in fine style, and the adventure altogether was of quite a romantic character,' wrote the *Derby and Chesterfield Reporter*. For the players, the game was much as it had been in previous years, with the difference that the police and the military provided the opposition.

PC Fearn and his colleagues finally caught up with play close to the village of Normanton, now a suburb to the south of Derby. The ball was with a group of All Saints' men, and a PC Messenger produced a fine rugby tackle to bring down the man in possession. But as he fell the man managed to sling the ball over a hedge. PC Fearn retrieved it but was quickly set upon by the All Saints' players. They grabbed the ball, threw Fearn himself bodily back over the hedge, then set off across the fields, finally 'goaling' the ball at the old mill wheel as darkness fell.

The footballers of Derby had defied the combined forces of the police, the special constables and the Army. But they knew it was all over. Allen and fourteen others were arrested shortly afterwards and Mayor Mousley sternly lectured them that 'it was only in consideration of their contrition, and promise not to offend again' that they were spared transportation to the colonies. Instead they were bound over to keep the peace. The authorities now meant business. For the next few years soldiers were brought into the town every year on the eve of Shrove Tuesday. And although crowds again gathered in

1847, they were cowed and no attempt was made to play the game.

By 1856 the *Derbyshire Times and Chesterfield Herald* was able to report that football in all its forms had been 'well nigh . . . discontinued' in Derby, other than the occasional 'knot of lads' who might be seen 'keeping up the old custom' on the outskirts of the town. The same pattern was repeated throughout the country. Football was in danger of extinction.

My maxim is hack the ball on when you see it near you,
and when you don't, why then hack the fellow next to you!

Public schoolboy, 1860

2

Muddied Oafs

Oxford v. Cambridge, Eton, 30 November 1863

A CRISP LATE NOVEMBER DAY, A FEW MILES TO THE WEST OF LONDON. A muddy field, overlooked by the Gothic, ivy-covered splendour of Eton College. A slight mist rolls off the nearby Thames and, in the distance, Windsor Castle can just be seen through the trees, magical in the slanting sunlight.

Twenty-two young men are ambling on to the field, hands shoved deep into pockets, shoulders hunched against the cold. Half are wearing red shirts, the other half blue. Other than that there is little to indicate they are about to take part in a sporting contest. They are wearing caps, full-length trousers and heavy boots, without studs. Sawdust has been sprinkled on to the field to help them keep their footing.

A fashionable crowd has gathered – parents and relatives of pupils at the school, returning old boys, and a smattering of the local gentry from the Windsor area. Around them swarm hundreds of Eton schoolboys, dressed in their distinctive cut-away black jackets, white ties and tall beaver hats, hopping and skipping from foot to foot, in part from excitement, in part to keep warm, it being one of Eton's more absurd customs that boys are forbidden to wear their greatcoats in public, even in the depths of winter.

This is a gathering of the British ruling class at the height of its power and self-confidence. The mid-century had proved a watershed, the tense, hungry years of the 1830s and 1840s turning out to be not a prelude to revolution but the birth pangs of the new industrial society. The Great Exhibition of 1851 ushered in an era of steadily rising prosperity and the years between 1851 and 1873 were Britain's Golden Age. Its power was unrivalled and the wealth and dynamism of its new industrial economy were the wonder and envy of other nations. Britain ruled the world, and these people ruled Britain.

They had assembled to watch the annual St Andrew's Day 'Field Game' between students from the universities of Oxford and Cambridge. The game was unique to Eton and the two teams were comprised entirely of Eton old boys. The match was a 'tradition' of just a few years' standing which had piggy-backed on the far older and rather duller 'Wall Game', which had taken place on this day since at least 1820. Both were variants of football, and it was in this unlikely setting, and on the playing fields of other public schools, that the ancient folk sport was given a new lease of life in the mid-nineteenth century when it came close to dying out among the common people.

The men on show would go on to fill the upper echelons of the Church, the Army and the Empire. On the Oxford side the Follett brothers were sons of a former Attorney General, and the captain, James Round, was heir to thousands of acres in Essex and Middlesex. Within three years he'd be Conservative MP for East Essex and would hold his seat for almost half a century, without making any discernible impression on the course of British history. For Cambridge, J. R. Selwyn was son of the Bishop of New Zealand and would later be Chaplain to Queen Victoria. Many were old chums. Bridges, Tritton and R. W. Follett, for Oxford, and Pelham, for Cambridge, all played in the Eton Field XI of 1862, one of the finest the school had produced.

The pitch was roughly the size of a modern football pitch, although there were no markings, the parameters indicated only by flags. The goals were a lot smaller, slightly less than half the size of those used today, and there was no crossbar. The ball was also smaller and lighter. There were two umpires stationed at each end of the pitch next to the goals, and on their signal half a dozen players from each side confronted one another in the centre of the field. They locked arms, bent down and formed a scrum – or 'bully' as it was known. The ball was released between them and, with a cheer from the spectators, the game began.

In the hot, breathy confines of the bully there was a ferocious clattering of boots on unguarded shins. Men grunted and cursed. To kick a man deliberately was considered unsporting, but if a chap kicked you by accident, as inevitably happened, the convention was that 'you are bound to shin him back'. 'If anybody thinks I care about shinning let them give me a kick and try!' shrilled 'A Public Schoolboy of the Third Form' in a letter to *The Field* at this time. 'They'll find it a game two can play at and I shall not be at all likely to stop and look at the laws and see whether shinning is allowed, not I!' Rather less enthusiastically, the writer James Brinsley-Richards, who spent many a miserable afternoon on the playing fields of Eton in the late 1850s, recalled, 'I have had my shins hacked till they were all blue and bleeding, and caused me the most maddening pain, which of course had to be borne and grinned at.'

It was brutal stuff. But, like the rustic game from which it was descended, it had its own subtlety. The key feature of the game was an astonishingly complex offside law which effectively outlawed passing – forwards, backwards or sideways. The men sweating and heaving in the pack were not even allowed to hook the ball out of the scrum to a team-mate. Instead, they had to try and break through their opponents' lines into open space. If unable to, they would try to force their way over the top of the ball, exposing it for the 'flying man' or the 'behinds' to run on to. These rear players then kicked the ball forward and the bully would break and set off in pursuit.

Once the forwards had the ball at their feet they had only one object in mind: to make a beeline for the opposition goal. Some kicked it far ahead and relied on their pace (Tritton on the Oxford side was particularly fast). Others were renowned dribblers and would infuriate their colleagues by weaving delicate patterns while the enemy regrouped. The ideal – as in modern football, as indeed at Eton still, where the Field Game is played to this day – was the man who could run at pace with the ball at his toes. His own pack would follow him en masse, forming a V-shaped phalanx, smashing its way through the opposition defence. 'Combination in a massed body is the key note of the Eton Field Game,' wrote a contemporary. 'The more closely they keep the ball in a combined and wedge-like body ... and the straighter towards the enemy's goals that their course can be, the more successful will be their play.' Should the man at the point of the wedge lose possession, those backing him up were expected to take possession and continue the charge. Players could use their hands to stop the ball, but not to catch or carry it.

If a defender managed to pluck the ball from the toes of the forward and hoof it upfield it forced the pack into a sudden, comic about-turn. 'The scene was extremely interesting,' remarked one uninitiated observer at Eton that day. 'The 22 players ... rushed across the field with the ball flying in their front, and then stopped and kicked the reverse way, causing the immediate confusion and prostration of many of the players.'

It was fast, vigorous, exhausting stuff. But there was a basic problem with the Eton Field Game which the spectators shivering in the cold beneath the grandeur of the college buildings soon became aware of: the small size of the goals combined with the strict offside law meant that players rarely scored.

Over the years a unique solution to this problem had evolved: the Eton 'rouge'. This involved getting the ball beyond your opponents' baseline and touching it with your hands – similar to a try in modern rugby, except the ball didn't have to be on the ground. But there was a catch. Before crossing the line the ball had to hit a defender. Much of the game therefore consisted of hovering close to the (unmarked) baseline, trying to bounce the ball off your opponents and into touch, and then grabbing it before a defender could get to it.

Just one 'rouge' was scored that day, by Oxford, and it would only count towards the final result if the goal tally was even. But it entitled Oxford to a kind of penalty which was the most bizarre feature of the Eton Field Game. The ball was placed in the goalmouth just a yard from the line. The Cambridge team packed the goal. The Oxford forwards then formed themselves up in single file, one behind the other, facing the ball. 'Left, right, left, right,' they chanted, gripping one another's waists and engaging in an extraordinary war-dance, or knees-up, in order to establish a collective rhythm. They then charged forward like a battering ram towards the ball, the rest of the team following up. A fearsome collision ensued, resulting, in the words of one observer, in a 'writhing, crawling mass . . . executing all sorts of contortions to get the ball'. But Oxford were unable to force the ball through. Shortly afterwards the game ended, goalless, Oxford's single rouge giving them victory.

'The peculiarities of the game now played at Eton . . . were never seen to greater advantage than during this contest,' wrote the sporting newspaper *Bell's Life*. 'Both the victors and the vanquished retired from the field, covered with honour, much dirt, and many kicks and bruises, but there were no broken legs.' The last point was worth making. 'I think there was a broken leg or collar-bone in the school at least once a year,' recalled the morose Brinsley-Richards. 'Sprained ankles and partial concussions of the brain, causing sick, nervous headaches, were of daily occurrence.'

So far as the public schoolboy founders of modern football

were concerned when they wrote their memoirs at the end of the century, this was the sport's Garden of Eden. The Gothic towers, the slim figures flitting back and forth in the misty sunlight – it was on the playing fields of Eton and England's other great public schools that the coarse folk game was tamed and civilized, before being handed back to the working class, cleansed and pristine, to become the mass sport we know today. 'The game of football, as originally played at the Wall at Eton, was the author of every sort and condition of football now played throughout the United Kingdom,' wrote *The Etonian* in 1884.

It's a crudely simplistic and self-serving vision, but it continues to be repeated in most modern histories of football. The truth is more complex. Games like the one played at Eton that day performed a vital role in the evolution of the sport, but it was not always a positive one. To understand it fully we must first delve a little more deeply into the extraordinary and somewhat alarming world of the early nineteenth-century public school.

The violence of public-school football reflected the culture of the institutions themselves. The majority of public schools were initially set up as foundations by either royal or religious patrons for the education of the poor – hence the term 'public'. Eton was established in 1440 by King Henry VI. From the beginning they were allowed to accept small numbers of paying pupils to supplement their income. But wealthier parents soon began to take advantage of the excellent facilities on offer and by the eighteenth century Eton, by far the largest and most prestigious, was dominated by the aristocracy.

This created a series of fundamental problems. The staff were, in most cases, the social inferiors of the boys. The boys had very little interest in learning. The bald fact was this: if you were born an aristocrat in the eighteenth century you were going to run the country no matter how useless and incompetent you were. The schools were useful to upper-class families primarily as a form of social networking, and this didn't depend on anything the teachers had to offer.

Throughout the eighteenth and early nineteenth centuries the great public schools were the scene of a constant power struggle between pupils and masters. Between 1768 and 1832 there were twenty-one full-scale revolts, six of them at Eton. Many involved the use of weapons and gunpowder, and at Rugby in 1797 and Winchester in 1818 the militia had to be called in with swords drawn and bayonets fixed to restore order. The masters responded with a savage disciplinary regime. At Eton in the 1790s the headmaster once flogged seventy boys in succession, ten strokes each, 'exercising himself so violently that he was laid up with aches and pains for more than a week'. His successor in the early 1820s flogged the entire sixth form and upper fifth for cheating in the composition of Latin epigrams. 'It was a grand scene in the library,' recalled a witness. 'The floor was covered with victims; the benches and tables with spectators; upwards of a hundred present. The Lower Boys were delighted to see their masters [the older boys] whipped . . . and jests and laughter accompanied the execution.'

The two sides eventually reached a crude compromise. The teachers would have full control during lessons, but outside school hours (and by 1830 boys at Eton spent only eleven hours a week actually in class) the students were in charge. The result, inevitably, was a *Lord of the Flies* environment where the older, larger boys wielded absolute power over younger, weaker ones. This was formalized in the infamous 'fagging' system, under which boys in the lower forms were obliged to act as servants to the fifth and sixth forms, as immortalized in the novel *Tom Brown's Schooldays*, set in Rugby in the 1830s.

One young Etonian, in a letter in 1824, described being tormented by a boy called Rolles, who could have been the prototype for *Tom Brown's* unforgettable villain Flashman. Rolles would put on a pair of spurs and 'ride' his fags around the dorm, forcing them to jump a gap 'positively impossible to be leapt over with a person on your back'. When 'we cannot accomplish it', the boy wrote, 'he spurs us violently. My thigh is now quite sore with the inroads made by that dreadful spur.' New arrivals at Eton (often as young as eight) were known as 'Jews' and subjected to the ritual of 'blanket tossing', whereby older boys flipped them up in the air, attempting to bump them against the high roofs of the dorms. In 1832 this almost resulted in a fatality when a boy fell on to the edge of an iron bedstead and 'was completely scalped as with a tomahawk, the scalp hanging down over the neck and back suspended only by a small piece of skin'. Miraculously he made a full recovery.

Originally at Eton scholarship students were obliged to share beds, and sexual relationships, voluntary or otherwise, were common. Most of the interminable public school memoirs of the era draw a discreet veil over this aspect of school life. But there is one exception. In 1889 the poet John Addington Symonds wrote an account of Harrow in the 1850s that was so frank and revealing that reading it is like suddenly stumbling across Joe Orton and it remained unpublished until the 1960s.

He was at the school at precisely the same time as a number of the men who went on to form the Football Association.

'Every boy of good looks had a female name, and was recognized either as a public prostitute or as some bigger fellow's "bitch",' he wrote. 'The talk in the dormitories and the studies was incredibly obscene. Here and there one could not avoid seeing acts of onanism, mutual masturbation, the sports of naked boys in bed together.' One boy was known as 'Bum Bathsheba because of his opulent posterior parts'. Another, 'a red-faced strumpet, with flabby cheeks and sensual mouth', effectively became the house prostitute and was subject to cruel abuse. 'Whenever he appeared in the mean dining room,' wrote Addington Symonds, they 'squirted saliva and what they called gobs upon their bitch, cuffed and kicked him at their mercy, shied books at him, and drove him with obscene curses whimpering to his den.'

Addington Symonds, who was homosexual, was repelled by 'the animalisms of boyish lust' and remained celibate, taking refuge in a fantasy world of idealized platonic love. 'During my first half year the "beasts", as they were playfully called, tried to seduce me,' he wrote. 'But it was soon decided that I was "not game".' The poor boy's adolescent confusion was made worse when he discovered the school's revered headmaster, Charles Vaughan, was having a sexual relationship with one of his friends (Vaughan's penchant for personally thrashing boys across the bare buttocks until he drew blood using a rapier-thin cane freshly made for each occasion ought to have set alarm bells ringing).

It was indicative of the anarchic temper of the public schools that during the winter months these real-life Flashmans chose to fill their ample leisure time with a sport as rough and disreputable as football. There are references to it at a number of schools as early as the sixteenth century, but it really took off early in the nineteenth.

Initially the boys adopted the folk game played in the countryside around the schools and in the home areas they came from. But under the peculiar conditions of the English public school it quickly evolved, taking on a distinctive form at each school. Many games involved dozens of players on each side, the fags obliged to take part, and there was a strong ritualistic element, designed to reinforce the domination of the older boys. 'I seldom saw much of the ball, but frequently saw and felt the nailed shoes of my adversaries,' recalled one younger boy at Eton in the late 1820s. At Winchester the fags were required to form a human wall along the touchline, their only function being to knock the ball back in when it went out of play. Until the middle of the century two boys were also obliged to stand with their legs apart, acting as goals. More often fags had to play as defenders, standing shivering on the goal-line, waiting to be flattened by the hordes of older boys who took the more exciting attacking roles. At Shrewsbury football was so bound up with the fagging system that it was actually known as 'douling' – 'doul' being the Shrewsbury word for fag, derived from the Greek word for slave.

With its roots in this brutal, repressive social system, the game that evolved was, if anything, more violent than that played by the common people. The description 'beastly fury' surely applied here if anywhere. 'My maxim is hack the ball on when you see it near you, and when you don't, why then hack the fellow next to you!' declared one Rugby schoolboy. The boys at Rugby wore boots called 'navvies', the iron toe of which 'much resembled the ram of an ironclad', and the games played at other schools were only marginally less savage. Most had rigid offside rules, of which Eton's was only the most extreme, ensuring the game remained confined to two hostile packs, squaring off against each other and attempting to force the ball forward through sheer strength. To pass the ball to a man in a forward position was considered positively unmanly and was known at Eton as 'sneaking'. Scrums (variously called 'hots', 'scrimmages' and 'squashes' as well as 'bullies') were a key element and dribbling highly prized. Football encouraged 'egregious selfishness', commented one observer at Shrewsbury. Charging was a vital element; at Winchester honour required that you charge face-on, without turning your back. Like the great Shrove Tuesday games, this was essentially a mock medieval battle, the older boys taking the part of knights, the fags that of the hapless peasant *levée*.

Public school football was also shaped in its early stages by lack of space. When the Duke of Wellington famously declared that 'the Battle of Waterloo was won on the playing fields of Eton', he should have said 'playing *field*'. Schools began to acquire substantial grounds only in the middle of the nineteenth century, and in the very early days football was played mostly in schoolyards and cloisters. This continued to be the case at Charterhouse and Westminster, cooped up in the centre of London, well into the nineteenth century.

As anyone who learned their football in a small school playground will know, the game quickly adapts itself to the peculiarities of that particular environment – an obstacle that juts out here, a space that provides a convenient goal there. The most striking example of this was Eton's Wall Game, played along the length of a high wall in the school grounds. The pitch was just five or six yards wide and the goals were formed at one end by a doorway, and at the other by a goal of exactly the same size chalked on to an old elm tree. It was notoriously difficult to score. By one calculation there were just three goals a century, although players were entitled to a 'shy' at goal under certain, complex circumstances.

Football was predominantly a kicking game at all the public schools at the start of the nineteenth century, perhaps reflecting the fact that it was originally played on hard surfaces. If a man is running with the ball in his hands then you have to tackle the man not the ball, and this is only really practical on grass. Dribbling was also generally valued over the ability to kick a distance, which possibly reflects a lack of space.

Rugby was the first public school to acquire large playing fields, in 1816, and, significantly, it was the only school at this time to develop a more expansive game which allowed players to run while holding the ball. The story of William Webb Ellis being the first boy to do this in 1823 is a myth invented by a group of Old Rugbeians in the 1890s, but it's certainly true that the practice became more common at Rugby during the 1820s and 1830s and it was incorporated into the rules in 1841. By the time other schools began to acquire larger playing fields their own kicking games were firmly established. Rugby, a newer establishment, may also have been more adaptable than older, ultra-conservative schools such as Eton and Winchester, where tradition was everything. The kicking or 'dribbling' game, as it became known, therefore remained the norm, and the Rugby game the exception.

A football culture was firmly established within the public

schools by the 1830s. But it was under threat. Those same earnest middle-class reformers who had suppressed bull-baiting and cock-fighting, and would soon drive football from the streets of Derby, had their sights on the Godless, lawless world of the public schools, and they had a direct, vested interest in its reform. The new rich spawned by the industrial revolution wished to join the elite and to see their sons educated alongside the aristocracy at Eton, Harrow, Rugby and Winchester. But they wanted a modern education, incorporating maths, science and French. The huge classes of up to two hundred boys, endlessly droning the grammatical rules of long-dead languages, presided over by a teacher impatiently tapping a birch on the palm of his hand, filled them with horror. Bullying, buggery and stale Latin may have been sufficient foundation for the aristocratic dilettante of the eighteenth century, but they weren't going to get you far in the competitive world of the Victorian era.

Reforming headmasters began to appear at some of the major schools from the start of the nineteenth century, and football was an early target. The game was 'fit only for butcher boys . . . [not] young gentlemen', declared Samuel Butler, headmaster of Shrewsbury from 1798 to 1836. Between 1827 and 1830 he banned it. His assistant, the Reverend Arthur Willis, would patrol the grounds on a chestnut pony trying to hunt down illegal games. At Eton too the Wall Game was forbidden for a time after a particularly vicious brawl during a match in 1827. But both bans were ineffective. It was one thing to stamp out the pastimes of factory workers and farm labourers, quite another to dictate to the sons of the aristocracy how they could spend their free time.

It was Thomas Arnold, headmaster of Rugby from 1828 to 1842, who finally cracked the puzzle of how to reform the public schools without provoking an aristocratic backlash. Rather than challenging the power of the older boys, he co-opted them, allowing them to retain their privileges but turning them into instruments of the school authorities, making them 'prefects' or 'monitors'. Like the Empire abroad, he worked through the indigenous ruling class, and Rugby quickly became the model for other public schools to imitate.

Arnold was indifferent to games, but he saw no purpose in needlessly antagonizing the older boys and allowed them to continue. Soon, though, it was seen that sports, far from being an evil to be tolerated, could actually make a positive contribution to the reforms. Firstly, they encouraged the boys to remain 'within bounds' rather than roaming the countryside poaching, fishing and engaging in the traditional pastime of tormenting the locals. They also helped break down the tribal groupings that formed among the boys. From the 1840s numerous football games were organized along such random lines as 'light hair v. dark hair', 'first half of the alphabet v. second half' and, at Eton, 'organ v. pulpit', which divided boys according to where they sat in chapel. Finally, because they were run by the boys themselves, sports encouraged them to take responsibility and develop organizational skills. Most importantly, they reinforced the control of the prefects over the lower forms.

Football, then, continued, much as it had always done. As in the folk game, there was a division between larger, more ritualistic games, which involved huge numbers of fags, and smaller, more controlled games, often eleven-a-side, like that contested by Oxford and Cambridge at Eton in 1863. The latter became more common as the century progressed, but the mass games continued, as violent and chaotic as ever, a purgatory for the small boys. 'In the house-games there are often twenty-five a side,' wrote Brinsley-Richards, describing football at Eton in the late 1850s. 'I have been pitched head-long with my face in the mud, and backwards along the rouge line, with such force that I almost turned a somersault; I have lain in front of goals flat as a fried sole, with a score of sprawling fellows above, all squeezing the breath out of me . . . I have suffered all these things in jolly games with big fellows, and have seen other small boys suffer worse.'

Public school football had become no more civilized. But it was now accepted by the school authorities, and this was the key change in the mid-nineteenth century. Eton began actively to encourage football from 1841, and over the next few years most of the major schools wrote down their rules for the first time. By the late 1850s an organized system of house teams, with house colours, was emerging, often playing for cups donated by the masters.

It was the start of an extraordinary transformation. Having been scorned and even outlawed in the 1820s, games generally – not just football – became a positive obsession at the public schools. Driving this was the 'healthy mind, healthy body' philosophy of 'muscular Christianity', propagated by writers such as Thomas Hughes and Charles Kingsley, which was increasingly influential from the 1860s onwards. 'Cleverness – what an aim! Cleverness neither makes nor keeps man or nation,' wrote one extreme disciple, and at many schools the athletes formed an elite caste, entitled to strange privileges – at Charterhouse, for instance, only the 'bloods', as they were known, could walk arm in arm. For many this new 'cult of athleticism' was as coarse and vulgar as the aristocratic anarchy it had replaced. 'Flannelled fools at the wicket and muddied oafs at the goals,' wrote Rudyard Kipling, mocking the new philistinism.

But in the 1840s and 1850s its significance was more limited. For football, it meant simply that the sport now had a thin veneer of respectability, and this had one key effect. Where before it had been assumed that you left the game behind once you left school, now, for the first time, it became a sport that men of the respectable classes continued into adulthood.

From the late 1830s small groups of enthusiasts began to gather together at Cambridge University. Immediately they encountered an obvious problem: they all played different rules. At Harrow the game was played with an extraordinary ball shaped like a church cassock. The rules on handling were the opposite of Eton – you *couldn't* stop the ball with your hands, but you *could* attempt a clean catch, which would entitle you to a free kick, and the players wore white string gloves to give them better grip. Winchester's game was played on a small, narrow pitch where, uniquely, dribbling was banned and shots on goal had to remain below shoulder-height unless they were taken on the volley. Rugby's game, of course, was the most distinctive of all. Not only were players permitted to run with the ball in their hands, it also required boys to kick the ball over, rather than under, the bar, and generally involved far larger numbers than games at the other schools. 'The result was dire confusion,' wrote H. C. Malden, one of the early players at Cambridge. 'Every man played the rules he had been accustomed to at his public school. I remember how the Eton men howled at the Rugby men for handling the ball.'

In 1848 he and a group of other students from Eton, Rugby, Shrewsbury, Winchester and Harrow got together to try to hammer out a common code. 'We met in my rooms ... at 4 pm; anticipating a long meeting,' Malden recalled. 'I cleared the tables and provided pens, ink and paper ... Every man brought a copy of his school rules, or knew them by heart, and our progress in framing new rules was slow ... We broke up five minutes before midnight.' This, and other meetings, resulted in the first attempt at a uniform set of rules. There was no place for the Eton 'rouge' and catching was to be permitted, provided a player kicked the ball immediately and did not run with it. A string was to be placed between the top of the goalposts and the ball had to pass beneath this for a goal. As at most of the public schools, the offside rule was strict, outlawing forward passing: 'No player is allowed to loiter between the ball and the adversaries' goal.'

Traditional histories of football see the game's evolution from this point on as being straightforward. Having supposedly tamed the wild folk game, public schoolboys had now codified it at Cambridge. From here the creation of the Football Association was but a short step. In fact the path from the Cambridge rules of the late 1840s to the creation of the FA in 1863 and a common code would be long and tortuous. And it soon became clear that there was no group of people less suited to the task of designing a universal set of rules than public schoolboys.

None of the public schools showed the remotest interest in adopting the Cambridge code. When, in 1858, a correspondent to *Bell's Life* tentatively suggested the schools try to agree 'fixed laws', there was a flurry of letters so vitriolic the editor declared, 'we consider them better unpublished, and the correspondence ... closed'. Eton men regarded the Rugby game as 'plebeian' while the Rugby men viewed Eton's game as 'effeminate'. The antagonism between Rugby and the rest is understandable since their games were so obviously different, but the hostility was just as intense between Eton and Harrow. 'In my opinion ... owing to the wide difference between the games at present existing, no combination can be framed with anything like equal fairness,' wrote an Old Harrovian to *The Times*.

The problem was partly snobbery. There was a clear pecking order among the public schools, with Eton at the top and newer schools such as Shrewsbury and Rugby at the bottom. As late as 1866 Westminster refused a challenge from Shrewsbury on the grounds that it did not even recognize it as a public school ('The Captain of the Westminster Eleven has yet to learn the first lesson of a true public school education, the behaviour due from one gentleman to another,' retorted the Shrewsbury captain). And God help lesser schools that had the temerity to challenge their social betters to a game. 'Eton we know, and Rugby we know, but who are ye?' sneered Harrow in response to a challenge from Mill Hill. Schools would never accept any rule change which implied deference to somebody else's code.

But there was more to it than petty rivalry. Difference and uniqueness were the very essence of public schools. Each had grown organically from its own particular point of origin and, over the centuries, developed institutions, customs and even language unique to itself. Public schools were mystical, almost magical clubs, deliberately incomprehensible and exclusive. Sports were an important part of this mystique, and the memory of school sports exerted a powerful emotional grip on old boys throughout their lives. 'My dreams have often taken the form that I am still at Eton, happy and careless – now that it is my turn to go in at cricket in Upper Club, now bathing in the Weir; or that I am running down with the ball in the field, or going in for shies at the wall,' wrote Alfred Lubbock, who was at Eton in the 1850s and 1860s, in his old age.

Cricket had always had a common set of rules. But football was different, and the idea of abandoning the ancient games in favour of a one-size-fits-all 'mongrel' version, which was everyone's game but no one's, was anathema. If it meant that the schools could play only within themselves or against panting, wheezing teams of old boys, so be it. As one correspondent to *Bell's Life* observed perceptively, 'prejudices are the very basis of our public schools'.

The new Cambridge rules were not even widely used at Cambridge. They ought to have made it possible for old boys from the different schools to play against each other, but no such matches are recorded. In fact, as football gained in popularity during the 1850s and the number of players increased, old boys at both Oxford and Cambridge found themselves able to retreat into their own footballing ghettos, like the two teams kicking lumps out of each other at Eton in 1863. The Old Etonian Football Club had been set up at Cambridge in 1856, imitating a similar one at Oxford, and the Old Rugbeians and Old Harrovians followed suit at Cambridge in 1857 and 1863, each using their own rules. If anything, the move towards integration was going backwards.

'It is impossible to report progress; the matter stands in precisely the same position as it stood years ago,' wrote the influential sports journalist John Cartwright in *The Field* in the autumn of 1863. Public school rivalry hung 'clog like, at the heels of football'. The public schools had perhaps saved football from oblivion, and provided a refuge for it at a time when the common people were largely confined to the chapel, the pub and the factory, but at the start of the 1860s there was no reason at all to suppose they were the springboard from which football would take over the world. The crowd of elegantly dressed men and women and babbling schoolboys that gathered beneath the towers of Eton that crisp November day in 1863 – rich, powerful and influential – might have seemed ideally placed to lead a renaissance of the old sport. In fact the public schools were a prison from which football would have to escape before it could be reborn.

> *It is desirable that a Challenge Cup should be established . . .*
> *for which all clubs should be invited to compete.*
>
> FA Minute Book, 20 July 1871

3

The Great Revival

Royal Engineers v. Wanderers, FA Cup Final, Kennington Oval, 16 March 1872

IF YOU HAD STROLLED DOWN THE KENNINGTON ROAD IN THE EARLY afternoon of Saturday, 16 March 1872, you might have been surprised to observe small groups of well-dressed people making their way towards the Oval in the warm spring sunshine. Odd, you might have thought. It's not the cricket season yet. Unless you were a particular football fan – a pretty small group at this time – you'd probably have been unaware that they were on their way to the very first FA Cup Final.

The match made little impact on wider society. The papers that weekend were busy reporting that 'a Mr Karl Marx' was to address a meeting of the Democrats of London to mark the first anniversary of the Paris Commune, and the equally alarming news that a large brown bear called Bessie had escaped and was on the loose in Cricklewood. On the sports pages most gave more space to the preparations for the forthcoming Oxford–Cambridge boat race than to the Cup Final, and *The Times* ignored it altogether. But in the history of the world's greatest sport, this was an event of seismic importance.

If you'd decided to follow the crowds and pay your shilling* (a price that excluded many working-class people) to get into the Oval you'd have been presented with an unprepossessing scene. Then, as now, the Oval was dominated by the ugly group of gasometers which stood at the north-eastern corner and made it so much less glamorous a location than Lord's. And it wasn't much by way of a stadium either. There were no stands, other than a small, squat pavilion. And even that wasn't being used. The football pitch had been set up in the outfield on the far side and the spectators were simply standing behind a rope around the edge of the pitch. Some of the wealthier ones had paid extra to bring in their carriages and were using these as a type of grandstand.

Unless you were from the upper echelons of society you might have felt a little intimidated. The character of the crowd was much the same as that which had gathered to watch the old boys from Oxford and Cambridge at Eton in 1863. In fact, a number of them were probably the same people. The turn-out wasn't a great deal larger either, perhaps two thousand. And, once more, they'd come to watch their own. Wanderers were drawn from the cream of the public schools and 'Varsity men

* In old money there were twenty shillings to the pound and twelve pennies to the shilling.

living in the capital (anyone else need not apply)'. Their opponents, the Royal Engineers, were a team of officers from the School of Military Engineering at Chatham Docks. Most of them were public school men too. Of the twenty-two players, eleven had been to Eton or Harrow.

Approaching the pitch, you'd have been confronted with the standard problem facing early football spectators: a solid wall of backs crowned with a forest of top hats, the bustled, petticoated dresses of the ladies providing the occasional splash of colour and an additional obstacle. If unconcerned by social niceties you might have elbowed your way to the front, ignoring the grunts of 'Really!' and 'I say!' Once there, around three o'clock, you'd have been rewarded with the sight of the two teams strolling on to the pitch, Royal Engineers in red and blue hooped jerseys with matching stockings, Wanderers some-what garishly outfitted in orange, violet and black. Looking up, you might have seen half-interested local residents in the upper windows of the surrounding houses, pausing briefly to look down on the novel scene. Then, with a polite round of applause from the gents around you, the game began.

For the modern observer there was still much about the match that unfolded over the next ninety minutes that was unfamiliar. Although the players had discarded their long trousers, they had on knee-length knickerbockers. The Royal Engineers wore a strange type of nightcap, or 'cowl', while a number of the Wanderers team were wearing brightly coloured caps. Their boots had no studs and they wore no shin pads. There was a tape rather than a crossbar and, as in the Eton Field Game, there were no markings on the pitch.

Heading played no part at all, and there was little passing, particularly from the Wanderers, the game consisting largely of concerted 'rushes'. Charging was still a central element, and the goalkeepers, although entitled to use their hands, tended to kick or punch for fear of being bundled through the goal. Goalkeepers could even be charged when not in possession; in the 1876 final the goal itself was demolished during one particularly ferocious onslaught. Knocks, given and taken in good spirit, were all part of the game. Lieutenant E. C. Creswell of the Royal Engineers was felt to have shown great 'pluck' in playing the full match despite the fact that he broke his collar bone after ten minutes.

Throw-ins were taken one-handed at right angles (as in modern rugby) by the first player to touch the ball after it went off. And the players were obliged to appeal to the two umpires if they felt there had been an infringement of the rules. The formations were the standard, default formations of the public schools once fags had been removed from the equation: 1-1-8 in the case of Wanderers, the Royal Engineers deploying a marginally more cautious 2-1-7. The two sides changed ends after every goal.

Despite these curiosities, there was much that was familiar. The goals were the same size as today, as was the ball. A referee had been appointed, although he was only called on to arbitrate when the two umpires couldn't agree. And, although the match occasionally degenerated into a 'loose scrimmage', particularly in front of goal, there were no formal 'bullies' or 'scrums'. There were no points awarded for touchdowns, the Eton rouge having been replaced with the modern corner. Handling had been outlawed altogether, other than for the goalkeeper, with the indirect free kick introduced as a penalty. And, most importantly, the rigid offside rules of most of the public schools, which had effectively outlawed forward passing, had been relaxed. Players were now onside so long as they had three opponents between them and the goal. Although still stricter than today's two-man offside rule, the change would have massive implications for the future of the game.

In short, this was recognizably the same sport we play today. Moreover, these rules were being applied in a national cup final organized by a national association. It was a dramatic advance. How had this happened in the space of fewer than nine years?

It all goes back to two brothers, or so the traditional histories of football would have us believe, probably because they were largely written by one of them. It's more complex than that, but this footballing Romulus and Remus are as good a place to start as any.

Their names were John and Charles Alcock, and they were the eldest sons of a wealthy shipbroker from Sunderland. In 1855 the two boys, then aged fourteen and twelve, were sent to Harrow when their father moved to London. Neither was academically gifted and on leaving school they went into their father's business rather than go on to university. But their real love was football, and in 1859 they established the Forest Football Club close to their home in Chingford, north-east London. According to Charles, Forest was 'the first club to work on a definite basis with the distinct object of circulating and popularising the game'.

It was from the Forest club that Wanderers, who would trot out on to the pitch at the Oval thirteen years later, evolved. Charlie Alcock always portrayed Forest as essentially a Harrow

Old Boys team. 'The trivial cause . . . was the humble desire of a few Old Harrovians, who had just left school, to keep up . . . the game at which they had shown some considerable aptitude,' he wrote in 1890. In fact analysis of the only surviving team photo, dated 1863, shows that just three of the eleven went to the school; most of the others came from well-to-do families in the local area. But the Harrow influence was strong and early match reports suggest they played something close to Harrow rules. John Alcock was the first club captain and Charlie himself was the club's star striker, ending as top scorer in the 1861–62 season.

Two other teams crop up in the sporting press around this time, the Crusaders and Dingley Dell (a place name taken from Dickens's *Pickwick Papers*), both drawing on men from various public schools living in and around London. Soon afterwards we begin to see the names of Barnes, Crystal Palace (no relation to the present club), Civil Service, War Office, Surbiton and the No Names of Kilburn. A modest footballing culture was taking shape in the capital.

Press reports suggest matches were genteel social occasions. A game between Forest and Barnes in February 1863 was played in 'a large field with a noble avenue of trees running through it which made a pleasant promenade for spectators and attracted many of the fairer sex', according to *Bell's Life*. While public schoolboys dominated these clubs, a lot of the players, although middle class, were not from the social elite and had learned the game outside the public schools.

As at Cambridge University, the emergence of these clubs created pressure for a uniform set of rules, and by the start of the 1863–64 season a fierce debate was raging in the sporting press. In the autumn of 1863 this led to the historic series of meetings at the Freemason's Tavern in central London at which the Football Association was created. The story has been told many times of how the representatives of the London clubs clashed over whether players should be allowed to run with the ball in their hands, and whether 'shinning', or 'hacking', should be allowed – both key elements of the game played at Rugby. Ebenezer Morley from the Barnes club warned, 'If we have "hacking", no one who has arrived at the years of discretion will play at football and it will be entirely relinquished to school-boys.' Francis Campbell of Blackheath retorted that if they banned hacking he would be 'bound to bring over a lot of Frenchmen who would beat you with a week's practice'. Ultimately, the Rugby faction was overruled and withdrew from the Association, leading to a split between the two codes which has lasted to this day.

But what is generally not understood is that the great division between the Rugby and non-Rugby codes was the only important, tangible result of these meetings. Other than that, they were a complete disaster. For the first four years of its existence, the Football Association and its new code of rules were almost universally ignored. And by 1867 the FA had just ten members, some of whom were begging to be allowed to play under different rules. At the FA's annual general meeting that year Ebenezer Morley, the chairman, even suggested that the organization be dissolved. What had gone wrong? The back stories of many of the men in the crowded gas-lit room at the Freemason's Tavern in 1863 provide vital clues.

John Alcock was present, one of the leaders of the anti-Rugby faction. Morley, then acting secretary, also played a key role. A 'pretty and effective dribbler' for the Barnes club, he was a solicitor and came from an evangelical background. But perhaps the most intriguing character is Arthur Pember, the FA's first president. Brought up in Clapham, South London, he came from a wealthy stockbroking family and, like Morley, was a member of the Barnes club. He too was intensely religious, but Pember was a 'sacramentalist', a wing of the Church of England which attached huge importance to ritual. Sacramentalists believed mystery and symbolism were the only way the working class could be drawn to religion, and Pember was a social and political radical. In 1867, four years after the meetings at the Freemason's Tavern, he emigrated to the US where he lived in comparative poverty as a left-wing journalist, often taking on undercover assignments to explore the seedy underbelly of American life. Illustrations survive of him variously disguised as a beggar, a boatman and as an 'extra' in the circus. He also wrote firebrand political tracts with titles like 'The Coming Revolution in England'. 'The days of arrogance and selfishness in politics are numbered . . . the days of justice to all are fast approaching,' he wrote in one – not the sort of stuff we've heard a great deal of since from presidents of the FA.

It's not surprising that the public schoolboys, with their fine nose for these things, instinctively sensed there was something not quite pukka about these chaps. Pember's political views aside, neither he nor Morley had been to public school, and even the Alcock boys, although Harrow men, were very definitely 'trade' and had not been to Oxford or Cambridge.

The public schools were invited to the meetings at the Freemason's Tavern but remained aloof. The attitude of many was summed up by a letter to the *Sporting Life* in November 1863 which stated: 'I do not think the meetings in London are attended by people or clubs of sufficient influence to cause their suggestions to be generally acted upon . . . [Who] are they to dictate rules to Eton, Harrow, Winchester, etc?' These simmering class tensions could be observed within the FA as well in the dispute over Rugby rules. Campbell, the Blackheath representative, felt the proposal to outlaw hacking came from 'those who liked their pipes and grog or schnapps more than the manly game of football' and blamed it on the fact that so many members of the London clubs had not learned their game at public school. As late as February 1868 *The Field* was complaining that the FA Committee could 'only boast of two public school men'.

Ultimately the presence of non-public school men made the London club scene a far more fertile environment for the evolution of a common code than Cambridge. They were not bound by public school prejudices. And, combined with the fact the public school men in London were that bit older, and so further removed from their school days, it meant there was a greater spirit of compromise than among the university students. The flip side was that the FA lacked authority.

But it was not just snobbery that led to the new FA rules being so widely ignored. There were also problems with the rules themselves. Take a look at them (Appendix 1, p. 276) – this isn't football. There is no crossbar, or tape, and the ball can pass between the posts at any height for a goal. There are still touch-downs, and these are to be followed by something very similar to the modern conversion in rugby. If you catch the ball cleanly and make a mark with your heel you are entitled to a free kick.

And the forward pass is outlawed. The only significant advance is the width of the goal, which is the same as today. This is a hybrid; precisely the sort of 'mongrel' game public schoolboys were wary of. Despite the split with the Rugby clubs the FA hadn't had the confidence to break completely with the Rugby code and the result was a game no one recognized as their own. A committee of more upper-class public school men might have had the confidence to be bolder.

It was from outside London that the impetus now came to drive football forward. Sheffield Football Club (no connection to modern Wednesday or United) was the only non-metropolitan member of the FA. Its role in the birth of modern football was for years largely ignored by historians. But in the late 1860s it moved centre stage.

The club was formed in October 1857, a couple of years before the Alcock brothers set up the Forest club. The account in James Walvin's *The People's Game* (1994) typifies the traditional elitist view of the origins of football: 'The Sheffield club was established under the influence of Old Harrovians who persuaded local village footballers not to handle the ball, allegedly by providing the players with white gloves and florins to clutch during the game.' In fact, Sheffield had nothing to do with Old Harrovians or, for that matter, with 'local village footballers'. It was established by the sons of local businessmen and industrialists in the steel trade, the product of a proud, provincial elite. Analysis of the fifty-seven men on the club's first membership list shows just one had been to public school, and he went to Rugby. So where had they learned the game?

The club's first secretary was Nathaniel Creswick, chairman of the local Silver Plate Company, a colourful character who later acquired something of a reputation for getting involved in punch-ups during games. In a speech at the club's Golden Jubilee Dinner in 1907 he said he had written off to the country's leading public schools to get copies of their rule books and then combined the best elements from each to draw up their first code. But people don't normally learn a sport from a book, and certainly not from books as deliberately confusing and opaque as the public school rule books. Common sense suggests these men must have played football before setting up a football club. Seventeen of them had gone to the Sheffield Collegiate School, the most prestigious in the city, and it is quite possible they had played together there. But football was not taught at the school and only one of the masters was a public school man, which still begs the question of where they learned the sport.

The answer may lie in the countryside around Sheffield. Although folk football had declined dramatically over the previous hundred years, it had not died out altogether. Here it is important to grasp a simple but vital truth about Victorian Britain: there were far, far more poor people than there were rich people. There were just seven public schools in the country in 1840, from which just a few hundred boys emerged each year. Even if the numbers playing folk football in 1850 were a mere fraction of what they'd been in 1750, working-class footballers would still have outnumbered public school footballers. Just because public school men attached no significance to football outside their own social circle doesn't mean it wasn't important.

Recent research has shown that folk football lingered more strongly in some parts of the country than others. And one of those areas was South Yorkshire, particularly the hill country around the villages of Penistone, Thurlstone and Holmforth, just a dozen miles north-west of Sheffield. There, matches between local teams were being organized well into the 1850s, often sponsored by publicans. Press reports make clear these were small-scale structured games rather than wild village romps. 'An excellent match of football took place at Thurlstone lately, between six of the celebrated players of that place and six from Totties, which ended with neither party getting a goal,' wrote *Bell's Life* on 12 February 1843. Another report specifies that the game being played is 'foot-ball, and not hand-ball'. The founder of Hallam FC, the Sheffield club's first local rival, was born in Penistone, and the first captain of The Wednesday (not known as Sheffield Wednesday until the 1929–30 season) was from the same area. It's surely no coincidence that Britain's first modern football culture outside London should have emerged in a city so close to this hotbed of the folk game.

The truth is that the public schools were part of a small but diverse football culture in the mid-nineteenth century that included elements of the old rustic sport. And there was more cross-fertilization within this culture than public school men cared to admit. Many boys arrived at public school having already played football with the village boys at home ('I love football so and have played all my life,' declares the hero of *Tom Brown's Schooldays* on his first day at Rugby). And football was also common at many grammar and prep schools, catering for the middle class. It's from this mix that the game in Sheffield emerged, rather than being handed down by Old Harrovians to the local peasants.

What, then, was the code the men of Sheffield decided to

play by? In many ways it resembled the crude game played at various public schools. But there was one glaring difference: they had no offside rule, sacrosanct to public school men. Whether this reflected the local folk game we just don't know. But if the villagers of South Yorkshire did have an offside law it's unlikely it was as complex and restrictive as those at the public schools, honed as they were in constant, daily games. Although an offside rule was later introduced in Sheffield it merely required the man receiving the ball to have a single player – the goalkeeper – between himself and the opposition goal.

By the early 1860s Sheffield's football culture, like London's, was expanding. Many of the teams were formed from existing cricket clubs – something that would become a common pattern. Hallam were still Sheffield's principal rivals and games between the two were fiercely contested. The Hallam men were from backgrounds almost as elite as those of Sheffield. But a match between the two sides at Bramall Lane cricket ground in December 1862 descended into a riot. The trouble started after Nathaniel Creswick, Sheffield's club secretary, was fouled by a Hallam man called Waterfall. Creswick shook his fist in Waterfall's face. Shortly afterwards Waterfall fouled Creswick again, at which point Creswick hit him so hard he made his mouth bleed. Waterfall then 'threw off his waistcoat' and charged at Creswick, which prompted a general mêlée involving both players and spectators.

Despite incidents like this Sheffield were regarded as the aristocrats of the local game. They were known in the city as 'the gentlemen', and one of the advantages Sheffield had over London was that the founding club's rules were accepted unquestioningly by all other teams. Free from public school prejudices and rivalries, the game also evolved more quickly. The use of hands died out faster than in London, and Sheffield pioneered the use of corners, free kicks and crossbars. There was just one area where it was more backward: the Sheffield goal was about the same width as the Eton one, and in the early 1860s a form of the Eton rouge was introduced to counter the proliferation of 0–0 draws.

By the mid-1860s football in Sheffield was filtering down from the social elite. Most of the new clubs were middle class, but by 1867 there were suggestions that players should be compensated for time lost at work if injured during a game – a clear indication of working-class involvement and the first hint of professionalism. Crowds were also growing, and in 1867 Thomas Youdan, a local entrepreneur, instituted Britain's first knock-out cup competition outside the public schools. On 5 March a crowd of three thousand paid threepence each to watch Hallam beat local rivals Norfolk 2–1 on rouges in the final.

Youdan owned the local Alexandra Music Hall, whose glittering chandeliers and raucous stage acts were a Mecca for the working class of Sheffield on Saturday nights, and in many ways he embodied the coming age. Youdan saw that the working class could provide a market as well as a work force – one of the defining realizations of the late Victorian era – and that this applied as much to the leisure industry as any other. He was one of the first to exploit the possibilities this opened up. The following year another local music hall entrepreneur instituted the rival Cromwell Cup, which was won by the newly formed Wednesday.

By this time Sheffield was competing against teams from Leeds, Nottingham and Lincoln, where similar rules were used. Nottingham in particular was effectively a footballing satellite of Sheffield, and it's easy to imagine football might have divided along north/south lines at this time. Fortunately the Sheffield men were fiercely loyal to the FA.

At the FA's AGM of 1867, William Chesterman, Sheffield's delegate, trekked down from the North to find himself one of just six people who'd bothered to turn up. But he brought with him a letter describing the advances in the Sheffield area and expressing firm support for the Association – a much-needed morale boost. Ebenezer Morley described Sheffield as 'the greatest stronghold of football in England'.

The FA was also able to draw on energy closer to home. In March 1866 a representative London eleven, captained by Arthur Pember, played Sheffield in Battersea Park. By all accounts it was a rough old game, the gentlemen from the North showing they could mix it with the meanest of the public schoolboys. 'Some of the London team got rather severely kicked and knocked about,' reported *Bell's Life*. But the result was significant: London won by 'two goals and four touch downs' to nil, which reveals that, although the FA was struggling, football generally in the capital was thriving.

This is backed up by analysis of the sporting press at this time. A total of 122 games were played in and around London in the last three months of 1866. By the same period in 1867 this figure had risen to 170. Given the problems with the code of laws drawn up by the FA in 1863 this presents an obvious conundrum: what rules were these teams using?

The answer seems to be that they had developed their own.

There was now a critical mass of footballers in the capital who *needed* to find a common code if they were to continue playing the game they loved. And, in the absence of a firm lead from the FA, they had gravitated towards the other point of authority in the capital: the local public schools. On 26 January 1867 *The Field* printed a long list of metropolitan teams that were now effectively playing the same game, and it identified the rules as being essentially those used at Charterhouse and Westminster. It may be there was a two-way process going on and the two schools were themselves influenced by the evolution of the club game in London. Either way, it just so happened they had rules that were closer, in key respects, to Sheffield and the modern game than any other public school. At Charterhouse you were onside so long as you had four or more opponents between yourself and the goal, while Westminster had a three-man rule – more restrictive than the modern two-man rule, but better than the alternatives. They had no touchdowns or conversions (making them more advanced than Sheffield in this respect), and Charterhouse made little use of bullies or scrums.

This rapid evolution of the club game in London and Sheffield left the FA in a strange position. Quite separately, in two different places, the uniform code it had been seeking had come into being, largely independent of its efforts. Not for the last time, it was lagging behind trends in the game. The challenge facing it was essentially an administrative one. It needed to catch up, and here the two Alcock boys re-enter the story.

At the start of 1866 Charlie replaced his big brother John on the FA Committee. It meant for the first time the FA had on board someone who was recognized as a top-class player.

It was also a happy day for the Association in other ways. John quickly faded out of football and went on to have a spectacularly uninteresting professional life (taking over his father's firm) and a spectacularly interesting private one. In 1867 he married Catherine Rowse, the daughter of a respectable coffee-house keeper. Six years later the marriage fell apart in a divorce for which the term 'messy' scarcely seems adequate. John made the astonishing claim that Catherine was a prostitute when he met her (which rather begs the question of how he met her), that he'd tried to reform her but that she had hit the bottle and returned to her 'vicious' ways. She in turn claimed John had beaten her up, at times pursuing her around the streets of Twickenham, where they lived, lobbing bricks at her and hitting her with a poker. Victorian Britain being what it was, the court confined her to a lunatic asylum while John was able to waltz free and shack up with a woman fifteen years his junior. By the time Catherine died in 1891, still incarcerated, John had moved on to partner number three, having got married in 1886, at the age of forty-five, to an eighteen-year-old. None of this prevented John becoming a local Conservative councillor and living on to a respectable old age.

Charlie, meanwhile, had a dull domestic life – he remained married to the same woman all his life and spawned eight children – but a professional life of such importance that he has been rightly referred to as 'the father of modern sport'. He was first of all an excellent footballer. Almost fourteen stone and close to six feet, he played all his life in the robust style he'd learned at Harrow. His close friend the cricketer W. G. Grace once said, 'The way Alcock used to knock over a fellow when he was trying to pass him I shall never forget . . . Alcock made Catherine-wheels of those fellows.' The Sheffield footballer William Clegg, writing in 1930, claimed referees would not have allowed Alcock to stay on the pitch more than five minutes in a later period. He was a prolific goalscorer, and in the 1870s, when internationals started, he was regularly picked as captain of England. Besides Forest, he also played for a range of leading clubs, as was common at this time, including Wanderers (formed in 1864), Upton Park, Crystal Palace and various Harrow Old Boys teams. In later life he refereed or umpired a number of FA Cup Finals.

Alcock was also a successful journalist, a profession he'd turned to in the mid-1860s after deciding his father's ship-broking business wasn't for him. He worked initially for *The Field* and *The Sportsman*, and from 1868 he edited the *Football Annual*, going on to write a number of books on both football and cricket. He was also secretary of Surrey County Cricket Club from 1872 until his death in 1907, revitalizing the club and providing the inspiration for the first Test match held in England, against the Australians at the Oval in 1880.

But it is for his work as a football administrator that he is best known. He was a man of enormous energy, and he entered the FA in 1866 like a bolt of electricity. It's probably no co-incidence that his very first meeting, the AGM in February 1866, was one of the most important in the history of the organization. Held at the Freemasons Tavern when the FA was at its lowest ebb, and attended by just a handful of people, it has been largely ignored by historians. But the decisions made that day laid the foundations of the modern game. They introduced a tape at a height of eight feet between the posts, and stipulated the ball must pass beneath this for a goal. They removed the right to a shot on goal, or conversion, following a touchdown (although they kept the touchdown). They removed the right to a free kick following a clean catch. And, most importantly, they introduced Westminster's three-man offside rule. Reports on the meeting make clear they came very close to abolishing the offside rule altogether; it may only have been a desire to placate schools such as Eton, Harrow and Winchester that prevented them doing this.

'Perhaps, now that sweeping reforms have been introduced, clubs that have hitherto withheld their support from the Association will think fit to become members,' wrote *The Field*, somewhat forlornly, in a report possibly contributed by Charlie Alcock. Unfortunately, the prestige of the FA had fallen so low by this time that no one really noticed. It wasn't until the AGM of 1867 that things really began to move. The touchdown was abolished and additional limitations were placed on handling. And after the meeting the FA secretary, R. G. Graham, was instructed to write to clubs throughout the country to publicize the new code. The new rules, he told clubs, were 'as far as possible, free from unnecessary danger, yet retaining all that is most scientific and interesting'.

The rule changes of 1866 and 1867 represented a final, definitive break with the Rugby code. 'It had become evident that to amalgamate the two classes [of football] was impossible, and the Association decided to throw in its lot entirely with the opponents of Rugby,' Secretary Graham wrote later. It worked. 'Great satisfaction was expressed by the whole body of players at the working of the rules . . . and their simplicity and efficacy met with universal approval,' read one match report. By the start of 1868 FA membership had risen to twenty-nine clubs, including Charterhouse and Westminster. And at the AGM that year, at Alcock's suggestion, the FA Committee was expanded to include a number of leading public school men, the most important among them the Old Etonian Arthur Kinnaird, who played a vital role in the Association from then on.

The revision of the core rules was completed with an outright ban on handling in 1870 (a law so sweeping that the following year it had to be clarified that the goalkeeper was exempt) and the introduction of the corner and the free kick at the start of 1872. By then Sheffield had abandoned the rouge and the two codes had converged in all areas other than throw-ins (Sheffield had 'kick-ins' instead) and the offside law. But Sheffield's role in the Association was so important that it was given special dispensation to retain its own rules for the time being.

By 1871 Charlie Alcock was FA Secretary, and on 20 July that year, in a meeting at his office at *The Sportsman*, it was agreed 'that a Challenge Cup should be established . . . for which all clubs should be invited to compete'. Inevitably the idea, inspired by the Cock House competition at Harrow, came from Alcock himself. And it was Alcock who led out Wanderers as captain at the Oval in the final the following March, enormously proud of what he'd achieved since he and his brother, fresh from Harrow, had set up the Forest club thirteen years earlier.

It was a good day for him. The Royal Engineers were 7–4 favourites. They were unbeaten in two years and hadn't conceded a single goal in the four matches they'd played en route to the final. But Wanderers came tearing out of the traps and laid into them with a ferocity that startled both their opponents and the crowd. Within a quarter of an hour they'd broken Creswell's collar bone and gone one up, Old Harrovian Morton Betts tapping the ball in after R. W. S. Vidal had 'middled' the ball from the wing.

Ends were now changed and Wanderers found themselves kicking into both the sun and the wind, with the gasometers at their backs. But there was no let-up, and within five minutes Alcock had scored, only to see the goal disallowed for handball. Shortly afterwards they hit the post, and it was only the acrobatics of Captain Merriman in the Royal Engineers' goal which prevented the score steadily mounting. Even in old age Alcock believed Merriman's performance that day was one of the finest he had ever seen.

It had been predicted that Wanderers would tire more quickly than their military opponents but they kept up the pressure to the end, making 'full use of their weight forward', according to *The Field*, and preventing the Engineers launching the 'rushes for which they are noted'. The Engineers managed only one attempt on goal and the papers the next morning were full of praise for the 'faultless . . . kicking' of Wanderers' two backs, Lubbock and Thompson. When time was called shortly after 4.30 Alcock and his men were victors by one goal to nil.

'Thus ended one of the most pleasant contests in which the Wanderers have ever been engaged,' commented Alcock's own paper, *The Sportsman*. Other papers were more effusive, and it was generally felt to have been one of the finest games yet played under Association rules. Alcock was awarded the Cup four weeks later at a dinner at the Pall Mall Restaurant in Charing Cross. The Wanderers players also received a silk badge and an inscribed gold medal worth £2 10s.

The modern game was effectively born that warm spring afternoon at the Oval. A national organization and a national set of rules were now in place. And in the Cup competition the FA had stumbled across a spectacularly successful formula. Over the next few decades it would acquire a popularity and mystique that would endure until the end of the twentieth century. Indeed the FA Cup would do more than anything else to spread Association rules and raise the profile of football.

The sport had been able to move forward because it had moved away from the public schools and begun to acquire its own separate momentum in the hands of adult footballers, only some of whom had been to public school. Association football was now essentially a fusion of the Charterhouse/ Westminster-influenced game played in London and the more folk-influenced game that had emerged from Sheffield. Both had taken it away from the game played at Eton, Harrow and Westminster, particularly with regard to the offside rule.

Alcock would later refer to this period as 'the great football revival'. But in 1872 there was still a long way to go. Organized football remained largely confined to fairly small groups of middle- and upper-class men. It was dwarfed in popularity by cricket (twenty thousand had watched the first day of the Eton v. Harrow match at Lord's the previous summer, ten times the number who watched the FA Cup Final) and there were still large areas of the country where the FA code had not penetrated. Most importantly, although the rules had evolved, tactics remained primitive. Reading match reports at this time you are struck by a sense of men adapting to a game they are still not entirely familiar with. Games were interrupted by endless handballs. There was confusion over whether you could score direct from free kicks and corners (you couldn't). And players had still not fully woken up to the possibilities of the new offside rule. The likes of Alcock and Kinnaird were still playing the crude charging game they had learned at school. Football awaited its *artistes*, and once more the impetus to take it to the next level would come from outside the public schools.

Individual skill was generally on England's side.
The Southrons, however, did not play to each other so well as their
opponents, who seem to be adepts in passing the ball.

The Graphic, Scotland v. England, 1872

4

How Glasgow Invented
the Beautiful Game

Queen's Park, 1867–80

WHEN CHARLIE ALCOCK WROTE TO THE *GLASGOW HERALD* ON 3 November 1870 to try to stimulate interest in an international, he described Scotland as having once been 'the land of football'. He was flattering them slightly, but the sport was certainly every bit as popular there as it was south of the border and had been played passionately for centuries.

As in England, we know about it through attempts to suppress it. In 1424 James I, concerned it distracted from military exercise, commanded 'that no man play at football under the pain of four pennies'. Even his own descendants ignored this. In 1497 in the royal accounts we find a record of two shillings given to a 'James Dog to buy footballs for the

King', James IV. And in 1568 Mary, Queen of Scots, imprisoned in Carlisle Castle, watched twenty of her retinue play football for two hours, 'very strongly, nimbly, and skilfully, without foul play – the smallness of their ball occasioning the fairer play'. A ball fitting this description, dating from around 1540, was found in the 1970s during renovation work in the roof beams of the Queen's Bedchamber at Stirling Castle and is now on display there – the world's oldest football.

Again as in England, there was a division between smaller, more structured games of the type Mary, Queen of Scots observed and mass-participation mob football played at festivals and on popular holidays. At Carterhaugh in Selkirkshire on 4 December 1815 Sir Walter Scott observed one of these more raucous games 'betwixt the Ettrick men and the men of Yarrow' and composed an ode in honour of the occasion:

> Then strip lads and to it, though sharp be the weather,
> And if, by mischance, you should happen to fall,
> There are worse things in life than a tumble on heather,
> And life is itself but a game at football.

Folk football lingered in Scotland longer than in most of England, although in more middle-class form. In 1824 a student called John Hope founded what has been claimed as the world's first football club at Edinburgh University, complete with detailed rules, subscriptions and an expenses book which has survived. For the season 1824–25 we find them paying two shillings for '4 bladders', one shilling for 'leather and pipes' (presumably to blow up the bladders, which could be an unpleasant task if done with the lips) and 10s. 6d. for the hire of a park. The club continued until 1841 playing a version of the game where kicking predominated, and John Hope was still organizing football in the city in the 1850s.

By the 1860s the game was rare enough that had you been walking in Queen's Park in the south of Glasgow on a summer's day in 1866 you might well have lingered, intrigued, to watch a group of lads kicking a ball around in a quiet corner close to the railings along Langside Avenue. They were from the local YMCA and were playing a typical hybrid kicking/handling game. After a few minutes you'd probably have strolled on. But this group has entered football folklore. Legend has it that they were the origin of all football subsequently played in Scotland.

In fact, this is a strange misunderstanding and may reflect a later eagerness to associate football in Scotland with traditions of muscular Christianity. Modern Scottish football did originate with a single group of players in Queen's Park, but they were not the YMCA boys. Instead we must tilt the camera a fraction to the right to a group of immigrants from north-east Scotland who were practising their traditional sports of hammer throwing, shot-putting and tossing the caber on the next patch of grass. From time to time the YMCA lads' ball rolled into their territory and they kicked it back. The two groups struck up conversation and agreed to play a game. This so inspired the men from the North-East that they decided there and then to form a football club. After this the YMCA boys disappear from history, although it is possible one or two of them joined the new club.

Drawn mainly from Morayshire, Banffshire and Aberdeen, the men behind the new club were respectable middle-class businessmen employed in offices and warehouses in the city.

They possessed formidable energy and were obsessively well organized. The club's inaugural meeting was held in Dick's Public House at 3 Eglinton Terrace at 8.30 p.m. on 9 July 1867. They elected a president, a captain, a secretary, a treasurer and a committee of thirteen and decided to call themselves Queen's Park, rejecting the alternatives The Northern, The Morayshire and The Celts. They then gave 'a hearty vote of thanks to Mr Black for his able conduct of the chair' before breaking up for the evening. All of which seems a little excessive for a bunch of guys agreeing to kick a ball around a park.

For a number of years that was all Queen's Park were. There were almost no other football clubs to play against and, like the original Sheffield team, they played among themselves, organizing games along such lines as 'smokers v. non-smokers' and 'lights v. heavy weights'. But they were keen and practised three times a week and soon opponents began to emerge.

Their first competitive match was against a team called Thistle from Glasgow Green on 1 August 1868 (for the first couple of seasons Queen's Park treated football as a summer game – perfectly reasonable in the Scottish climate). The letter sent by the Queen's Park secretary, Robert Gardner, to clarify the rules survives. He proposed they play twenty-a-side for two hours ('quite long enough . . . in weather such as the present') and he asked Thistle to bring their own ball 'in case of any break down'. Queen's Park won 2–0.

It was their only competitive match that year. The following summer they defeated Hamilton Gymnasium in a fifteen-a-side game, the scoreline of four goals and nine touchdowns to zero reflecting the fact that they still played an idiosyncratic form of the game. The 'club poet' wrote a piece celebrating the victory which refers to the ball being driven towards the Hamilton goal 'with fist and hand, with kick and whack'.

In 1870 the club, already fiercely ambitious, joined the Football Association and adopted FA rules. When the FA Cup was established the following year they contributed a guinea towards the cost of the trophy and were one of just fifteen entrants. Charlie Alcock was always keen to encourage the spread of football and they were awarded byes until the semi-final in recognition of the distances they had to travel.

On Monday, 4 March 1872 they lined up at the Oval against Wanderers to play for the right to meet the Royal Engineers in the final. It's at this point that the legend of Scottish football begins. Captained by Charlie Alcock, Wanderers were 'well known in England as the most influential and powerful of all the Association clubs', wrote the *Glasgow Herald*. The burly public schoolboys were also, for the most part, a couple of inches taller and a stone or two heavier than their opponents and it was assumed they would wipe the floor with what was essentially a park team. But an hour and a half of fierce football later the match ended 0–0. FA rules required that Queen's Park return to the Oval for the replay. Their trip south had been paid for by public subscription and they had no money left so they had to scratch, enabling Wanderers to go through. But Queen's Park, a team which had still not played more than a dozen competitive matches, had come within a whisker of contesting the first FA Cup Final.

How do we explain this extraordinary result? Partly it reveals a very simple fact: the early Southern teams weren't terribly good. How good is your school's Old Boys team? Because that's essentially what most of them were. It's revealing that throughout the 1870s and into the 1880s FA Cup-winning sides continued to play against the First XIs of the leading public schools, and frequently lost.

But there was more to it than that. During those hours and hours of concentrated practice in Queen's Park this group of dour, somewhat obsessive Scots had stumbled across a secret ingredient, a magic formula that gave them an immediate advantage. Contemporaries called it 'combination play'. The Queen's Park men passed the ball to one another.

'They dribble little, and usually convey the ball by a series of long kicks, combined with a judicious plan of passing on,' wrote *The Field*. The *Glasgow Herald* noticed the same phenomenon. 'The play of the Glasgow 11 was most creditable, as their forwards worked well together, and their backs kicked with great accuracy. On the other hand, the Wanderers dribbled and played skilfully . . . but collectively they hardly showed so well as their antagonists,' it wrote. The Wanderers men were left chasing shadows, their crude charging neutralized by the fact that their victims had normally passed the ball to a colleague by the time they were sent sprawling to the ground. 'Very much to the astonishment of the Londoners, who expected to carry it without much effort, [the game] ended in a draw,' the Queen's Park secretary wrote smugly in the club's meticulously kept minute book.

The match opened Charlie Alcock's eyes to the quality of football north of the border. Ever an innovator, he had been keen to organize international games for some time and five 'pseudo internationals' had taken place between 1870 and 1872. These were all in London and the Scottish team had consisted of London-based men whose connection to Scotland often amounted to little more than a fondness for Scotch whisky. It had been in a bid to drum up a more genuinely Scottish team that Alcock had written to the *Glasgow Herald* in November 1870. Now he saw his chance. It was agreed a match would be played later that year in Glasgow, and Queen's Park were invited to organize the Scotland team.

The match that is now recognized as the world's first international took place at the West of Scotland Cricket Ground in Partick on 30 November 1872 in front of just over two thousand spectators. Like the Oval, the ground was little more than an enclosed field, the crowd kept back from the pitch by a thin rope. The Scots wore dark blue shirts with the lion rampant emblazoned on the left breast while the English wore white shirts with the three lions as their emblem, colours and badges which have remained unchanged ever since. Walter Arnott, later a great full-back for both Queen's Park and Scotland, remembered walking five miles to watch the game as a boy only to find he couldn't get in because he hadn't realized you had to pay. He persuaded a cabman to let him climb up on his vehicle to look over the fence and never forgot the intense excitement of the crowd. 'I was so impressed with everything I saw, that to this day I can vividly recall it all,' he wrote.

Robert Gardner, now Queen's Park's captain, had been given the job of choosing the Scottish XI, and he'd simply picked the Queen's Park team, which was probably an accurate reflection of the strength of Scottish football at the time. The FA took an all-star XI north, comprising the pick of the English club sides. 'The English team was by far the heavier one,' recalled Arnott. 'What a treat it was to see Clegg or Ottaway getting the ball near their own goal, and making off at a great pace down the field, and only being robbed of it by someone in the last line of the Scotch defence!' The Scots, though, held their own and just before half-time almost scored, Leckie hitting the tape, prompting wild cheers from a section of the crowd who thought the ball had gone under. In the second half the English had the advantage of a slight slope and for the last quarter of an hour the Scottish goal was besieged, William Ker in the Scottish defence playing superbly. But once again the game ended 0–0, and again it was the passing of the Scots that caught the eye. 'Individual skill was generally on England's side,' wrote *The Graphic*, 'The Southrons, however, did not play to each other so well as their opponents, who seem to be adepts in passing the ball.' The English forwards 'played an individual game', recalled Arnott, whereas the work of the Scottish forwards 'was done in pairs'.

This was a revolution in football, one born directly from the change in the offside rule in 1866. Suddenly the magical, shifting kaleidoscope, the beautiful geometry of the modern game, became possible. You could make the ball do the work. You didn't have to charge through your opponents to get to their goal. Drilled in the old public school games (of the 158 men who played as gentleman amateurs in the first dozen FA Cup Finals, forty-eight learned their football on the field at Eton) the established, English sides continued, mechanically, to play in the old style. But none of the Queen's Park men had been to public school and they were alive to the possibilities the new offside rule opened up.

The Queen's Park players quickly found their style required a second, key innovation. The Southern teams generally played with a goalkeeper, a back, a half-back, and then eight forwards who hunted the ball in a pack. But the minute they started passing the ball the Glaswegians realized they needed to spread players around the pitch more. As early as the game against Hamilton Gymnasium in 1869 the Queen's Park captain, Gardner, had distributed cards to his team before the match showing each man where he must play. By the time of the first international the Scots were using a radical 2-2-6 formation.

The Scots were not entirely alone in developing 'combination play'. Charlie Alcock claimed the Sheffield teams were the pioneers. Their more relaxed offside rule 'gave rise to a loose and disjointed game, which directly encouraged . . . a certain kind of passing', he wrote in 1890. *The Field*'s report on the 1872 Wanderers v. Queen's Park game commented that the Scots played 'much after the fashion of Sheffield', noting as well that both had adopted the peculiar practice of 'driving the ball with the head'.

But the Sheffield teams were nothing like as methodical as Queen's Park, and theirs was more of a long-ball game while the Scots specialized in short passing. The main effect of the Sheffield offside rule was to encourage goal-hanging, just as the public schoolboys feared. The most notorious offender was the Wednesday forward Frank Butler. Just five feet four inches tall and bow-legged, Butler would stand chatting to the opposing keeper. Then, when the ball came upfield he'd suddenly turn round and start roughing him up, it being perfectly legal to charge and obstruct the keeper even when he wasn't in possession.

More important than Sheffield as innovators were the Royal Engineers, Wanderers' opponents in that first Cup Final and the only one of the Southern teams to have seriously explored the possibilities of passing in the early years. This probably reflects the fact that, like Queen's Park, they endlessly practised together whereas the Old Boys teams rarely met up other than for matches. Formed in the early 1860s, the Royal Engineers were drilled by their captain, Francis Marindin, who was also the brigade major, a position he cheerfully exploited to arrange the transfer of skilled footballers to the naval base at Chatham where they played. They were a 'club' in a sense that many of their opponents never were and attributed their style to a military *esprit de corps*. 'Individually, as most of us knew, we were sometimes up against better players than ourselves, but, collectively, we felt equal to any club,' wrote Major General Sir Richard Ruck, who played in the Cup Final of 1875. 'We were a veritable band of brothers.'

The Royal Engineers were already beginning to experiment with the passing style by the time of the FA Cup Final of 1872. But it was a tour of the North at the end of 1873 that proved a watershed. 'We were very much surprised that between one season and another they had considered "military football tactics",' wrote William Clegg, whose Sheffield team was hammered 4–0. S. W. Widdowson, whose Nottingham Forest team lost 2–1, claimed that 'combination was the key-note of the Engineers' success'.

Between 1871 and 1875 the Royal Engineers lost just three games out of 74, scoring 244 goals and conceding only 21. The record of Queen's Park was even more impressive: they didn't lose a game until 1876, nine years after their formation, and didn't even concede a goal until 1875. The obvious superiority of the new style of play was reflected most clearly in the annual England v. Scotland matches. In 1873 the Scots incorporated in the side a handful of exiles from Southern public school teams. The newcomers completely broke their rhythm and they lost 4–2. They didn't make the same mistake again. Thereafter the Scotland team was dominated by Queen's Park men, and between 1874 and 1886 they lost just once – 5–4 at the Oval in 1879 – winning nine and drawing three. As late as the international of 1882 Charlie Alcock commented that 'the disinclination to pass at the proper time settled England's chances as effectively as it has done from the very first of these International contests'.

So why were the old, Southern teams so slow to adapt to the new passing game? It's the great conundrum of public school football in the 1870s and 1880s, and it can be best disentangled by picking apart the career of one man: Arthur, later Lord, Kinnaird, the greatest footballer of the age.

Born in 1847, Kinnaird was the scion of an ancient Scottish family. He was raised in England and always lived there. But in 1887 he inherited twelve thousand acres of rambling estates in Perthshire connected to Rossie Priory, a grand aristocratic pile nestling in the Sidlaw Hills. He was also fabulously wealthy through banking interests and his father was a godson of the Duke of Wellington.

Kinnaird attended Eton and then went to Trinity College, Cambridge where he captained the Eton Football Club. When Wanderers toured the university in the autumn of 1867 he played both for and against them and he was soon turning out regularly for various London clubs, despite still being a student. Somehow he also found time to excel at tennis, swimming, sprinting, canoeing and fives.

By the time he graduated in 1869 he was already a member

of the FA Committee. And in the *Football Annual* of 1873 Charlie Alcock described him as 'the best player of the day, capable of taking any place in the field, is very fast and never loses sight of the ball, an excellent captain.' He scored the first of Wanderers' goals in their 2–0 victory over Oxford University in the 1873 FA Cup Final following a spectacular dribble and went on to play in nine FA Cup Finals for Wanderers and the Old Etonians (a record which still stands), picking up five winners' medals. With his flowing red beard he was football's answer to W. G. Grace and cut a distinctive figure, insisting on wearing a cricket cap and full-length white flannels, in the old Eton style, long after other players had switched to knickerbockers.

Kinnaird's responsibilities at his bank don't seem to have been particularly onerous – he was able, for instance, to go off on a lengthy tour of India during the 1872–73 season – and, like a number of his contemporaries, he could dedicate almost as much time to football as later professionals. Writing in old age, Charlie Alcock captured the breezy style of these early amateur sides:

> They were glorious days in the way of enjoyment, those of the late Sixties and throughout the Seventies. Then it was the game pure and unadulterated . . . I can vividly recall a visit I made to Gresham Street one Friday afternoon to get a goalkeeper to play against Queen's Park at Glasgow the following day.
> 'Can you play tomorrow, G—?' was my salutation.
> 'Yes,' was the reply: 'where?'
> When I responded 'At Glasgow,' he said cheerily:
> 'All right! When do we go?' It was then late in the afternoon.

'From Euston at eight.'

'I shall be there,' he returned with a smile.

The code by which a man was judged suitable or not for these teams was never explicitly stated, but widely understood. Alcock described the recruitment process for the Butterflies, a cricket team he helped run which was very much the summer equivalent of Wanderers: 'Someone would come into our study and say, "I say, you fellows, can I be a Butterfly?" Whereupon, if he was a good fellow, we used to say, "My dear fellow, you are one"; the election being instantaneous.' Alcock and his chums instinctively knew if a chap was one of them.

Like Alcock's, Kinnaird's playing style was robust. As early as 1861 his schoolmate at Eton, Alfred Lubbock, recalled him being 'hard as nails, never tiring, and capable of running the whole day if necessary'. Alcock was once forced to confront him during a match between Old Etonians and Old Harrovians at the Oval and demand, 'Now, Kinnaird, are we to have hacking or are we not?' 'Oh, let us have hacking, by all means,' replied Kinnaird with a grin. Kinnaird's mother once supposedly told Alcock she feared that 'one day Arthur will come home with a broken leg'. 'Do not fear,' replied Alcock, 'for if he does, it will not be his own.'

By the mid-1870s even the Eton- and Harrow-dominated teams Alcock and Kinnaird played for were beginning to adapt their style. The game was 'in transition', wrote Alcock in the *Football Annual* of 1875, and Wanderers began using the 2-2-6 formation from 1876. But they were behind the curve, and accounts of Wanderers' matches reveal they still relied heavily on a brutal, charging game. Playing alongside Kinnaird was

Alfred Lyttelton, another golden boy from Eton and Cambridge, who was notorious for his 'bunting'. His brother, Edward, described watching Lyttelton play a game against the Royal Engineers: 'I saw him make a run down from one end of the field to the other and floor four men on the way, the last two having charged him simultaneously from opposite sides, and both rebounding on their backs.' Lyttelton played the game 'in exactly the right state of irascibility', Edward wrote, 'except when a successful "bunt" dissolved him into a loud merry laugh, in which the prostrate victim not infrequently joined'. Lyttelton's style sounds positively terrifying. 'When things grew to be exciting his ardour waxed to a formidable heat, and he would come thundering down with the heavy knees far advanced and all the paraphernalia of a Homeric onset,' wrote Edward – a type of charge that was actually illegal, even in the 1870s.

The likes of Kinnaird and the Lyttelton brothers regarded their style of football as character forming. Their great concern as football moved away from the public schools in the 1860s and 1870s was that it was becoming less 'manly'. Paradoxically, this was partly to do with the switch from boys to adults. It was generally accepted that boys' games were rougher than men's, boys being more supple and resilient and better able to afford time off injured. But for the traditionalists there was something more pernicious at work, which was to do with the democratization of the game.

Although historians would later claim the public schools civilized football, when the rules were being debated in the early 1860s it was widely acknowledged that the public school games were more violent than the folk game. 'The savage "rouge" or the wild broken bully, would cause a vast sensation among our agricultural friends,' wrote an Old Etonian to *The Field* in October 1861. 'We cannot quite picture to ourselves John Bull, fresh from the plough, as post in a rouge, standing unmoved with the ball between his legs, to resist the approaching rush of the heavy brigade.' A couple of years later a correspondent from Sheffield warned that it was vital to outlaw hacking if 'agricultural labourers . . . and the operatives of some towns and villages' were to be attracted to the game.

The changes introduced since meant football had 'lost its zest', some felt. The offside rule in particular came in for stick. The old rule at Eton had 'made Eton football a synonym for all that is manly and straightforward in the game', wrote an Old Etonian in the *Football Calendar* of 1877–78. It had obliged forwards to charge through their opponents in a pack, rather than pass around them. But the new FA rule actively encouraged 'sneaking' and a player lurking close to the opposition goal was 'sure rather to come in for a cheer than the hiss he properly deserves'.

There was, then, an element of aristocratic disdain for the new, more subtle trends entering the game. For the first international against Scotland in 1872 the FA had selected Charles Clegg, a Sheffield man who was the only player in the side not to have been to a public school. Clegg was one of the leading footballers of the day and had begun to experiment with combination play in games with his brother, William, also a prominent player. But he found his team-mates reluctant to pass the ball, or indeed to speak to him at all. 'Every man seemed centred in himself,' he said later. 'I longed to be responsive. But my sensitive nature was chilled by the atmosphere of haughty indifference which pervaded our team. Under such circumstances, I could not play my game.'

In the late 1870s another Sheffield man, Billy Mosforth, became the first working-class footballer to play for England. He found his colleagues' reluctance to pass even more exasperating, and during the 1877 game against Scotland he finally exploded at Alfred Lyttelton. 'I am playing for my own pleasure, sir,' responded Lyttelton.

But the reluctance of the public school men to adapt to the new passing game reflected more than just snobbery and conservatism. To fully understand the sheer aggression of public school football in the mid-Victorian era we must probe the careers of men like Arthur Kinnaird off the pitch.

Kinnaird was intensely religious. It was a religious age, so in this he was not unusual. Of the 158 gentleman amateurs who played in the early FA Cup Finals sixteen went on to a career in the Church and many more were involved in religious causes. But Kinnaird had the wealth and power to promote his religious ideas and was a fervent evangelist. He was also an active Liberal, and much of his energy was dedicated to alleviating poverty. He, like many others, saw football and other outdoor sports as morally uplifting and was keen to extend the benefits enjoyed by public schoolboys to the working class. 'Manly outdoor sports not only develop the physical nature of men, but react in a pure and healthy way on their intellectual and moral characters,' he told workers on his estates in Scotland in 1900. With his old school chum Quintin Hogg he helped establish the London Polytechnic in the 1860s for the education of the poor. And in 1875 he was instrumental in setting up Hanover United for students there, a club which would play a key role in stimulating football in the capital. Kinnaird regularly turned out to play alongside the Poly boys until well into his forties.

None of which explains why he and his pals were such violent footballers. But if there was one thing that exercised Kinnaird more than poverty, it was sex. When John and Charlie Alcock were at Harrow in the 1850s the authorities were apparently indifferent to the frenzied orgies unleashed in the dorms each night, described so vividly by Addington Symonds. When a boy called Dering was caught sending a note to a handsome youth known as 'Leila' informing him he 'had a good bed ready' and inviting him to visit, the headmaster merely lectured the school on the inappropriateness of female nicknames. But in the 1860s and 1870s, as the reform movement gathered pace in the public schools and religious revivalism gripped the country at large, this changed. By the early 1880s 'social purity' organizations were sprouting like pimples on an adolescent's face, and wherever the fight against vice and depravity was at its fiercest Kinnaird was there in the thick of it, sword (or rather cheque book) in hand. He was president of the YMCA and later Lord High Commissioner of the Church of Scotland, and he bankrolled a whole range of groups, including the Pure Literature Society, the Central Vigilance Society for the Repression of Immorality, and the National Vigilance Association. This last, of which he was vice-president, was one of the most militant. In 1889 it rejoiced at getting jailed for three months the seventy-year-old English publisher of the 'obscene and lewd' novels of Emile Zola, Gustave Flaubert and Guy de Maupassant; it also campaigned fiercely against the writings of Rabelais and the novels of Balzac. In 1895 Kinnaird responded to the prosecution of Oscar Wilde with an impassioned plea at the Association's AGM for 'something further in the way of repression!'

Homosexuality, or 'beastliness' as it was known at public schools, was a major concern for these people. But what really terrified them was masturbation. It was blamed for almost every ailment that could afflict a young man, from epilepsy to curvature of the spine, and by the 1870s a vast body of pseudo-scientific literature had been produced justifying these views. 'Boys who indulge in these wrong acts invariably become weak and sickly, and unfit for playing games. They often die young or go mad or become idiotic,' the Social Purity Alliance told mothers in its booklet *Schoolboy Morality*. Dr Acton, in his *Functions and Disorders of the Reproductive Organs*, provided invaluable tips on how to spot the self-abuser: 'The pale complexion, the emaciated form, the slouching gait, the clammy palm, the glassy or leaden eye, and the averted gaze, indicate the lunatic victim of this vice.' One doctor was actually prescribing a terrifying implement called the 'spiked penile ring' to prevent unwanted night-time erections. (Acton had concluded that women, 'happily for them, are not very much troubled with sexual feeling of any kind', and they were largely spared the attentions of these quacks.)

Alfred Lyttelton's father packed each of his eight sons off to Eton with what must have been an excruciatingly embarrassing letter (he told them they must never mention it to him) warning against the perils of masturbation. 'This particular temptation can be resisted by anyone,' he wrote. He recommended 'plenty of healthy exercise and temperate habits . . . To go to bed rather tired and likely to sleep quietly is of great use.'

Alfred was later involved in the White Cross Society, which attempted to wean the working class off 'the solitary vice'. And Edward, who played alongside his brother in the Cup Final of 1876, became headmaster of Eton and wrote a series of pamphlets on the topic. Unusually, he felt physical exercise was of little help in combating so 'deadly' a habit, recommending instead 'cold baths' and warning, bizarrely, of the dangers of 'late suppers'. With that magnificent Victorian lack of self-awareness he urged masters to 'take in hand' the worst offenders.

But the general consensus was that healthy outdoor sports would reduce the sexual urge. The *Quarterly Journal of Education* argued as early as 1835 that 'A daily proper portion of bodily fatigue is the antidote to all wandering of the thoughts and dwelling on improper subjects.' And by the 1870s this was the standard view. Guilt-ridden and terrified of the spiked penile ring, it's scarcely surprising that teenage boys were huffing and puffing out on the playing fields, desperate to burn off surplus energy. And it's hard not to see this morbid fear and paranoia – from which the more libidinous working class was largely free – as contributing to the fevered atmosphere and extreme violence of public school football in the second half of the nineteenth century. It was *meant* to hurt.

Public schoolboys therefore continued to charge up and down the pitch like express trains, sending one another sprawling into the mud amid hearty guffaws long after everyone else had adopted a more scientific approach. What is surprising is that they got away with it for so long. Wanderers won the FA Cup five times between 1872 and 1878 and the other winners before 1883 – Oxford University, Royal Engineers, Clapham

Rovers, Old Carthusians (the Charterhouse Old Boys team) and Old Etonians (twice) – were all public schoolboys.

In part they were lucky. The Royal Engineers, with their passing style, might have dealt a more damaging blow to the old charging game if they hadn't suffered big-match nerves. Although they lost just three games between 1870 and 1875, all were FA Cup matches, two of them finals. They also lost the final of 1878. Wanderers, by contrast, seemed to rise to the big occasion.

The annual humiliation in the international game aside, the public schoolboys also managed to avoid playing the Scots too often. The story of how they did this is revealing. After their draw with Wanderers in the semi-final in 1872, Queen's Park struggled to find money to compete in the FA Cup. They again got a bye until the semi-final the following year but were forced to scratch and didn't enter the competition again until the 1880s. But they were keen to organize regular home and away games against Wanderers and the first of these took place in October 1875.

By this time Scotland had its own Football Association and Cup, both established in 1873. Rangers, Hibs and Hearts were all in existence, and there was a thriving football scene which was rapidly overtaking that in England. A total of forty-nine teams entered the Scottish Cup for the 1875–76 season, compared with just thirty-two for the FA Cup. Glasgow was buzzing with excitement ahead of the game with Wanderers and a crowd of more than ten thousand turned up at Queen's Park's new Hampden Park stadium, a figure which dwarfed anything so far seen in London. For more than an hour before the match 'crowds of people thronged into the park, and well laden buses and cabs kept rattling out of Crosshill Road', wrote the *Glasgow Herald*. Wanderers were captained by Charlie Alcock, and Arthur Kinnaird was in the side. Once more they were bigger and heavier than the Scots. But they were hammered 5–0, the Londoners' archaic 1-2-7 formation and heavy charging game no match for Queen's Park's slicker style. The Scots were 'very sorely tumbled about', said one report, but the English 'found it was no use knocking them over, as they just rolled on to their feet again'. Their star striker, James Weir, in particular delighted the crowd by shrugging off charges from both Alcock and Kinnaird, then calmly placing his foot on the ball before firing home. 'The enthusiasm was unbounded, many of the on-lookers, not content with cheering and waving their hats, tossed their head-gear into the air in the ecstasy of their admiration,' the *Glasgow Herald* added.

The return came at the Oval the following February. It was a bitterly cold day and a crowd of fewer than a thousand turned up. For the Scots the match was a national disaster, Queen's Park going down to their first ever defeat, 2–0. The club 'had met its Flodden', wrote its historian. Charlie Alcock, who was an umpire, described it as 'one of the most brilliant displays ever seen at the Association game'. But Scottish reports described the pitch as a quagmire and pointed out that their star, James Weir, played despite the fact he was injured.

In November 1876 revenge was taken with a spectacular 6–0 win, again at the Oval. Alcock wrote that Queen's Park 'passed, without exception, unselfishly and at the right time, and they never hesitated to transfer the ball when a chance was given'. The *Glasgow Herald* observed the Queen's Park men were 'very much superior in the difficult art of "playing together"' and commented bluntly that the 'English were somewhat fat, and decidedly short of practice'.

And there the sequence of games between the clubs came suddenly to a close. The Scots were keen to arrange a return game in Glasgow. But Wanderers dragged their feet. Sensing the problem might be financial, the Queen's Park secretary was instructed to offer, 'in as delicate a manner as possible', a sum of £60 to cover expenses (which they presumably hoped to recover in gate receipts). Without any delicacy at all Wanderers wrote back demanding £100, an extraordinary amount for the time: Queen's Park had managed to get down to London for the November 1876 game at a cost of just over £2 a man. Queen's Park dug their heels in and that was that. The two premier sides of the age never met again.

You can't help but feel the English simply didn't fancy it. Rail travel had made possible the take-off of a national football scene, but it was still an eleven-hour journey between London and Glasgow and, with hard seats and no restaurants, toilets or heating, early trains were far from luxurious. Writing to his cousin, Mary Gladstone (William Gladstone's daughter), Alfred Lyttelton described a trip to Scotland in August 1876 as 'nearer to physical pain than a very heavy kick on the leg at football, or a cricket ball in the eye'. Why put yourself through that simply to be belted by a bunch of diminutive Scots? Thereafter, the winners of the Scottish Cup regularly challenged the winners of the FA Cup, and always won. These games aside, matches between the Scots and Southern English teams were few and far between, and the public schoolboys were able to maintain their dominance of the domestic trophy.

But their days were numbered. New teams continued to rise

up closer to home. Most were middle-class sides, very much on the model of Queen's Park and the original Sheffield club. In Nottingham, Notts County had been formed in 1862 and Nottingham Forest in 1865. 'The County were . . . representative of the Shire and superior persons, who assumed that they were people of importance, while the Foresters were essentially a city or a town club which appealed more to the middle classes,' wrote a contemporary journalist. Stoke City were also formed in the mid-1860s, by Charterhouse Old Boys working for the North Staffordshire Railway Company. And 1875 saw the formation of Blackburn Rovers by a combination of public school and grammar school boys. The Wednesday in Sheffield were also part of this group, which represented a transitional stage between the old teams of Southern gentlemen and the working-class, professional clubs that were to come. Culturally, they aped the values of the older public school sides. But the bulk of their members had not been to public school and they played mostly in the new passing style. They were few in number, but the public schoolboys were aware of the steadily rising tide, progressing further each year through the rounds of the FA Cup.

Nottingham Forest and Blackburn Rovers were particularly strong. Forest were defeated in the semi-final in both 1879 and 1880, to the surprise of many. Then in 1882 Blackburn Rovers stormed through to the final, beating The Wednesday 5–1 in a semi-final replay. There they met Old Etonians, led by Arthur Kinnaird, now a grizzled veteran of thirty-five.

Rovers had enjoyed an extraordinary season. They were undefeated in 35 games and had scored 192 goals, conceding just 32. Like Queen's Park they had a club poet, and they were so confident of victory that he turned up at the Oval clutching numerous copies of his 'Ode to Victory' for sale after the game.

> All hail, ye gallant Rover lads!
> Etonians thought ye were but cads,
> They've found at football game their dads,
> By meeting Blackburn Rovers.

But on the day their football was no better than their poetry. Like so many teams since that have swept all before them, they wilted at the last. Charlie Alcock felt they were simply exhausted: that year, for the first time, the season had crept beyond the traditional 1 October – 31 March boundaries (instituted to protect the sacred cricket season). Alcock also criticized Rovers for overdoing the short-passing game 'to the point of extravagance in front of the opposition goal'. Old Etonians won 1–0 and Kinnaird, who'd played a 'truly fine game, his speed and tackling being superb', delighted the crowd by performing a handstand in front of the Oval pavilion at the end.

It was a gesture that captured the man and the era he dominated. And it was a last hurrah. The dam was about to break, and when it did the likes of Arthur Kinnaird would be swept away for ever.

FOLK FOOTBALL

Street football in 1721. The respectable classes saw football as barbaric and modern historians have followed their lead. But many smaller-scale games were surprisingly civilized.

The Shrove Tuesday game at Kingston, Surrey. These annual games often involved hundreds on each side and created chaos and mayhem. This image dates from 1846, the year the Shrove Tuesday game in Derby was repressed by the authorities.

PUBLIC SCHOOLS

Right: Harrow football First XI, 1867. Football found a refuge in the public schools when it came close to dying out among the common people in the middle of the nineteenth century.

Left: The Eton Field Game. Each public school played its own variation of football, and most were just as violent, if not more so, than the old folk game.

Left: The Wall Game at Eton. Goals were scored on average three times a century.

Below: Rugby was the only public school to develop a game which involved running with the ball ih your hands. It soon became the more popular of the two codes and Association football did not overtake it until the 1880s.

EARLY SIDES

Above: Forest Football Club in circa 1863. Charlie Alcock, later Secretary of the FA, stands in the middle, immediately behind the chair. His brother John is on his right in dark trousers.

Right: Another early London team, possibly the Crusaders. The bearded figure on the left is Arthur Kinnaird, who still holds the record for FA Cup Final appearances.

Below: An early Sheffield representative XI. Sheffield pioneered football in the north of England and was a key influence on the evolution of the early rules. Top left are the two Clegg brothers, Charles and William. Bottom right is Jack Hunter, who would later go on to captain the Blackburn Olympic side that won the FA Cup in 1883.

Arthur Pember, first President of the FA, disguised as a beggar during his subsequent career as a radical undercover journalist in America.

Illustration from *Beeton's Football*, the world's first football manual, published in 1866. Handling was still allowed at this time. 'A very serviceable "dodge",' *Beeton's* told its readers, 'and one very puzzling to the enemy, is to stop suddenly, and strike the ball backward with the hand between the legs.'

1870s

The very first international between England and Scotland, played at the West of Scotland Cricket Ground in Partick on 30 November, 1872. The Scots had adopted a cunning new tactic – passing. They were also among the first to head the ball.

Queen's Park with the Scottish Cup in 1874. Founded in 1867, they were the pioneers of the game north of the border and provided the bulk of the early Scottish teams. *Back row, left to right*: A. McKinnon, Dickson, Lawrie, Campbell, Neill. *Front row*: Leckie, Taylor, McNeil, Thomson, Weir, W. McKinnon.

The England team for the international against Scotland in 1876. This photo was only discovered in 2008. All were gentlemen amateurs. *Back row, left to right*: Field, Buchanan, Smith, Green, Maynard. *Front row*: Savage, Turner, H. Heron, Bambridge, F. Heron. *On floor*: Jarrett.

Football at the Oval – England v. Scotland, 1879. England won 5–4, their only victory against Scotland between 1874 and 1887. The Oval also hosted FA Cup Finals from 1872 until 1892.

Arthur Kinnaird. The top gentleman amateur of the 1870s played in full-length white flannels to the end of his career, in the old Eton style. He was later President of the FA from 1890 to 1923.

The father of modern sport – Charlie Alcock, at his desk at the Oval. Alcock devised the FA Cup, based on the Cock House competition at Harrow, his old school, and he held the FA together during the dispute over professionalism in the 1880s. He was also the driving force behind the first cricket test match played in England in 1880.

Blackburn Olympic, the first working-class side to win the FA Cup. They defeated
Arthur Kinnaird's Old Etonians 2-1 in 1883. *Back row, left to right*: Bramham
(Secretary), Warburton, Astley, Hacking, Astley, Yates, Gibson. *Middle row*: Beverley,
Hunter, Dewhurst, Ward. *Front*: Wensley?, Matthews.

The 1883 FA Cup Final at the Oval.

The Invincibles. Preston North End, double winners in 1888–89, pictured here in 1886. Billy Sudell, the chairman/manager and the inspiration behind the team, is given pride of place. Sudell was later arrested for embezzlement and falsification of accounts.

Jack Ross, captain of Preston North End. 'His teeth were discoloured, almost green near the gums, and he hissed through them as he played. He was [a] demon,' wrote the journalist Jimmy Catton.

'Darkie' Wharton, Preston's goalkeeper for the 1886–87 season and one of the first black players to play in England. 'Is the darkie's pate too thick for it to dawn upon him that between the posts is no place for a skylark,' wrote one newspaper.

This was indeed the Triumph of the Democracy!
Jimmy Catton, *The Real Football*

5

The Hole in the Wall Gang

Blackburn Olympic v. Old Etonians, FA Cup Final
Kennington Oval, 31 March 1883

HAD YOU FOUND YOURSELF WALKING DOWN KENNINGTON ROAD
once more, this time on the afternoon of 31 March 1883, you'd
again have been struck by the crowds making their way to the
Oval. By now you would probably be aware it was Cup Final
day. But there were subtle differences with the scene from
eleven years earlier.

The crowd was rather larger. And not all of them were quite
so well dressed. Amid the top hats there was now a smattering
of flat caps. Small, excited groups of men scurried between the
carriages, dressed in their Sunday best for the big occasion, but
in clothes of a rougher cut than the gents'. If you'd glanced
down you'd have noticed some were wearing clogs. They were

more raucous, and a little bleary, in some cases because they'd enjoyed a drink or two over lunch, but primarily because they'd spent the entire night travelling. Their accents betrayed them too. These men had come down from Lancashire, and not only were they Northern, they were unmistakably working class. Intrigued, you might have followed them and once more paid your shilling (no longer quite such a prohibitive price for working people) to get into the Oval, by this time effectively England's national stadium. It was run by the ubiquitous Charlie Alcock as secretary of Surrey County Cricket Club, who must have spent a lot of time writing letters to himself in his various capacities. Not surprisingly, those from the Football Association always received a favourable response from the Oval and the ground staged FA Cup Finals and internationals. It was also the home ground of a number of the Old Boys teams, and it hosted a range of other sports, including rugby, cycling and even baseball. In winter the pitch was often a quagmire, but on this day the weather was fine and the turf in good condition.

You'd have needed to be fairly aggressive to elbow your way to the front this time. There were around seven thousand people squeezed inside – still smaller than the crowds that turned out for football matches in Glasgow, but the largest attendance so far in the capital. A small stand had been erected opposite the pavilion especially for football matches, with covered seating for a few hundred people; it was in use for the first time this year. Alcock had also had small earth banks built up all round the perimeter to form a primitive terracing – the standard solution to rising crowds in early cricket and football stadiums. Every vantage point was occupied, and those local residents who'd gazed down, half interested, on the 1872 final may already have been making money hiring out their apartments to spectators.

Shortly before 3.30 the two teams trotted out and the clash of cultures this final represented was immediately apparent. In the light blue were the Old Etonians, the Cup holders, led as ever by Arthur Kinnaird, now thirty-six and ten years older than anyone else in his side. But it was their opponents who caught the eye. In Victorian Britain there was no cruder manifestation of social class than physical size, exposing the cruel inequalities in diet and standard of living. And the Etonians dwarfed their opponents.

The finalists this year were Blackburn Olympic, local rivals of Blackburn Rovers and very much their poor relations. The Olympic goalkeeper – the eccentric Tom Hacking, identifiable in photos by his bizarre tam-o'-shanter hat – was a dentist's assistant. Other than that, the team was solidly working class. There was Albert Warburton, team captain and full-back, who was a plumber; beside him in defence, Jimmy Ward, a cotton operative who'd turned eighteen just the week before, a celebrated athlete who performed feats for money and was said to be able to jump the Leeds–Liverpool canal; in the half-back line, William Astley, who kept a newsagent's, and tough little Tommy Gibson, an iron-moulder and the club's oldest serving player; among the forwards, Tommy Dewhurst and John Yates, both weavers, Jimmy Costley, a cotton operative, and Arthur Matthews, a picture-framer. There were also two outsiders, both from Sheffield: George Wilson, the team's centre-forward, and Jack Hunter, the engine of the side at centre-half, who had played seven times for England. Hunter doubled as the team's trainer and as a veteran of thirty-one was very much Kinnaird's counterpart. But while Kinnaird represented football's past, Hunter represented its future. His profession was listed as landlord of the Cotton Tree pub in Blackburn; Wilson's occupations were described as 'various'. In reality, both played football for a living.

'They looked a tiny set as they entered the field and few fancied that they would defeat the Etonians,' wrote one journalist. 'We should think that the Olympic averaged about 5 ft 6 in, and scaled about 10 and a half stones,' wrote another, 'while the Etonians were probably two or three inches taller, and from a stone to 21 lbs heavier per man.' It was a battle, he added, of 'the humble and the weak against the mighty and the strong'.

Olympic had been formed five years before from an amalgamation of two local neighbourhood sides. Their home ground was a sloping mudbath of a pitch behind the Hole i' th' Wall pub – so called because bootleg liquor used literally to be sold through a hole in the wall – which stood at the top of a windswept hill called Shear Brow, overlooking Blackburn's densely packed terraced houses and factory chimneys. Their rise had been almost as meteoric as Queen's Park's. But unlike the Scottish side they had not emerged miraculously from a footballing vacuum. They were the product of a vibrant football scene centred on the triangle between the cotton towns of Blackburn, Bolton and Preston which had already eclipsed Sheffield and was fast catching up with Glasgow. Olympic were not even regarded as the best of the local teams. Blackburn Rovers had beaten them four times the previous season and it had been a surprise when they defeated Accrington, another working-class team like themselves, in the first round of the Cup that year. So where had this, England's first working-class football culture of modern times, suddenly sprung from?

Football in Lancashire was born from two clubs: Darwen, created in 1870, and Turton, created in 1871. Both were the products of the sons of local mill-owners returning from Harrow and dragooning local villagers into a football team so that they could continue to play the sport. Darwen, located just south of Blackburn, was set up by the sons of Nathaniel Walsh, owner of the Orchard Mill. Turton, just north of Bolton, was established by the Kay family, who had made a fortune pioneering innovations in the flax-spinning industry and set themselves up as local squires. The Kays were 'loved by [the] tenantry', according to a sycophantic contemporary history, and took a paternalistic interest in club members, providing a 'reading room' for their self-improvement. Turton played Harrow rules in its early years.

Other elements of the local establishment in Lancashire were also keen to push football. Schools encouraged the sport. St John's in Blackburn, which Olympic's goalkeeper Hacking attended, was a particularly rich source of early footballers. The churches, keen advocates of the cult of muscular Christianity, were even more enthusiastic. Bolton Wanderers, originally established in 1874 as Christ Church FC, were one of numerous teams with a religious background (although they soon chafed at the control of the local vicar and broke their ties).

Many teams were funded by local mill-owners. Blackburn Rovers received generous backing from John Boothman, who also encouraged football among his own work force at Hollin Bank Mill. 'Councillor Boothman took out ten of his work-people ... to play a match against eleven workpeople from Messrs. Meadow's Bridge Mill,' reported the *Blackburn Times* in

November 1880. 'The jovial Town Councillor was to be seen keeping goal for his side, arrayed in velvet knickers and waist-coat, with a Turkish cap to crown all.' Olympic's own sugar-daddy was Sydney Yates, who owned an iron foundry in Birley Street close to Jack Hunter's Cotton Tree pub. These men stepped up their funding of football following a lengthy and very bitter textile strike in the spring of 1878, which was marked by rioting in a number of towns; it may be they saw the game as a useful distraction. That was certainly the view of many early socialists who tended to see football as a fiendish upper-class plot to divert the masses from revolution.

But the workers were nobody's fools and the rise of football in Lancashire was driven from below as well as from above. Lancashire, like Scotland and South Yorkshire, was an area where the old folk game had lingered longer than elsewhere. Darwen in particular was renowned as a footballing centre in the early nineteenth century, and as late as 1845 a visitor to the town commented on how, as soon as the lunchtime whistle sounded at the mills, the streets were full of 'young men and boys, dressed in fustian' kicking a ball about – their 'favourite sport'. It's unlikely that when, twenty-five years later, the young squire gathered round the local people and showed them a football he was introducing them to an entirely new game. Close analysis shows that the initiative for the host of school, church and works teams that sprang up in these years came as often as not from the members themselves as from middle-class benefactors.

This pattern of top-down, bottom-up development would soon be repeated elsewhere. Football had already filtered down the social scale in Glasgow. And from the Bolton–Blackburn–

Preston triangle it would spread through the English working class like a virus, first to the Black Country, then to the North-East, then to Liverpool, then to Manchester and finally to London. By the end of the 1890s it was the country's first truly mass sport.

One factor above all explains the extraordinary explosion in the popularity of football in the years after 1875: the Saturday half-holiday. Working hours had been edging downwards since the middle of the century and women and children in the textile mills had enjoyed a statutory two o' clock finish on Saturdays since 1850. But among adult men progress was patchy before the 1870s. Then, with the economy booming, and under pressure from the trade unions, employers caved in and, quite suddenly, between 1872 and 1874 the five-and-a-half-day week became the norm for the mass of British workers. There was now a window, outside the Sabbath, for organized recreation.

Working people were finally starting to reap the benefits of the industrial revolution in other ways too. Wages were rising, leaving just that little bit extra to spend on something other than basic necessities. Music halls took off, as did weekend excursions to the coast, made possible by the new railways. The working-class culture we would be familiar with from the first half of the twentieth century was taking shape, and Saturday afternoon at the football was a central part of this. Working people were also better fed. There is an air of listlessness in descriptions of pre-nineteenth-century sports. So many of them involved either sitting around doing ghastly things to animals or forcing animals to do ghastly things to each other – a lethargy that was the result no doubt of the dreadful, low-protein diet of the mass of the population. Now the workers had an appetite for more active sports, and there is an unmistakable sense of unleashed energy about these teams of feisty little canal-jumpers who suddenly came pouring out of the North and Midlands in the late 1870s and 1880s.

The take-off of football in Lancashire can be dated to a specific moment: the second half of the FA Cup quarter-final between Darwen and Old Etonians at the Oval on 13 February 1879. It was Darwen's second visit to London that year. In a previous round they had defeated a lesser-known public school outfit, the Remnants, 3–2, after which one of their small band of supporters, a woman carrying a baby, had been heard to mechanically repeat, 'Fancy a lot o' working lads beating a lot of gentlemen!'

Darwen turned up for the Old Etonians game wearing trousers cut off at the knee in place of knickerbockers and 'shirts . . . of all sorts', according to one spectator. 'The two men who wore "sweaters" were evidently the "Brummels" of the team,' he sneered (a reference to the famous Regency dandy Beau Brummel). A number of the players were wearing braces. Old Etonians, with Kinnaird at half-back, were overwhelming favourites, and in front of a crowd of just two hundred they raced to a 5–1 lead by half-time. But in the second half Darwen's superior fitness began to show. The score remained unchanged for half an hour, but then, in the last fifteen minutes, Darwen scored four times, their Scottish forward James Love equalizing with almost the last kick of the game.

Exhausted, Old Etonians declined extra time, somewhat ungallantly forcing Darwen to return to London for a replay. Much was made of the fact that they contributed £5 to their costs, which seems a paltry amount for such wealthy men. Darwen don't appear to have been enjoying much patronage from the Walsh family by this time: the trip was paid for by public subscription, consisting mainly of hundreds of tiny contributions from local working people.

The replay ended 2–2. This time Old Etonians agreed to extra time but this failed to break the deadlock and Darwen were forced to return to the Oval for a third match. Worn out by so much travelling (most of them, remember, were having to work full shifts in the cotton mills in between), they succumbed 6–2. But they'd put Lancashire football on the map. 'The pluck shown by the Darwen eleven . . . justifies the belief that Lancashire will soon be regarded as one of the chief strongholds of the dribbling game,' wrote Charlie Alcock in that year's *Football Annual*.

It was at this point that the local press in Lancashire suddenly began to pay attention to football. The following year a crowd of ten thousand turned out to watch the final of the Lancashire FA Challenge Cup between Darwen and Blackburn Rovers, which was rapidly becoming the first truly intense local rivalry in English football. The hillsides around were black with people enjoying a free view as Darwen won 3–0.

By this time the first murmurings of middle-class unease at the monster they had unleashed could be heard. In November 1880 an even larger crowd turned out to watch a friendly between Darwen and Rovers which ended in ugly clashes on and off the pitch. The trouble started after a vicious foul by Rovers player Fergie Suter, who had defected from Darwen shortly before, on his old team-mate Tom Marshall. Marshall told him 'not to do it again, or he might fare worse' (although you suspect not in quite those words) and then lifted Suter up by the legs and held him dangling in the air for some time with his head in the mud, prompting a pitch invasion. 'In the North of England . . . the game is often played in a very different spirit, and at times the anxiety to win leads to much unpleasantness,' wrote *The Field* shortly afterwards.

Darwen's defeat by Old Carthusians in the FA Cup semifinal of 1881 marked the high point of their brief period of glory; by 1883 Olympic had replaced them as Blackburn Rovers' chief local rivals. Jack Hunter, their trainer-cum-centre-half, who'd joined the previous summer from Sheffield Heeley, epitomized the new breed of Northern footballer.

Hunter's decision to cross the Pennines was controversial and was sparked, indirectly, by events six thousand miles away in South Africa. On the morning of 22 January 1879 a Zulu army of twenty-five thousand men had swooped down on a detachment of fewer than a thousand British troops camped at the base of Isandlhwana mountain and all but wiped them out. In the hours that followed a smaller Zulu force laid siege to the British border post at Rorke's Drift, an event immortalized in the film *Zulu* starring Michael Caine. The British sent reinforcements and the Zulus were defeated at the Battle of Ulundi six months later. But the war left close to two thousand British dead.

In Sheffield a bunch of patriotic footballers decided to do something for the widows and orphans. That November they organized a charity game against a Sheffield representative XI, the twist being that they played the game dressed as Zulu warriors in black jerseys and stockings, with feathers round their heads, beads around their necks and their faces blacked.

They even brought along shields and Zulu spears recovered from the battlefields of South Africa, although these were left on the touchline before the game began. They took Zulu names too, and among them was Jack Hunter, or rather Ngobamalrosi. The game against the Sheffield XI drew two thousand people and ended in a 5–4 victory, and over the next few months the 'Zulus' toured the North playing a number of other exhibition games.

By the start of 1880 the Sheffield FA had begun to take a dim view of these frolickings. Its secretary, William Peirce Dix, had decided it 'was calculated to degrade the game and bring discredit upon those connected with it'. More importantly, he suspected 'that these players were receiving payment for playing', violating their amateur status. He imposed a ban, and when, the following Christmas, the Zulus defied this the entire team was suspended, including Hunter.

The suspensions came at a vital stage of the season and passions were soon running high. A few weeks later Peirce Dix had the misfortune to referee a local cup semi-final in which Sheffield Heeley, missing Hunter and another player, lost 7–2 to The Wednesday. He was hooted and whistled (which may partly have been to do with his refereeing style: he tended to be somewhat stationary, and unfurled an umbrella when it rained) and at the end the crowd invaded the pitch and he was jostled and kicked. Eventually the Zulus apologized and were reinstated, but the affair soured relations between Hunter and the football establishment in Sheffield and he made the move to Olympic at the end of the following season.

In Blackburn he was soon shaking things up. Hunter was

responsible for introducing a radical innovation at the club – training. This was something rarely indulged in by the old public school teams; indeed it was seen as positively unsporting by most of them. *Beeton's Football*, the world's first football manual, published in 1866, had merely recommended that players abstain 'from food and habits which are injurious to the wind and general powers of endurance'. It was assumed playing itself provided sufficient physical exercise and attitudes had not changed by the early 1880s. This was one of the reasons Old Boys teams frequently lost to the First XIs at the public schools, who maintained ferocious levels of fitness as a result of their daily, compulsory games.

A number of the newer teams held practice sessions. But Hunter took things to a different level. Prior to the FA Cup semi-final against Old Carthusians he whisked the entire team off to Blackpool for a week of intensive preparation, paid for by Sydney Yates. The schedule was scarcely exhausting:

6 am – Glass of port wine and two raw eggs followed by three
  mile walk along the sands.
Breakfast – Porridge and haddock.
Dinner – Two legs of mutton (one for each end of the table).
Tea – More porridge and a pint of milk each.
Supper – Half a dozen oysters each.

Between times they took light exercise, and there were also a couple of friendlies against a local Blackpool team. The purpose was as much to keep the players out of the pub as anything. But it was novel enough that 'a great many folks . . . thought it unwise', according to the *Blackburn Standard*. 'They are afraid . . . that they may overdo the training and become stale before the week is out.'

Hunter's tactics were vindicated. Against Old Carthusians in Manchester on 17 March they romped home to an unexpected 4–0 win in a match delayed by half an hour because no one had thought to bring a ball. The *Athletic News* dubbed the game 'Patricians and Plebeians'. The Charterhouse team, it said, 'were all educated gentlemen and undoubted "swells" when compared to their rough and ready opponents, every man of whom has inherited the primeval curse and has to earn his bread by the sweat of his brow'. But the Olympic side, it observed, although smaller, was more skilful. Other newspapers commented on their fitness. The *Sporting Chronicle* thought the Lancastrians still 'as fresh as newly painted butterflies' at the end.

It was only now that people really began to sit up and pay attention to Olympic. And it was observed that they had introduced another key innovation, a tactical one that also coincided with Jack Hunter's arrival at the club: they'd pulled back one of the two centre-forwards from the standard six-man forward line and converted him into a centre-half, Hunter himself filling the position.

This new 2-3-5 formation was one a number of Northern teams, including Darwen, The Wednesday and Nottingham Forest, had been experimenting with since 1879. It marked the final stage in a slow-motion readjustment that had been going on ever since the introduction of the three-man offside law in 1866. But it had never before been used in a Cup Final. It would soon be adopted by all teams and would remain the standard system for forty years, until the introduction of the modern offside law in 1925 prompted Herbert Chapman to withdraw the centre-half still further and convert him into a centre-back (although the old name has lingered).

This, then, was how Olympic lined up as the clock ticked towards 3.30 at the Oval on 31 March 1883. They were fresh and 'in the very pink of condition', according to *The Sportsman*. Hunter had again taken them off to Blackpool for a week beforehand and they had travelled down to London on the Thursday, avoiding Rovers' mistake the previous year of coming down on the Friday and leaving themselves tired for the final. The Olympic team had spent the Friday sight-seeing and Hunter had treated himself to a new top hat.

As the Old Etonians watched the sinewy Northerners limbering up in front of them they were astute enough to realize they were faced with an entirely new force in football. But it was a challenge they were resolved to confront in their traditional manner – by attempting to knock them over.

The match marked the end of an era in a number of ways. At a meeting of the English, Scottish, Welsh and Irish FAs (the latter two established in 1876 and 1880) the previous December the modern throw-in had been introduced. Until then throw-ins could be taken one-handed. But the rule change didn't come into effect until the following season for domestic games, and in the 1883 final, for the last time, specialists like Arthur Kinnaird were still launching one-handed howitzers into the goalmouth from huge distances, which made the game much faster.

Like Wanderers eleven years earlier, Old Etonians came tearing out of the traps. They had doubtless read reports of Olympic's fitness in the semi-final and were keen to finish them off before the Lancastrians' superior condition began to show.

There was 'bully after bully in front of the visitors' goal', reported *The Sportsman*. The Etonian forwards Goodhart, Macaulay and Dunn all came close as the public schoolboys exploited their greater size to the full. Goodhart was described as 'a very heavy and very bony man, who, without even appearing to charge, simply ran over anyone who came in his way'. The *Blackburn Standard* described Dunn as being like a 'steam engine', ploughing repeatedly into the Olympic back line. 'No matter how many of his opponents he had to face he would not pass the ball.'

The Etonians employed a type of flying volley, cultivated in the Field Game, which was executed at full speed with both feet off the ground, and the Blackburn men frequently found themselves staring at the oncoming soles (still mercifully unstudded) of their opponents' boots. Olympic were wearing shin pads (another Northern innovation, worn outside the socks and scorned by the public school men) but these provided little protection against this type of assault. Their right-winger, Matthews, received a nasty kick in the jaw and played the rest of the game with a badly swollen face. The centre-forward, Wilson, identified as Olympic's danger man and closely marked by Kinnaird, soon joined him in the ranks of the walking wounded.

After half an hour the ball broke from a ferocious bully in the Olympic goalmouth, involving every single one of the Etonian forwards, and Goodhart slotted it home. Olympic managed to hold on without conceding a second till half-time (which lasted just a few minutes and was spent on the pitch), but after the break the Etonians resumed the assault. Hacking, just five feet six inches tall and known as the 'india-rubber man' because of his versatility, performed heroics in the Blackburn goal.

Then two events occurred in quick succession which transformed the game (newspaper reports differed over which came first). Dunn, the Etonian forward, was brought down by young Jimmy Ward at the end of one of his steamrollering runs and didn't get up again, having to be carried off. And Olympic scored, the injured Matthews firing home a powerful shot from the right wing.

The Etonians had failed to deliver the knock-out blow, and now they were wilting, badly. Goodhart went down with cramp and Macaulay was also injured. There were no substitutes allowed. Only the veteran Kinnaird and the full-back, French, seemed still able to 'raise a gallop'. Olympic poured forward. Now their passing game came into its own. Like most of the Northern teams, Olympic played in the Scottish style, but with a variation. The journalist William Pickford, later a president of the FA, described it as a combination of 'short passing and dribbling with long passing from wing to wing'. It was these sweeping cross-field balls which particularly confused the Etonians and they found themselves pulled out of position, puffing and panting after the ball as it sailed back and forth over their heads. 'Their tactics simply wore the Etonians off their legs,' Pickford wrote.

There was a hard edge to Olympic's game as well. Though small, the Lancashire men could give as good as they got and were soon charging into their tiring opponents with gusto. 'The sinewy plebeians played skittles with the much more formidable looking sons of the aristocracy,' wrote one journalist. Over the next few days the metropolitan press, apparently blind to the assaults on Matthews and Wilson in the first half, were positively spluttering with outrage at the performance of Olympic in the second period. 'Their play . . . was very rough, and on more than one occasion did the spectators (even their own friends) express their disapprobation at the charging from behind, holding, and tripping tactics employed,' wrote *Bell's Life*. Its reporter claimed he had heard a 'burly Lancastrian' comment, 'T'lads moost ha' made a mistake, and think they were playing Roogby Union.' *The Field* said it was only Olympic's 'rougher kind of play' that had thrown the Etonians off their game. Even the *Manchester Guardian* felt it was 'to be regretted that the Blackburn men fouled them so repeatedly'. More than twenty years later Kinnaird wrote, 'I carry their marks to this day.' You sense there was an edge to this game, which most observers agreed was not a footballing classic.

Exhausted, battered and bruised, the Etonians somehow held on. Then, with seconds remaining, Kinnaird brought the ball out of defence, exchanged passes with Bainbridge, and delivered a long ball into the path of Macaulay. Although limping, he was clean through. The Etonians had always had a reputation as a lucky side, and just for a moment it looked as if they were about to pull off another unlikely victory. But once more the goalkeeper Hacking came to Olympic's aid, and moments later the final whistle blew.

Kinnaird's men flopped down on the grass, utterly spent. They were in a 'truly pitiable' state, wrote the *Blackburn Standard*, and with Olympic still full of bounce it was clear to everyone present that extra time would be a mere formality. But it was not until ten minutes from the end that the *coup de grâce* was finally delivered. Dewhurst took the ball down the right and crossed it into the box where Jimmy Costley, the smallest man on the pitch, poked home from close range. 'Then ensued a scene . . . without parallel in the football world,' wrote William Pickford. 'The Olympic and their supporters went wild with excitement.'

The match ended 2–1 and the Blackburn supporters poured on to the pitch. In previous years the Cup had always been handed to the winning captain at a private dinner some weeks later. Now, for the first time, the presentation formed the climax of the match itself. But first the players retired to the cricket pavilion to wash and get changed and the crowd had to wait patiently while a table was prepared in front of the grandstand where Colonel Marindin, the old Royal Engineers captain and now president of the FA, would perform the ceremony.

When finally the Blackburn players appeared, scrubbed and clean and dressed in their Sunday best, they were met with cheers from their own supporters but boos and hisses from the cockneys and college boys in the crowd – much to the disgust of the provincial press. Colonel Marindin made a gracious if slightly rambling speech, complimenting Olympic on becoming the first Northern team to win the Cup, and expressing the hope they would make a gallant defence of it the following year. The Blackburn team had taken seats around the table and, in mid-speech, Marindin leant across and handed the captain, Warburton, the Cup with the words, 'Here it is.' In this slightly low-key way, history was made.

The Blackburn team made their way from the Oval to St James's restaurant in Piccadilly where the town's political establishment had laid on a sumptuous banquet. The players themselves declined to make speeches, but there was much collective back-slapping from Blackburn's industrial and political elite. 'This has not been a match between two teams who have had equal advantages,' said the local Conservative MP, William Coddington. 'It has been a match today between gentlemen of undoubted position on the one side – gentlemen who have everything they want to assist them – and of working men on the other (loud cheers). The working men of Lancashire have proved themselves the best football players in England.' But he also urged the players to remain sober and 'keep the honour you have this day acquired . . . London is a very seductive place and probably many of you have seldom, if ever, visited it before'.

In Blackburn there were no such inhibitions. Updates on the score had been delivered by telegram to Hunter's pub, the Cotton Tree, every ten minutes. After Blackburn equalized large crowds began to gather in the street, and when news finally came through of the team's victory there were wild celebrations lasting till late in the night. The team returned home two days later and it seemed the whole town turned out to greet them at the station. A huge cheer went up as the train drew in and the players paraded through the streets in a wagon drawn by eight horses, accompanied by three brass bands playing 'See the Conquering Hero Comes' and 'For He's a Jolly Good Fellow'.

At the centre of all the hysteria was the FA Cup itself, held aloft by Warburton. Some were a little disappointed. It was just eighteen inches high and had cost the FA only £25 back in 1872 – a reflection partly of the Association's poverty in those days, and partly of the public schoolboys' dislike of show and gaudiness. The Lancashire FA's own Challenge Cup, for which the local millocracy had stumped up £160, was far more impressive. 'Is that t'Coop?' shouted one man in the crowd. 'Why, it's like a tea kettle.' 'Ey, lad,' replied Warburton, 'but it's very welcome in Lancashire; it'll have a good home and it'll ne'er go back to Lunnon.' Since this particular version of the Cup was stolen in 1895, he turned out to be right.

In London, meanwhile, a post-mortem was underway. The Southern press was not only critical of Olympic's physical tactics, but also of their trip to Blackpool before the game. 'We must say that going into actual training was never contemplated by those who initiated the Cup competition,' wrote *The Field*. The *Eton College Chronicle* felt it was 'strange that a football eleven composed of mill-hands and working men should be able to sacrifice three weeks [an exaggeration] to train for one match, and to find the means to do so too' – a clear insinuation that Olympic were not true amateurs. It said Old Etonians had been too casual; 'It was their very confidence that lost them the match. Had they only been non-favourites the result would have been different.' But a correspondent to the *Chronicle* was more perceptive: 'Some of the chief points necessary to make good players at the Association game are palpably wanting in Old Etonian elevens, notably unselfish "passing",' he wrote. Tellingly, the *Chronicle* revealed that, twenty years on from the formation of the FA, many members of the Old Etonians club were still not entirely familiar with Association rules and did not greatly care for them.

As for Arthur Kinnaird, he was gracious in defeat. Man of the match for the Etonians and a powerhouse until the very end of extra time, despite his age, he afterwards acknowledged that his side had taken 'a fair and honourable beating'. As the sun set 'on that last day of March in 1883 he and his team-mates slipped quietly out of the Oval and into history. No team of gentleman amateurs would ever again appear in the FA Cup Final.

*Preston are all professionals, but if you refuse to legalize them
they will be amateurs. We shall all be amateurs,
and you cannot prove us otherwise.*
Billy Sudell, FA meeting, 19 January 1885

6

Billy Sudell and the
Revolution of 1885

Preston North End, 1880–85

ONE DAY IN 1875 A SMALL, SPRIGHTLY FIGURE HOPPED OFF THE
train at Preston and, suitcase in hand, stepped out into the
bustle of the town centre and a new life. His name was Jimmy
Catton, and he was just fifteen. He was a Southerner, born in
Greenwich. But the North would be his home for the next three
decades and he was about to take a ringside seat for the rise of
one of the most remarkable teams in British football history.

Catton was no sportsman. Just five feet tall, he soon acquired
a distinctive, plump, football-like shape. But he was part of a
new breed – the sports journalist. Until the 1870s sports
coverage in Britain was dominated by papers such as *Bell's Life
in London and Sporting Chronicle* and *The Field*, which

described itself as 'The Country Gentleman's Newspaper'. Coverage of football was squeezed between page after page of hunting, fishing, racing and cricket. The football reports they did carry were generally contributed by participants, often provoking heated correspondence from opponents disputing their version of events, including, sometimes, the score.

The year of Jimmy Catton's arrival in Preston saw the birth of an entirely new type of paper, a weekly called the *Athletic News* which, in winter, dedicated itself primarily to football. Published in Manchester, it had a circulation of close to two hundred thousand by the mid-1890s and soon faced competition from other similar papers, like the *Football Field*, published in Bolton from 1884. The mainstream press was also dedicating more and more space to the sport, and from the early 1880s Saturday-night specials began to appear in a number of towns, carrying football results from around the country. Initially some papers used homing pigeons to gather local scores; others used messenger boys, dashing through the streets on their bicycles. But the introduction of the telegraph in the mid-1880s, and later the telephone, transformed the speed with which results could be reported, and in the absence of TV and radio, the Saturday night 'pink 'uns' and 'green 'uns' – sometimes written in local dialect – were awaited by crowds at newsagents.

Catton was on his way to take up an apprenticeship at the *Preston Herald*, where he would work at first as a general reporter. He later recalled the great textile strike of 1878, 'when Dragoons and Lancers were patrolling high roads in Lancashire', as the most terrifying experience of his career. But he quickly began to specialize in football and cricket, assuming the nom de plume Tityrus. He eventually rose to become editor of the

Athletic News and the most influential football journalist of the early twentieth century.

Where Catton went to school is unknown, and he had clearly not gone on to university. But he was well educated and, in the style of the day, liked to pepper his football reports with both classical and Shakespearean references. Describing a local derby in Nottingham in 1890 he wrote:

The fierce partisans of each side rubbed their shoulders together, and as I looked round the parallelogram the words of Hecate, in *Macbeth*, were brought vividly to mind:

> Black spirits and white,
> Red spirits and grey,
> Mingle, mingle, mingle
> You that mingle may!

And by the standards of the time, his style was positively chatty.

Once settled in Preston, Catton soon moved into the orbit of a group of enthusiastic young sportsmen who played for the North End Club. Initially established as a cricket team in the early 1860s, by the late 1870s it was diversifying into rugby and athletics and at the start of the 1880–81 season it set up an Association football side for the first time. Preston North End, as they soon became known, were thrashed 6–0 by Turton and 16–0 by Blackburn Rovers in that first year. But they made remarkable progress, and in the 1882–83 season they lost just three games out of 35, scoring 211 goals and conceding 61. By the summer of 1883 they were generally recognized as the strongest team in the town.

There was clearly an energy buzzing away at the heart of Preston North End. Like Blackburn Rovers, the club had been established by the well-to-do sons of local businessmen. But it had an anti-elitist ethos. It kept its annual subscription low and actively set out to attract the local working class, both as players and spectators.

Dominating the club was one individual, Billy Sudell, its chairman since 1874, who quickly became a close friend of Catton's. Born in 1850 and privately educated at a Cheshire boarding school, Sudell came from the middle ranks of society. His father ran a cotton warehouse and was part of the new managerial class which had sprung up in the industrial North as a buffer between the factory owners and their work force. As a child Billy played with the children of the upper class (he would always have the knack of making useful connections); at the age of twelve he skated the length of the frozen Preston–Lancaster canal in the company of W. Ashworth, who went on to become a key figure in the elite Preston Cricket Club. But he started his working life as a humble cashier for the Goodairs, one of the great cotton families of Preston.

'A good-looking, nicely-built, athletic young man' according to Catton, Sudell possessed enormous drive and ambition. In his job he displayed such financial acumen – he was said to be able to add up three columns of figures simultaneously – that he quickly rose to become general manager of the Goodairs' two mills. He was also active in the Liberal Party and, encouraged by the Goodairs, joined the local Volunteer Force, forerunner of the Territorial Army. By 1881 he was already a lieutenant and later became a major, the title by which he was often known in football circles. Both the Liberal Party and the

Volunteers provided him with a valuable opportunity for networking, and Preston North End served a similar purpose. He was a genuinely enthusiastic sportsman and played rugby, cricket and football for the club. But above all it gave him a chance to cut a figure in the town, and he drove the club forward relentlessly. 'Everyone knew Billy Sudell, the life and spirit of the North End,' wrote Jimmy Catton.

Almost from the first Preston North End was a money-making enterprise. Sudell had negotiated the hire of their Deepdale ground as early as 1875, and the switch from rugby to football occurred because Sudell had observed the financial success enjoyed by Darwen, Bolton Wanderers and Blackburn Rovers just a few miles to the east. In the summer of 1883, with domination of the Preston football scene achieved, Sudell was determined to take the club to the next level, and he made a momentous decision: to create the world's first unashamedly professional football team.

The payment of players had been creeping into the game since the mid-1870s as attendances took off. It was an insidious process which began with the remuneration of expenses, progressed to the payment of wages for time lost at work, and then to the offer of employment at local factories and workshops to encourage players to turn out for a particular team. The line between being paid to play football and being paid to do a not particularly onerous job, with plenty of time off in which to play football, was obviously a thin one. But these arrangements could easily be hidden. It was only when clubs began to import players from other regions that it became obvious what was happening and objections began to be raised.

The early 'professionals', in the sense of men who travelled for financial reasons to play football, were almost all from Scotland, where the game had taken off among the working class just that bit earlier than in England. The first was probably James Lang, a shipyard worker from Glasgow, who came south to play for The Wednesday in Sheffield at the start of the 1876–77 season. He was given a job at a local knife-making firm but 'his time was chiefly devoted to football and reading the news of the day in the papers', according to The Wednesday's first historian. 'I am not going to say that I crossed the border to play for nothing, because you would not believe me if I did,' Lang later confessed in an interview. He also revealed that he had played his entire career half blind having lost an eye in an industrial accident on the Clyde in 1869 – a fact he always somehow managed to conceal.

Lang was one of the Sheffield Zulus, alongside Jack Hunter. He escaped suspension, but the firm line taken by the Sheffield Football Association over that affair, combined with the comparatively small size of the local football scene, meant the mass importation of players never really took off in Sheffield.

It was Lancashire that became the seed-bed of professionalism. The first Scottish 'professors', as they were known, to emigrate to the county were two Partick players, Fergie Suter and James Love, both of whom played for Darwen against the Old Etonians in the epic Cup ties of 1879. Suter was a stonemason and was given a job locally. But, according to Jimmy Catton's wry account, he discovered 'that the stone was much harder than he had been accustomed to in Scotland, that his hands and arms were swelling, and that he must have a rest'. He and Love did little but play football. When Suter later defected to Blackburn Rovers he was said to have been given a sweetener of £100.

Suter and Love were followed by others, and the trickle soon became a flood. Clubs took little trouble to conceal the fact they were paying players. 'Football player (a good full-back) wanted for a club in Northeast Lancashire, to act as captain' ran an advert in *The Scotsman* in October 1882 – 'To a really good man . . . who can teach well, liberal wages will be given.' A month earlier the *Athletic News* had suggested that Bolton Wanderers should 'now wear kilts' and change their name to 'Caledonians', there were so many Scots in the side. By 1884 there were fifty-five Scottish players in England, almost all of them in Lancashire, and that year they gathered together to organize a Christmas party for themselves. These men played a key role in spreading the Scottish passing game through northern England.

Inevitably the Scottish clubs were none too happy to see their players poached. Then, as now, antagonism was focused on the role of agents. 'What Scot worthy of the name would be so base as to deliver a fellow-countryman into abject relations of total humiliation and subservience?' thundered the newspaper *Scottish Sport*. The fact that many men were lured south with the offer of a job as landlord in a pub fuelled the resentment. Football was 'a wile of the serpent', declared one Free Church of Scotland minister. But the logic of the market was too strong to resist.

When Billy Sudell conceived his grand design for Preston North End in the summer of 1883 it was towards Scotland that he looked. But rather than turn to Glasgow and the mill towns and mining villages around, already being exhaustively plundered by the other Lancashire sides, his main focus was Edinburgh. Here his connection with Jimmy Catton came into play. In the composing room at the *Preston Herald* were two brothers from Edinburgh, Tom and Jock McNeil. Jock had played for Hearts, and they now became Sudell's link men with the football scene in the Scottish capital.

His first signing was his most important: Jack Ross, the twenty-year-old captain of Hearts, who crossed the border on 17 July 1883 and quickly became the powerhouse of the team. As late as 1926 Jimmy Catton regarded Ross as the greatest full-back he had ever seen, and there is an unmistakable whiff of Roy Keane about contemporary descriptions of him. He was a quality footballer and a deep thinker about the game. But he also possessed a ferocious temperament and could be a terrifying opponent.

In one match against Blackburn Rovers he developed a grudge against Rovers' Jimmy Brown and the entire crowd could hear him howling 'dire threats' against him as he pursued him about the pitch. He finally caught up with him shortly before the end and Brown did not play again for two months. The secretary of Everton, whom Ross played for briefly later in his career, described him as 'an unfair if not cruel player, and more liable to bring disgrace than honour to his team'. According to Catton, Ross's 'teeth were discoloured, almost green near the gums, and he hissed through them as he played. He was [a] demon.'

But other descriptions stressed his speed and the quality of his passing. 'Ross was probably the best full-back that ever lived,' wrote one journalist in 1906, 'because he not only could do everything to perfection that a full-back ought to do, not merely because he knew everything that a back ought to know, but because he had the faculty of winning matches. He possessed the indefinable something, that magic quality which, for lack of a better word, we call genius.'

He was followed at the start of the 1883–84 season by Geordie Drummond – 'a wonderfully clever player anywhere . . . a trickster with his feet', according to Catton – and Sandy Robertson, another hard man, both poached from Edinburgh St Bernard's on the recommendation of Ross. Then came David Russell from Stewart Cunningham, who combined football with a career as a music hall comedian; Jack Gordon from Port Glasgow Athletic, a great winger and fine header of the ball; Johnny Graham from Ayrshire, a tough and reliable left-half; and Sam Thomson from Lugar Boswell, a stylish left-winger.

It was said Sudell could judge the quality of a player by watching him kick a sardine can. In a matter of just a few months he assembled the nucleus of a team that would stay together for almost a decade and become perhaps the greatest football side Britain saw until the rise of Arsenal in the 1930s.

The task was completed with the signing of Jack Ross's younger brother, Jimmy, and John Goodall, who would form a prolific strike partnership. While Jimmy Ross shared his brother's temper and was 'cunning as a monkey', Goodall was a gentle, mild-mannered man and a wonderfully intelligent footballer who would become the most important member of the team after Jack Ross. There was just one prominent amateur in the side, the inside-left Fred Dewhurst, who was a schoolmaster at the local Catholic grammar school and one of the few Prestonians. As was typical of amateurs from the more genteel classes, his style lacked the subtlety of his professional teammates. Catton described him as 'a big, vigorous . . . player and talented, but he had not the science of his colleagues . . . He could simply walk over his opponents – and did.'

All were officially amateurs. 'We were supposed to have trades of course,' Drummond recalled later. 'I was reckoned to be a painter, Jack Ross did a bit of slating, and Jimmy Ross a bit of plumbing . . . But work never interfered with football. We could always get off when we liked – when we did work.' Sandy Robertson, supposedly a decorator, spent ten leisurely months doing up the house of a local supporter, which also served as free lodgings for new arrivals from Scotland. The imports were paid between £1 and £2 a game.

Catton recalled watching a game at Notts County in 1885 where a 'young swell' turned to his friend and said, 'What a stwange accent these Lancashaw fellahs have!' His elder companion answered, 'Very stwange. It's awfully like Scotch!' The crowd barracked Preston for their dependence on Scottish mercenaries, but the players were indifferent, Geordie Drummond dancing a Scottish reel with a team-mate 'to show that the remarks of the crowd had no effect on them'.

Sudell's strategy was soon paying dividends. As early as September 1883 Preston defeated Turton 6–0. 'So disgusted were some of the Turton "lady" spectators that they threw off their shawls and . . . let the players know the power of their tongues,' reported the *Preston Herald*. That autumn they beat both Wednesbury Old Athletic (a leading Black Country team) and West Bromwich Albion – their first significant victories against non-Lancashire opposition. And by the New Year they had progressed to the fourth round of the FA Cup.

Their opponents in the cup were Upton Park, a team of London-based public school men. It was this game that was to change the face of football. It was played at Deepdale on 19 January 1884 and drew a crowd of over ten thousand. The Preston ground at this time contained just two small stands down one side of the pitch with the rest enclosed by shallow terracing. It was packed to bursting. The club put up canvas screens to prevent people getting a free view, but many still climbed trees around the ground. Preston scored after just three minutes and looked set to run away with the game. But early in the second half Upton Park equalized and, after the referee disallowed what appeared to be a perfectly good Preston goal, the match went to extra time. Upton Park packed their goalmouth and, to the fury of the crowd, Preston had a second apparently valid goal disallowed two minutes from time. The game ended 1–1 and Sudell's team prepared for a replay.

The bombshell fell the following morning. Preston received a letter from Charlie Alcock at the FA, dated 18 January, the day before the game. 'I beg to inform you,' wrote Alcock, 'that I have this morning received a protest from the Upton Park Club against your club on the ground of professionalism. It will be placed before the committee at their next meeting.' Preston were accused of violating the FA's rule 15: 'Any member of a club receiving remuneration or consideration of any sort above his actual expenses, and any wages actually lost by any such player taking part in any match, shall be debarred from taking part in either Cup, Inter-Association, or International contests and any club employing such player shall be excluded from this Association.'

The protest was something of a mystery. Upton Park denied that they had lodged it. When Sudell and other members of the Preston committee appeared before the FA the following week

'the Upton Park officials showed them every kindness and consideration, and expressed their regret that they had been made
the channel' for the complaint. It may have come from a
Scottish club, resentful at Preston's endless poaching of their
players, or, more likely, a local Lancashire rival. Sudell was
grilled for an hour and a half in closed session and it quickly
became clear a leading FA official had been busy collecting
evidence against Preston in Scotland for some time before the
Upton Park game. Sudell won admiration by frankly admitting
that Preston imported players and found them jobs – although
he disputed that this contravened rule 15 – and was praised by
Major Marindin, the president of the FA, for his conduct. But
Preston were found guilty and thrown out of the FA Cup,
although the committee drew back from fully implementing
rule 15 and expelling them from the Association.

The move caused outrage in Lancashire. If Preston were
guilty, so were almost every other major Lancashire team, if not
to quite the same extent. A correspondent to the *Preston Herald*
claimed Burnley were employing eight imported players,
Halliwell ten and Bolton Wanderers fourteen. Sudell and the
Preston committee felt 'that whoever prompted the action
against North End [was] a contemptible fellow', according to
the *Herald*, and they were determined that 'come what will, the
English Cup . . . shall find [its] way to the proud town'. The fact
that the FA refused to release the evidence against Preston only
compounded the anger in Lancashire. 'Our notion of what
constitutes fair play may differ from those held in the South of
England,' wrote Bolton's *Football Field*.

The action against Preston brought to a head a conflict over
professionalism that had been simmering for some time. The

FA had set up the first of numerous sub-committees to investigate the issue in October 1882. But the Lancashire clubs had simply presented it with false accounts, and early in 1883 it had solemnly reported that it could find no evidence of professionalism. 'Not guilty, but don't do it again,' wrote one critic, caricaturing the FA's weakness and vacillation.

Now the issue could no longer be dodged. On 11 February 1884 a meeting of the FA Committee was called to consider the question. Charlie Alcock, ever far-sighted, put forward a proposal that 'the time has come for the legalization of professionalism'. This was narrowly carried. But by the time of the Association's AGM on 28 February the forces of opposition had mobilized. Alcock's proposal was overturned and instead a sub-committee was set up to look into ways of repressing professionalism. This reported in June, proposing a series of tough measures to stamp out the creeping payment of players.

From a modern perspective the controversy is bewildering. What was the problem with men being paid to play football? Obviously those Scottish clubs that were losing their players and the smaller Northern clubs who could not compete financially wanted to see amateurism enforced. But why should so many without a direct, vested interest have been so hostile? The answer went to the very core of how late Victorians viewed both football and the broader society they lived in.

Critics put forward two arguments. Firstly, once money was involved the spirit of the game would be destroyed. 'Football is a sufficiently dangerous game already, without the employment of hired professionals, who, to maintain their credit and earn their wage, must necessarily feel bound to exhibit unnecessary energy,' *The Graphic* had written in February 1882. 'Rough and unfair play, a disregard of the rules, disgraceful rows, and abuse of the umpires and referees, can all be traced, directly or indirectly, to the presence in certain teams of paid professional players, to whom a love of the game and fair play are of very small importance as compared to the absolute necessity of winning a match and dividing the gate' was the view of the *Hull Packet and East Riding Times* two years later. Critics also found the 'unfair partisanship' of Northern crowds distasteful, and 'spectatorism' generally was thought to be unhealthy. The hunched-shouldered, chain-smoking crowds who passively watched professionals playing in Lancashire were the antithesis of the muscular Christian ideal of manly participation. Many Southern clubs took positive pride from the fact that no one turned up to watch them.

The second argument was that professionalism would lead to corruption. If a man could be paid to win a game he could be paid to lose it. 'If professionalism is allowed it will only be placing greater power in the hands of betting men and encourage gambling,' argued one critic. Boxing had gone into sharp decline from the 1820s precisely because the combination of professionalism and gambling led to widespread fight-fixing, and many feared the same fate for football.

But gambling and professionalism had existed happily side by side in cricket for many years in the late eighteenth and early nineteenth centuries. And the charge that professionals were dirtier footballers than amateurs did not stand up. Professionals, after all, depended for their livelihood on remaining free of injury, and it was obvious to the most casual observer that the public school game was far rougher than that played by teams such as Preston and Blackburn Olympic (although amateurs firmly maintained that the pros, while shunning manly charges, were much more prone to sly trips and nudges).

Underlying these arguments, of course, was a far more fundamental issue – that of class. 'Let those who sneer at foot-ball "professionalism" over their walnuts and wine . . . consider for a moment what it is for a working man who has to be thrown on his own resources,' wrote the *Football Field*, a fierce champion of Preston and the other Lancashire clubs. The pro-fessionals, to a man, were working class. When people referred to amateurs it was taken as given that they meant men of the middle and upper class who could afford to play without pay.

In other sports the class nature of the professional/amateur divide was explicit. The Amateur Rowing Association defined a professional not just as a man who received payment for rowing, but as anyone who 'has been by trade or employment for wages a mechanic, artisan or labourer, or engaged in any menial duty'. As late as the 1920s the Olympic gold medallist Jack Kelly was barred from Henley simply because he had once worked as a bricklayer. In football the class prejudices were only marginally more subtle. The new 'class of "professional" foot-ballists is distinguished neither for refinement of manners or language', wrote *The Graphic*. Another critic complained that 'the employment of the scum of the Scottish villages has tended, in no small degree, to brutalise the game'. Until now, the gentleman amateurs had dominated the sport. The rise of professional players and clubs threatened their control, and it was this that lay at the heart of the convulsion that almost tore the football world apart in 1884–85.

The rise of professionalism in football fitted with broader

trends in society. The Civil Service and the Army were being steadily prised free from the grip of nepotism and opened up to merit. In 1884 the Third Reform Act massively increased the number of men eligible to vote in parliamentary elections. And the end of the 1880s saw the beginning of a fresh wave of militant trade unionism. The age of democracy was dawning and the more intelligent officials at the FA could see the need for compromise over the issue of professionalism. 'I object to the argument that it is immoral to work for a living, and I cannot see why men should not, with that object, labour at football as at cricket,' declared Charlie Alcock early in 1885.

What Alcock proposed – the legalization of professionalism, but under stringent conditions – was a compromise, and cricket was his model. In cricket it had looked briefly in the mid-nineteenth century as if the sport would be taken over by teams of travelling professionals. But then the amateurs had reasserted control and the county system had been set up. Teams like Surrey, of which Charlie Alcock was secretary, employed both amateurs and professionals. But the position of the professionals was clearly and firmly subservient. They ate separately, got changed separately, and even entered the pitch by a different gate. They were also expected to do work around the ground and put in time bowling to the amateurs in the nets. The fact that the 'expenses' claimed by a top 'amateur' like W. G. Grace dwarfed the earnings of professionals made explicit the fact that the division was not really about money. Alcock crushed a strike by professionals at Surrey in 1896, after which one of the ring-leaders complained, 'If I had played cricket as a "gentleman" I should have made sufficient out of my "expenses" to retire by now.' It was a humiliating position for skilled sportsmen to find themselves in, but one which fitted with the social mores of late Victorian England. And it was a system Alcock and others now wanted to extend to the world of football.

'I cannot be called a supporter of professionalism ... but until professionalism is legalized the deadlock which now exists will continue,' declared Alcock in early 1885. It was an unavoidable evil that had to be controlled. And in this attitude Alcock was firmly supported by Arthur Kinnaird, by now treasurer of the FA. Others were more intransigent.

One of the most hostile was Nicholas Lane 'Pa' Jackson, who had been the driving force behind the prosecution of Preston North End following the Upton Park game. It was he who had been busy in Scotland collecting evidence against Sudell's club before the hearing. A member of the Finchley club and a keen all-round sportsman and journalist, Jackson belonged firmly on the reactionary wing of football. He disliked the 'democratization of the game' and looked back to a golden age when football was 'confined to old public-school boys [and] the laws were strictly observed, any infringement, as a rule, being purely accidental'. He felt that since football had become 'the adopted sport of the masses ... good sportsmanship did not operate so freely'.

But, strangely, the firmest opponents of professionalism came not from among the Southern public school men, but from Birmingham and from the old football centres of Sheffield and Nottingham. Charles Clegg, the Sheffield man who had so resented the haughty attitudes of his team-mates during the first international in 1872, was one of the most fervent.

Clegg's playing days were over, but he would be the dominant figure in the generation of FA officials that succeeded Alcock, Kinnaird and Marindin, and it is important to understand his complex psychology. A successful solicitor, Clegg was from a powerful Sheffield family. His father was three times mayor of the city in the 1880s, a position his brother William – another successful footballer – also later held. And his sister was married to William Peirce Dix, secretary of the Sheffield FA and scourge of the Sheffield Zulus. A severe, upright man, Clegg was later president of the British Temperance League and had a reputation as a straight dealer. 'No one ever gets lost on a straight road' was his pet saying. But the Cleggs were what would today be called 'players', and Charles was a shrewd and often ruthless boardroom operator.

Clegg was fiercely hostile to professionalism. But he combined this with an equally fierce hostility to public school snobbery. All his life he made a point of speaking in a broad Yorkshire accent at FA Council meetings. This chippy, complex mixture was typical of many of the new, more middle-class officials entering the FA, including Charles Crump, the all-powerful president of the Birmingham Football Association. Less socially secure than the Kinnairds, the Jacksons and the Alcocks, and more directly threatened by the rise of professionalism (it was still unknown in the South at this time), these men lacked the social confidence to compromise. They now formed the backbone of the resistance.

By the summer of 1884 the opponents of professionalism had the upper hand and in early October the FA distributed a questionnaire to member clubs. It demanded they give full details of each man on their books, including any wages being paid and their length of residence in the district. From now on clubs would be obliged to prove their innocence and could face expulsion if they refused. The 'catechism', as Jimmy Catton called the questionnaire, was a declaration of war, and the Lancashire clubs knew it. Their 'very existence' was at stake, declared a Bolton Wanderers official.

On 10 October 1884 nine rebel clubs, including Preston North End, Burnley and Bolton Wanderers, met at the Commercial Hotel in Bolton with Billy Sudell in the chair. The Preston chairman and his allies were no longer interested in subterfuge or concealment; they were ready to go into battle over the very principle of professionalism. 'The clubs were determined not to bow the knee to the Southerners,' wrote Catton. At a series of meetings over the next few weeks they resolved not to answer the FA's questionnaire, to withdraw from the FA Cup, and finally to establish a breakaway, professional British Football Association. Twenty-five clubs immediately enrolled as members.

The crisis had now come to a head. A split similar to the one that tore apart the game of rugby ten years later loomed. Gazing into the abyss, the FA finally buckled. At a meeting in London on 3 November it was agreed to establish another sub-committee. Nine days later this sub-committee met in Manchester and finally recommended the legalization of professionalism. Crucially, Pa Jackson had been persuaded to bow to the inevitable. 'They had tried to crush out professionalism but could not. Were they to repeat the farce?' he asked. The Sheffield, Nottingham and Birmingham men remained opposed, along with a handful of the older Lancashire clubs. But the battle was to all intents and purposes won.

However, to become official FA policy the new rules had to be passed by a two-thirds majority at a general meeting, and the hardline amateurs fought a determined rearguard action. On Monday, 19 January 1885 more than two hundred delegates from all around the country gathered at the Freemason's Tavern in London, where the FA had been formed twenty-two years earlier. Major Marindin was in the chair and Jimmy Catton noted that the delegates arranged themselves tribally, 'Lancashire and the North on the right side of the gallant Major, and the Southern and Midland organisations on his left'.

It was Charlie Alcock who put the proposal that professionalism be legalized. He held up the game played in London just two days before between Preston North End and the leading amateur club, the Corinthians, as evidence that 'paid players play the game without undue roughness, and that gentlemen do not object to meet them'. The North End team had stayed on in London and were all in the audience, marshalled by Sudell to vote as proxies for other Lancashire clubs unable to attend.

Pa Jackson rose to second the motion, signalling that a key faction of the Southern gentleman amateurs was now on board. It was opposed by Charles Crump of Birmingham, who argued that 'the introduction of professionalism will be the ruin of the pastime'. He was seconded by Harry Chambers, one of the founders of the original Sheffield club, who sneered that Lancashire was a relative Johnny-cum-lately to football and had no right to dictate its views to the rest of the country.

Then Billy Sudell rose – to wild cheers. He was now recognized as the champion of professionalism and his speech was a moment of high drama. 'Gentlemen,' he said, 'Preston are all professionals, but if you refuse to legalize them they will be amateurs. We shall all be amateurs, and you cannot prove us otherwise.' He then accused his opponents of hypocrisy. 'He made more than one so-called purist wince when he boldly declared that he was prepared to prove that there were men who had played in Lancashire as professionals who were now figuring in Birmingham as amateurs, and the authorities of Birmingham must be aware of it,' reported the *Football Field*. The same, he said, was true in Sheffield. Attendances in Birmingham were almost as large as those in Lancashire; 'Where did the money go to?' he asked, pointedly. His comments provoked howls of protest, but these were undermined when William McGregor, of Aston Villa, frankly admitted that professionalism existed in the Black Country.

The arguments raged for two and a half hours. When the division came the advocates of professionalism won, but by just 113 votes to 108, well short of the two-thirds majority needed. 'Nothing therefore results from this great meeting, the whole time and trouble being wasted, and the committee left in an awkward position,' commented the *Glasgow Herald*.

Two months later delegates met again at the FA's AGM at Anderton's Hotel in Fleet Street. This time it was Dick Gregson, secretary of the Lancashire Football Association, who proposed the legalization of professionalism, seconded by Sudell. At Marindin's request speeches were kept short, the arguments having now been fully rehearsed. But W. H. Jope of Birmingham made a lengthy intervention in which he argued 'it was degrading for respectable men to play with professionals'. His speech drew boos and hisses and a furious response from Alcock, and it was clear the balance was now shifting in favour of the pragmatists. But when the division came the vote in favour of professionalism was 106 to 69 – still just short of a two-thirds majority.

As a way out of the impasse yet another sub-committee was established, containing Sudell, Jackson, Crump and six others. A few months later this reported, making much the same recommendations as the sub-committee the previous November, and by the time delegates gathered again at Anderton's Hotel on 20 July 1885 the opponents of professionalism had thrown in the towel. Just a handful turned up and the key vote was won by thirty-five votes to five. The meeting lasted only ten minutes. So the modern age of football dawned.

There were controls. Professionals could play for only one team in a season and they were to be barred from serving on any local or national FA committees, so driving home their subordinate status. Most importantly, they could play for a club in FA Cup matches only if they had been born within six miles of the ground, or had lived there for the last two years, which restricted the value of importing players. This was a sop to the Scottish Football Association which, still dominated by the amateurs of Queen's Park, remained fiercely opposed to professionalism.

Nevertheless it was a historic victory, and one that had been driven above all by Billy Sudell's determination to cut through all subterfuge and force the issue. 'He was above small deceits or any sinful games,' wrote his friend Jimmy Catton. The leaders of the FA may have wanted to squeeze football into the same stultifying, hierarchical straitjacket as cricket. But Sudell knew the events of 1885 represented a watershed and that there could be no turning back. He was now determined to push football forward to an era in which the professional element would be dominant. 'Professionalism must improve football,' he wrote, 'because men who devote their entire attention to the game are more likely to become good players than the amateur who is worried by business cares. No; purely amateur clubs will never be able to hold their own against a professional team.'

Preston would be his model. Most of Preston's Scots, hired in late 1883 and early 1884, would soon be eligible to play in Cup matches under the two-year rule. And, having revolutionized the FA, Sudell could now return to his real ambition: to create the greatest football team in the world.

There never was a team so clever in all sections, so
beautifully balanced, so excellently adjusted physically, and
so happily blended as Preston had in the middle 'eighties'.

Jimmy Catton, 1922

7

The Invincibles

Preston North End, 1885–95

IN JANUARY 1886 A MATCH WAS ORGANIZED AT PRESTON'S DEEPDALE
ground between 'Gentlemen and Players', which in the parlance
of the day meant amateurs and professionals. It was a model
taken from cricket, where the fixture was played from 1819
until 1962, and was intended to become a regular feature of the
football calendar. But Lancashire responded with a yawn. Just
three thousand people turned up and the Players put out a
weak team, losing 1–0. The *Athletic News* found the match distasteful. The FA, it commented, 'did their level best to make the
pros look like pros [still assumed to be a negative term]. Dark
blue jerseys savour more of the collier than anything else, and
the Gentlemen were clad in spotless white shirts.' In the same

year the Blackburn Rovers player J. H. Forrest, the first acknowledged professional to play for England, faced the indignity of having to wear a different coloured shirt from his amateur colleagues in the game against Scotland.

But this sort of thing soon died out and the Gentlemen v. Players game was abandoned after just a few fixtures. The boundless energies of proletarian football could not be confined and constrained in the same way as cricket. The surge of working-class teams emerging from the North and the Midlands was simply too overwhelming and footballers were just not prepared to tolerate the same petty humiliations. The shift in the balance of power was soon evident within the cramped confines of the FA's new headquarters at 51 Holborn Viaduct.

Throughout the dramas of 1884 and 1885 the FA Committee had continued to be dominated by Southern amateurs. But at the Association's AGM in August 1886 the Lancashire clubs staged a dramatic coup, organizing themselves into a caucus and sweeping the board at the elections. The Southerners fought back at a special meeting a couple of weeks later and a compromise was eventually reached which involved restructuring and expanding the FA Committee. But when the dust settled the Southern dominance had gone for ever and the Northern and Midlands clubs were in the majority.

Sudell and his colleagues had turned on their former allies. They had won in 1885 only because they had the support of a faction of the Southern amateurs. But now they were allied with their former opponents from Birmingham, Sheffield and Nottingham. Men such as Clegg and Crump had resigned themselves to the victory of professionalism and they now showed their other face, a chippy, provincial hostility to metropolitan domination, which they shared with the Lancashire men.

The issue of the timing of meetings was a petty but revealing bone of contention. Provincial delegates wanted them moved earlier so they could travel home in the evening and not stay overnight, but the London delegates wouldn't allow them to interfere with their work day. In March 1886 E. S. Morley, chairman of Blackburn Rovers and one of the more conservative Lancashire members, wrote to the FA to 'protest against the studied discourtesies and lack of consideration shown toward the Northern members of the Committee'. And William Pickford, later president of the FA, complained of the haughtiness of the 'Metropolitan or Old Boy type of member' towards representatives 'from the backwoods' – although he was careful to exempt Charlie Alcock from this criticism.

But even Alcock was an increasingly anachronistic figure. He stayed on as secretary until 1895, smoothing the transition between the amateur and professional eras. But his editorials in the *Football Annual* had a dusty, archaic feel, dwelling on matches between representative sides from the counties and local football associations long after these games held much relevance for the viewing public. For those paying at the gate it was the matches of the professional clubs that mattered now, and one club stood head and shoulders above all others: Billy Sudell's Preston North End.

Sudell was the first manager in the modern sense, although he was unique in that he combined the role with that of chairman. Under him, Preston 'studied football with chessmen set out on a billiard table and with diagrams on a blackboard', wrote Jimmy Catton. Their training routine was far from strenuous. 'We really had no training to speak of, except what we used to do ourselves, and this only amounted to a bit of a kick once or twice a week,' wrote the forward John Goodall. They nonetheless maintained surprising levels of fitness. And there was something about this group of players that clicked.

The word 'machine' crops up again and again in descriptions of Sudell's side, which quickly became known as 'The Invincibles'. 'They play with machine-like accuracy and rigid unselfishness,' the *Birmingham Daily Post* stated in its preview of the 1886–87 season. 'They have brought the "short-passing" game to the highest point of perfection ever seen.' 'The secret of our success,' Goodall remarked later, 'was the fact that the men seemed all to fit so well; I mean, that their style of play dove-tailed beautifully. No one stood out by himself, because every one was a star in his particular position. The game was there-fore made quite easy for all of us.' 'There never was a team so clever in all sections, so beautifully balanced, so excellently adjusted physically, and so happily blended as Preston had in the middle "eighties", wrote Jimmy Catton.

At times it seemed they could score goals at will. Goodall later recalled a match against Notts County where Preston were losing 2–1 with ten minutes to go. 'Now then boys, get us a goal or two!' came a shout from the bench. And they did. After the match the left-half Johnny Graham told Goodall it was one of the most extraordinary things he had ever seen. 'I simply stood behind you with my mouth open, for I could not say a word. It was wonderful football.'

The team represented the culmination of tactical trends visible in football since the change in the offside rule in 1866 and the development of the passing game by Queen's Park in the early 1870s. Sudell, writing in January 1887, attributed the team's success 'entirely to its being a professional combination . . . There is not a weak spot in the team, and we have been able to bring it to its present state simply by having the men always playing together.' Football, he said, would 'be played more scientifically and with less roughness and dash in the future', and his Preston side was the prototype for the new, model professional side. The fact that financial pressures forced Sudell to keep the squad fairly small and that the team remained largely unchanged for several years also helps explain their extraordinary mutual understanding. They even had a secret method of signalling to one another.

For three years, 1884 to 1886, Preston missed out on the FA Cup. Having been expelled in 1884 over the Upton Park game, they withdrew in pique at their treatment the following season. Then, in the third round in 1886, Preston and Bolton managed to get each other thrown out of the competition. This was an era when Cup ties were frequently followed by endless legal wrangles, and Bolton objected to the presence of Geordie Drummond in the Preston side, pointing out he was working in Edinburgh at the time and so technically in breach of FA residency rules. The complaint was upheld by the FA. Preston, who had won the tie 3–2, retaliated by making a similar complaint against a Bolton player, leading to Bolton's expulsion. In Preston's absence Blackburn Rovers won the Cup three years running. But by the end of the 1885–86 season it was generally acknowledged Preston were the best team in the country. That season they played 64 games, winning 59 and losing just two. They scored 318 goals against 60 and at the start of the following season were widely tipped to win the Cup. But the next two years were to be ones of frustration for Billy Sudell and the Invincibles.

The 1887 FA Cup was the final one in which Scottish teams were allowed to compete, and in the first round Preston drew Queen's Park. The Scottish club was still a major power and had won the Scottish Cup the previous season for the seventh time and been losing finalists in the English Cup in 1884 and 1885. Preston had played them for the first time the previous year and drawn 1–1. A friendly between the two teams was scheduled for 25 September 1886 and this Preston won 6–1 – a result seen as a national humiliation in Scotland and for which Queen's Park were keen to gain revenge in the Cup game.

The two teams met at Hampden Park on 30 October. Close to twenty thousand people were squeezed inside, including around five hundred who had travelled up from Preston, and the overlooking hillside was crowded with people, as were the windows and rooftops of the tenements around. The great trial of strength was something of a damp squib, Preston cantering to a 3–0 victory, but the game exploded five minutes from time when Jimmy Ross committed a savage foul on the Queen's Park player Harrower. The crowd erupted. When the final whistle blew spectators poured on to the pitch and surrounded Ross uttering cries of 'Knife him!' and 'Shred him!' Ross lashed out manfully with his fists and the Queen's Park players re-emerged from the pavilion to escort him from the pitch. But the mob was not satisfied and surrounded the dressing rooms, baying for blood. An attempt was made to smuggle Ross out in a long coat and hat but he was spotted and forced to flee back to the pavilion where he reportedly 'sank down in tears'. He eventually managed to escape through a window. But as the Preston team attempted to board their train home that evening a crowd gathered again, inflamed by false reports that Harrower was close to death. A major riot was averted only when the police announced that Ross had been arrested (in fact he'd fled to Edinburgh). Sudell apologized to the Queen's Park club for Ross's behaviour.

Unfortunately for Preston, in the third round they were again drawn to play in Glasgow, against Renton, and the match once more took place at Hampden Park. Queen's Park, as owners of the ground, hiked the price of admission to a shilling 'to keep out the rougher section of the masses'. But, according to the *Athletic News*, it was the officials of Queen's Park who were the problem. Preston won 2–0 and the behaviour of the Queen's Park 'nobs . . . would have disgraced a Billingsgate fishwoman,' the *News* wrote. 'They did not disguise their chagrin at the Renton boys being snuffed out. The shots they levelled at Mr Sudell . . . were in shocking bad taste.'

In the quarter-final Preston met Old Carthusians – one of the last times an Old Boys team would progress this far in the Cup. Because of international commitments the match was delayed and took place just three days before the date set for the semi-final. Preston had offered the Charterhouse men £100 to switch the tie to Deepdale but they refused and Preston were forced to traipse down to the Oval where they won a hard-fought game 2–1 in extra time. The match left them exhausted and, with Jack Ross absent through illness, they went down to a surprise 3–1 defeat in the semi-final against West Bromwich Albion, a team comprising primarily local boys earning a fraction of Preston's wages.

During this Cup run Preston used as their goalkeeper Arthur

'Darkie' Wharton, one of Britain's first black footballers. Born in Ghana of mixed Scottish–Ghanaian parentage, Wharton was living in England as a student. His style was eccentric. He would sometimes crouch by the side of the goal, only springing into action when the ball approached. Other times he watched the game from the crossbar, leaping down when danger threatened. This was partly to avoid heavy charges, but there may also have been an element of racist self-parody in this clowning, designed to ingratiate himself with the fans. He kept a clean sheet in four games during the Cup run, but many regarded him as too casual, and when he started to make mistakes at the start of the following season the press quickly turned on him. 'Is the darkie's pate too thick for it to dawn upon him that between the posts is no place for a skylark? By some it's called coolness – bosh!' wrote the *Football News and Athletic Journal*. He soon fell out of favour with Sudell and didn't play again for Preston after 1887.

In 1887–88 Preston again stormed through the early stages of the FA Cup. In the first round they beat the Manchester side Hyde 26–0, which remains an English record and led to the FA introducing qualifying rounds the following season to avoid such mismatches. They then beat Everton 6–0, Halliwell 4–0 and Bolton Wanderers 9–1 before coming up against Aston Villa in the fifth round.

Villa had won the Cup the year before, beating West Bromwich Albion 2–0 in the final, and it was widely assumed that the winners of this game would go on to lift the trophy. The match attracted an attendance of close to thirty thousand – the largest yet seen anywhere in Britain. Villa's Perry Barr ground was hopelessly inadequate for such numbers and, despite the efforts of two soldiers who mounted cab horses to try to keep the crowd back, people were soon spilling on to the pitch. The match quickly became a farce and it was agreed between the referee and officials from both sides that it would be treated as a friendly, the Cup tie being replayed at a later date – although this arrangement was kept from the crowd for fear of provoking a riot. Preston won 3–1. But then, when the issue came before the FA, Sudell went back on this agreement, claiming it was Villa's responsibility, as the home team, to ensure security. To the fury of the Villa officials the FA narrowly backed him and Preston progressed to the sixth round. Preston's John Goodall felt embarrassed and later described Sudell's actions as 'the greatest injustice ever meted out to a club'.

Preston breezed past The Wednesday 3–1 in the sixth round and Crewe 5–0 in the semi-final to reach the FA Cup Final for the first time. There they were once more confronted by West Bromwich Albion and, as in the previous year's semi-final, were firm favourites. So low was the confidence of the West Brom players that when the Preston men sidled up and offered to place bets on the result, they refused, no matter what the odds. But Preston went down to a 2–1 defeat, one of the greatest shocks in the history of the FA Cup. John Goodall later recalled standing motionless in the centre of the pitch for several minutes at the end of the game, unable to comprehend the result.

Preston may partly have been victims of their own role as pioneers of professionalism. The West Brom goal had been under siege throughout and there was fierce criticism of the referee, Major Marindin, president of the FA. An amateur of the old school, Marindin was a figure of amusement to the new professionals who referred to him, behind his back, as 'The Majaw', exaggerating the second syllable. He liked to lecture teams on fair play for a few minutes before each game and it was well known he was unsympathetic to professionalism. He particularly disliked the importation of Scottish players. After refereeing West Brom's victory against Preston in the semi-final the previous year he was reported to have gone into the West Brom dressing room and asked, 'Are you all Englishmen?' When they replied, 'Yes, sir,' he said, 'Then I have very much pleasure in presenting you with the ball. You have played a very good game and I hope you will win the Cup.'

No one ever suggested deliberate bias on Marindin's part, but his refereeing in this 1888 final was certainly erratic. At one point, just as Preston were about to score, he blew in response to an appeal for a foul, only to find no appeal had been made (it wasn't until 1894 that referees were granted the right to award free kicks without an appeal). After the game the Cambridge University captain Tinsley Lindley commented to Jack Ross, 'Well, Jack, you cannot expect to win when playing against eleven men and the devil.'

But Preston didn't help themselves. The Preston left-back that day, Bob Holmes, blamed their defeat on the fact that they had gone to watch the Boat Race that morning. 'We got starved to death on the Thames bank, and could not get warm again before the match began. The Invincibles entered the field at Kennington Oval that afternoon in a pitiful state. We were daft.' The West Brom captain, W. J. Bassett, said they deliberately set out to hustle Preston and stop them playing their normal passing game and felt Jack Ross 'lost his cool that day . . . that was key . . . I managed to keep cool, and the cooler I kept, the rasher Ross got.' Bassett recalled that Ross kept charging him and, towards the end, went flying over the top of Bassett's back and did a somersault. Ross picked himself up to watch Bassett slip the ball to Woodhall, West Brom's outside-right, who fired in the winner off the far post. 'I have seen all the best sides in football, but I have never seen a side to compare with Preston North End at their best,' wrote Bassett later. 'We beat them, but I do not pretend for a moment that we deserved to beat them.' It was Preston's first defeat in forty-three games.

Sudell was phlegmatic. 'A man who cannot lose is not fit to win, and though it would be useless to say I am not deeply dis-appointed, I shall have another try, and if I am knocked down next year I will try again and again . . . It will be our turn to win it some day.'

By the time Preston came to launch their next campaign for the Cup at the start of the 1888–89 season the football land-scape had been transformed. That summer the Northern and Midlands clubs took their most important initiative yet: the establishment of the Football League. The brainchild of William McGregor, a director of Aston Villa, the League was a response to the new, professional clubs' need for a regular, guaranteed source of income, besides Cup matches, to support their wage bills. Attendances had begun to plateau in the second half of the 1880s, spectators wearied by the endless diet of meaningless friendlies. It was clear they wanted competitive games and the League was set up at a series of meetings over the spring and summer of 1888. It initially consisted of just twelve teams, six from the North and six from the Midlands: Accrington, Blackburn Rovers, Bolton Wanderers, Burnley,

Everton, Preston North End, Aston Villa, Derby County, Notts County, Stoke, West Bromwich Albion and Wolverhampton Wanderers. Billy Sudell, who had suggested the name Football League (McGregor preferred 'Football Union'), was the first treasurer.

As the 1888–89 season dawned Preston North End found themselves gearing up not just for another Cup campaign, but also for a twenty-two-game League programme. Over the summer they had suffered a major blow with the defection of their captain, Jack Ross, to Everton following a row with Billy Sudell over money. There was also a general feeling that the great team of the mid-eighties was past its best. But on the first day of the season they defeated Burnley 5–2 at Deepdale. They then went on to register five more straight wins, their first six games yielding twenty-five goals for and just five against. The fickle Preston press, spoiled by success, was grudging in its praise, and Preston's 1–1 draw at home to Aston Villa on 10 November was described as 'a disgrace'. But the team steam-rollered on and had the title sewn up as early as 5 January 1889, four games from the end of the season, when they defeated Notts County 4–1 at home. They finished eleven points clear of second-placed Aston Villa without suffering a single defeat and with a goal difference of 74–15.

Now they could turn their attention to the Cup, still by far the more prestigious of the two competitions. They swept through to the final without conceding a single goal, in the process finally overcoming West Bromwich Albion, 1–0 in the semi-final. Then, at the Oval on 30 March, they confronted Wolverhampton Wanderers, who had finished third in the League.

Around twenty-five thousand turned up, the largest Cup Final crowd yet. By now the event was growing too big for the Surrey County Cricket ground. It had become the occasion for an annual invasion of London by what the *Pall Mall Gazette* called 'Northern barbarians . . . sharp of tongue, rough and ready, of uncouth garb and speech'. Many Northern and Midlands supporters now ran special 'Cup Final Clubs' to save up for the trip south, and the match was combined with a day's sight-seeing in the capital. Londoners remained largely oblivious. The Boat Race, generally held on the same day, still aroused far more interest and the cab drivers, all sporting either Oxford or Cambridge colours, would tease the Northern football fans, calling them 'lunatics' and asking, 'Does your mother know you're out?'

Anticipating a capacity attendance, Alcock had arranged for the pitch to be shifted closer to the centre of the enclosure. This meant the entire stadium could be brought into use for the first time, and the crowd was arranged as for a cricket match, well back from the pitch, although two rows of seats were placed a little inside the boundary ropes. The stands and the terracing were packed and the *Pall Mall Gazette* reported that 'every window which commanded a view was converted into a private box, and every roof had its little band of onlookers'. The cricket pavilion was also 'thatched with spectators'. 'A stream of excited beings was making its way towards the gates of the Oval from all quarters,' the *Gazette* added. 'Cabbies swore, bussies bellowed, the Brummies shouted, and as you fought your way along the foot-paths and the roads your ear caught many a racy remark from the sturdy Lancashire lads who had come up to see the fun, and to give three cheers for stalwart Sudell and his merry men.' The gates were closed long before kick-off and thousands were turned away, creating scenes of chaos in the streets around. 'The horses were frightened, the crowd was mad, and confusion reigned complete,' the *Gazette* reported, and the gates had to be reopened to prevent a riot. In the end around two thousand were left outside. When Arthur Kinnaird arrived to act as an umpire he was only able to squeeze in at the last moment.

Preston appeared in their customary white while Wolves wore red and white stripes. 'Both sets of men looked in the pink of condition, the Prestonians the heavier metal, "Wolves" dogged, thick-necked, crop-haired – both sets nasty-looking people to quarrel with,' according to the *Gazette*. As the game got underway Sudell paced the touchline in the manner of a modern manager, almost 'suffocating with emotion'. Like West Brom the year before, Wolves tried to harry Preston out of their game, but without success. After a quarter of an hour Jimmy Ross sent a stinging shot against the crossbar and Fred Dewhurst headed home the rebound. Then, shortly before half-time, the Wolves goalkeeper fumbled another shot from Ross, allowing it to roll between his legs, and Preston went into the break 2–0 up. Halfway through the second half Sam Thomson added a third, and long before the end of the game the crowd was creeping on to the enclosure, lining the pitch, waiting for the final whistle. When it came they surged forward and the players were mobbed as they struggled back to the pavilion.

Finally, Preston had done it, and they had done it in style, without conceding a single goal throughout the competition. Their feat of winning the League and Cup 'double' would be repeated just once in the next seventy years (by Aston Villa in 1897). Dewhurst, the Preston captain in the absence of Jack Ross, tried to persuade Billy Sudell to accept the trophy on the team's behalf. He declined, leaving Dewhurst to deliver a eulogy on all that Sudell had achieved at Preston. 'It is through his exertions that we have kept together for the last five or six years,' he told the crowd. 'Mr Sudell has been father to the team, and if it had not been for his exertions I do not suppose that we would have been able to win the Cup. I call upon the team to give three lusty cheers for Mr Sudell.'

Huge crowds awaited the players when they arrived back in Preston a few days later. This time Sudell was less modest, taking pride of place in the civic procession that was now part of the Cup-winning ritual, the trophy on his lap, while Dewhurst made do with the match ball. At the Town Hall, Sudell addressed a crowd of several thousand, praising football as the great working-class sport. He said 'he did not know a single amusement out of which the operative classes had got so much amusement at such a cheap rate as that of football. The richer classes could have their hunting, shooting, fishing and boating, not one of which was in the reach of the working classes, so that the latter had a right to any legitimate amusement within their reach.'

'The town has a right to feel proud of its champions, but the town need not go silly,' the *Preston Chronicle* commented sniffily as football hysteria spread. The *Manchester Guardian* simply described Preston as 'the greatest club in the world . . . by universal consent'. It was the pinnacle of Billy Sudell's career. At last, after so many years of frustrations and disappointments, he had achieved all he had set out to do in the summer of 1883. But from here there was only one way to go.

Jack Ross, unhappy at Everton, returned in the summer of 1889, bitter at having missed out on the Cup win. But the great side began to break up. Over the following season Sandy Robertson, John Goodall, Johnny Graham, Fred Dewhurst and Sam Thomson all either moved on or retired; they were followed shortly afterwards by David Russell and right-back Bob Howarth. It ought to have been easy to fill the gaps. In May 1889 the FA removed the residency requirements for FA Cup games. From now on professionals could be signed and play in the Cup almost immediately, without having to wait two years. The move was the culmination of the revolution begun in 1885 and the final failure of the amateurs to impose cricket-like constraints on professionalism. Fiercely opposed by Charlie Alcock, who felt the Association had broken a debt of honour to the Scottish FA, it prompted the resignation of Major Marindin as president of the FA and was followed by a renewed flood of Scottish footballers crossing the border – 230 by 1890. However, few of the best men ended up at Preston.

Billy Sudell had shown what could be achieved by the whole-sale importation of professionals. Others were quick to follow his lead, and the iron laws of football economics began to assert themselves. Small town teams such as Darwen and Turton had already fallen by the wayside and it had become clear middle-sized towns such as Bolton, Blackburn and Preston could support just one team (unable to compete with the financial muscle of Blackburn Rovers, Blackburn Olympic had folded in 1889). Now the balance began to shift towards teams from larger towns, initially Aston Villa and Sunderland. In the autumn of 1889 the press reacted with horror to reports that

Sunderland was paying a man £5 a game. 'That's a shilling a minute for playing football, and ten bob to spend afterwards!' wrote *Sports and Play*. 'Sunderland people seem mighty fond of chucking their money about.'

In their double season Preston had averaged home League attendances of 6,725 – second only to Everton, who averaged 7,400. But this figure remained more or less unchanged over the next few seasons while crowds at other clubs rose steadily, until by 1893–94 Preston's gates were among the worst in the First Division. They simply could not compete.

The team was also not as fit as it might have been. There was a drink culture among professional footballers from the outset, reflecting the working-class backgrounds they had come from (alcohol consumption in Britain peaked in the 1870s and was always heaviest among those who could least afford it). The problem of young men with money in their pockets and time on their hands, idolized by the local population, was one professional football clubs wrestled with from the start and they were forever pleading with supporters not to 'treat' players. Little Jimmy Costley, who scored the winning goal for Blackburn Olympic in the 1883 Cup Final, was just one who could never resist temptation. 'Wherever he went people would buy him a drink and he would come home drunk,' recalled his granddaughter many, many years later. He was saved from a life of alcoholism only when he signed the pledge and became a teetotaller.

Many of the Preston players certainly liked a drink. As early as November 1886 a game against Stoke was called off at the last moment, on the curious grounds of a loss of form. A correspondent to the *Lancashire Evening Post* gave a far more likely explanation: 'We have heard and read a lot about professionalism being an evil, but I think a greater evil exists in the temptations to drinking which are put in the way of professional footballers.' During Preston's pre-season tour of Scotland that year it was reported from Dundee that 'hotel proprietors in this town have had enough of football teams'. And at the start of 1891 an incident at Wigan station involving an attractive barmaid, some broken glass and a railway guard being kicked unconscious had an unpleasantly modern ring to it. The great Preston side of the mid-eighties had got away with playing hard – in every sense – and training little, but as football moved into the 1890s the lifestyle began to take its toll. During a defeat by Darwen in the semi-final of the Lancashire Cup in April 1891 the players were said to be 'sweating and blowing as if they had had no training for months'.

Nevertheless, Preston's decline was gradual. They were knocked out in the early stages of the FA Cup every year in the early 1890s but were League champions again in 1889–90 – albeit by a smaller margin than the previous season – and runners-up in 1890–91, 1891–92 and 1892–93. But by this time the club was in financial difficulties. Although officially just chairman of the committee, Sudell had run the club as an autocrat for more than a decade; there had not even been an AGM since 1889. In the summer of 1893 the members decided it was time to examine the books and an AGM was called for 20 July.

Sudell was in fractious and defensive mood. When R. P. Woodhouse, a member of the committee who had resigned shortly before, queried certain items in the accounts, he exploded. 'I must protest against this,' he said. 'I object to answer questions if my word is to be doubted.'

'I am asking a civil question' ... You should not take it offensively,' replied Woodhouse.

'Well I do take it offensively,' Sudell thundered.

He eventually wrung a vote of confidence out of the meeting, but it was a turning point. A decision was taken to convert Preston into a limited liability company – a path being taken by many clubs at this time – and after this Sudell's power was drastically reduced.

The following year the heart was ripped out of the team. In the autumn of 1893 club captain the pugnacious Jack Ross had begun to show signs of ill health. In early January 1894 it was reported he had pneumonia. The club, which had plummeted down the League and was struggling against relegation in his absence, sent him on a cruise to Madeira. But over the summer his condition worsened. He died of tuberculosis at his home in Preston on 7 August, leaving a wife and five children under nine. He was just thirty-one. Large crowds gathered for his funeral and blinds were drawn all along the route. 'He had the dual temperament of fire and water. His flame never danced and flickered. It glowed steadily and lit up all the scene,' wrote one journalist.

Preston narrowly escaped relegation that year. The following season they rallied and finished fourth in a League which had now grown to sixteen teams. But on 20 March 1895 the era of The Invincibles came definitively to a close. At 5.30 that afternoon, while walking along Waterloo Road, Billy Sudell was approached by Detective Inspector Gardner and arrested on charges of embezzlement and falsification of accounts.

Sudell had been entrusted with sole charge of the Goodair family's mills since 1886. It now turned out that since 1890 he had been systematically plundering the company, not for personal profit but to bolster the finances of Preston North End. In all he had taken £5,326 – a huge amount for the time.

It seems Billy Sudell had not been able to resign himself to the prospect of gradual decline. Originally a middle manager at a mill in a small provincial town, he had risen through football to a position of enormous power and influence. He had revolutionized the sport and built up the greatest team of the age. Preston were the Manchester United of their day, and in the late 1880s you challenged Billy Sudell at your peril (the 1888 ruling at the FA following the Aston Villa Cup tie was one of numerous slightly dubious decisions that went Preston's way). 'He was well known throughout the country,' said his counsel at the trial, 'and was elated with the universal esteem he was held in throughout England. He spent money royally on everyone who came near him. He entertained teams when they came to the town, and paid for drink for everybody who wished.' It was a lifestyle and a reputation he could not bear to relinquish.

Sudell sat with his head in his hands throughout the trial and 'appeared to feel his position most keenly', according to the *Liverpool Mercury*. He pleaded guilty, but the judge was unsympathetic. Sudell, he pointed out, enjoyed a generous salary from the Goodairs of £500 a year – far higher than anything he paid his own footballers. He had betrayed their trust, essential in a trading community, and the money he had taken 'had disappeared in riotous living; that is what it comes to'. He also felt the prisoner had not 'showed enough remorse'. Sudell was sentenced to three years in prison – a term that visibly shocked him.

J. J. Bentley, the president of the Football League, wrote to the *Athletic News* to raise funds for Sudell's wife who 'faced the world alone without a penny and with many hungry mouths to feed' (Sudell had nine children). 'Footballers will do well to remember that the unfortunate man was once one of the leaders in English football,' he wrote. He appealed to readers 'to support and not kick one down'. Otherwise the football community was unsympathetic. Sudell's behaviour had embarrassed them. It seemed to confirm all the worst prejudices about the way professional football was run.

When Sudell emerged from prison he and his family emigrated to South Africa and a legend later became established that he had killed himself in despair. But Sudell was not that sort of man. The truth was that he went on to pursue a successful career in sports journalism and died at his desk, much respected by the South African sporting establishment, on 5 August 1911 while writing a report on a rugby match. He was sixty-two. Sudell had always inspired affection in people and his paper, the *South African News*, described him as 'a true gentleman, a valued friend and co-worker, and a man of unselfish, kind-hearted, amiable character whose love of the game had won him the respect of thousands'.

Jimmy Catton was loyal to his friend to the last. 'I can never believe that he forfeited his honesty and self-respect. In disposition he was noble enough to have borne the burden of another man's misdeed,' he wrote, implying Sudell had taken the rap for someone else. Given that Sudell wielded absolute power both at Preston North End and the Goodair mills it's hard to see who this might be.

Sudell's disgrace meant that he was quickly forgotten, both

by Preston North End and the wider football establishment. But it is hard to overstate his importance to the history of the sport. Not only did he force the issue of professionalism, he also created a side that continued to inspire awe for decades afterwards. In 1926 Jimmy Catton still regarded them as 'the finest team I ever saw', and it was a view echoed by many others. As football became more frenetic and aerial in the years after the First World War Preston were seen as representing a lost ideal of cultured, 'scientific' football. As late as the early 1940s the voice of Bob Holmes, the left-back in 1889, could be heard bellowing across the club's training ground, 'That's not a balloon . . . Play it along the ground!'

Above all it was Sudell's management of the club that was revolutionary. He was the first to abandon all pretence of creating a local side, concentrating instead on the uncomplicated goal of assembling as much talent in one place as possible. His aim was the pursuit of excellence and success, pure and simple. Preston were the first sporting organization to leave the haphazard ways and convoluted ethics of the gentleman amateurs behind for good. In no other sport in Britain did this happen before the First World War, and Preston became the model for every professional football side around the world that followed. This was the great contribution of Billy Sudell – visionary, tactician, businessman and fraudster. His career marked the dividing line between football's ancient and modern eras.

8

The Corinthians

1882–1914

IF THERE WAS AN AMATEUR COUNTERPART TO THE STANDARD-BEARER
of the professionals, Billy Sudell, it was Nicholas Lane 'Pa'
Jackson, the FA official who had led the prosecution of Preston
North End back in 1884. Jackson was 'a velvet-gloved, hard-
hitting champion of amateurism . . . [who] delighted in
fighting "the Northerners" and, as a fighter, he made enemies,'
wrote the great all-rounder C. B. Fry.

Born in 1849, a year before Sudell, Jackson had been a
minor player for Upton Park and for Finchley, his local team. He
was a keen all-round sportsman and the editor of a number of
sporting publications, including *The Midland Athlete, Football*
(a joint venture with Charlie Alcock) and *Pastime*. In the early

1880s he began to make a name organizing 'scratch' teams to play matches for charity, and the story of how he acquired the nickname 'Pa' is revealing. Jackson believed professionals lowered the tone of football. But it seems the behaviour of these early amateur sides on the road was probably not so different.

The year was 1880, and Jackson was taking a Cambridge University team to play a match up in Manchester. They had hired a large saloon carriage, and while most of the team wanted to get some sleep one of the party was drunk and kept singing. The train made a stop and 'most of us got out for a drink', wrote Jackson. When the train restarted it was noticed 'the over-boisterous one' was missing. A few hundred yards out of the station they became aware of a tapping on the window. There, clinging to the outside of the carriage door, was 'our rowdy friend ... with a bottle of whisky protruding from his pocket and three or four bottles of soda under one arm!' After being hauled inside he smiled sweetly at Jackson and said, 'Now, Pa, don't be cross.' The name stuck and Jackson would be a father-figure to generations of gentleman amateurs.

For Jackson, the year 1889 was the great turning point. Even more than Alcock, Kinnaird and Marindin, he regarded the decision to remove residence qualifications for professionals as a betrayal. From that moment, he believed, football lost its soul. 'The last vestige of the "stringent conditions" under which professionalism was legalized had now disappeared; competition for the most renowned players was unrestrained and undisguised,' he wrote later. As the leader of the key Southern amateur faction that had switched sides to back professionalism in 1885 he felt duped and believed the character of the FA had changed irrevocably. 'Previously the members were mostly gentlemen who gave their time and ability to the management of the Association solely on account of their love of the sport.' Now the organization was under the control of 'a class of men who followed football as a business'.

For Jackson, the introduction of the penalty kick in 1891 had a totemic significance. There were still almost no markings on the pitch and until then fouls and handballs close to goal had simply been punished with a free kick. This encouraged defenders to commit what would later be called 'professional fouls' when a player seemed certain to score. Briefly, during the 1881–82 season, referees had been given the power to award a goal when this happened. But this proved unworkable. It was the Irish FA that came up with the penalty idea, initially awarded for any foul within twelve yards of the goal-line. Goalkeepers were allowed to advance six yards, and the Preston forward John Goodall wrote that 'some of the best goalkeepers make a practice of dancing about extravagantly and waving their arms in order to disconcert the kicker'. The top forwards quickly developed the skill of chipping goalkeepers who advanced too far.

For amateurs, the great problem with the penalty kick was that it implied a foul had been committed deliberately. 'It is a horrible blot on the game,' wrote Jackson. 'It should be taken for granted that no player would *intentionally* break the laws.' He blamed its introduction on 'that vast army of players who have not had the opportunity of imbibing the sporting spirit of the game at school'. His views were echoed by C. B. Fry: 'It is a standing insult to sportsmen to have to play under a rule which assumes that players intend to trip, hack and push their opponents and to behave like cads of the most unscrupulous kidney. I say that the lines marking the penalty area are a disgrace to the playing field of a public school.'

The amateurs were overruled, and from that time on Jackson went into a position of outright opposition to the new establishment, seeing himself as a sort of guerrilla leader fighting a valiant rearguard against the encroaching forces of professionalism. In this struggle his principal weapon was his most famous creation: the Corinthian Football Club.

Jackson had initially set up the Corinthians in 1882. He explained their original purpose: 'My reason for this venture was that our English teams were continually being beaten by Scotland, whose eleven was largely composed of Queen's Park players.' The Scots, he pointed out, 'were constantly playing together, giving them a combination altogether lacking in our elevens'. England had lost 6–1 in 1881 and 5–1 in 1882. The idea was to bring together the best English players to play on a regular basis and so give them a better chance of competing.

Jackson claimed his experiment 'was fully justified' by results, but this is questionable. It wasn't until 1888 that the tide turned in England–Scotland games, and although the English won five of the eight internationals between 1888 and 1895, this was largely because the Scots did not legalize professionalism until 1893 and refused to select Scottish professionals playing in England until 1896. In fact, the Corinthians quickly assumed a second, far more important function in the mind of Pa Jackson: only amateurs could play for them, and it was taken as given that this meant men who had attended either public school or one of the great universities. By the late 1880s the Corinthians were a shameless exercise in concentrating as many talented gentleman amateurs in one team as possible. 'Let me here tell a secret,' wrote C. B. Fry, who played for the Corinthians at the turn of the century. 'The main purpose of the Corinthian FC was to provide an amateur team *capable of meeting the leading professional clubs on equal terms.*'

Initially Jackson took a back seat. He had recently been appointed assistant honorary secretary to Charlie Alcock at the FA and was also heavily involved in the newly formed London FA, leaving him with little time. But it was soon clear a firm hand was needed. In their first couple of seasons the Corinthians made little impact, and in the autumn of 1883 Jackson took over as secretary.

He was an excellent organizer, 'the cleverest man who ever appeared in connection with the promotion of football', according to Fry. 'He gradually drew all the best players into his silken Corinthian net. Pa was a cute angler, and his bait was an international cap. Few young players could resist his charming manner, and he had a wonderful knack of conveying the impression that a favour done to him would be a stepping stone to future greatness.' Soon the Corinthians were *the* team to play for among gentleman amateurs.

Jackson was clever enough to avoid the mistakes of Wanderers, who in many ways were an earlier incarnation of the Corinthians. They too had gathered together the best amateurs of their day. But with the rise of Old Boys teams at the end of the 1870s Wanderers had gone into rapid decline, it being the convention that a man's school had first claim on his loyalties. Jackson decided the Corinthians would not enter the FA Cup – or any other competition – and would play most of their games in mid-week, so enabling the top players to play both for him and their old school team.

The Corinthians were above all a touring side. They would organize two trips, one at Christmas and one at Easter. The Christmas tour was the most important and generally involved matches in the North and Scotland against top professional sides, and it was during the Christmas tour of 1884 that the Corinthians established their reputation. Their first opponents were Blackburn Rovers, the FA Cup holders.

'I venture to predict them a pretty sound drubbing,' declared Bolton's *Football Field*, confidently, a few days before the match. But the Corinthians, clad in what would become their trademark white shirts (later imitated by Real Madrid, but originally simply cricket shirts), were ahead inside a minute. They were 4–0 up after little more than a quarter of an hour and ended 8–1 winners. 'It may be said with safety that such magnificent football . . . was never seen in Lancashire. It was simply marvellous all round – the dribbling, passing, tackling and kicking of the various players being as near perfect as possible,' wrote the *Athletic News*. 'The spectators could scarce believe their eyes,' wrote the *Football Field*. 'People who did not see the game and heard the result could not swallow it. The Rovers beaten by eight to one? Nonsense! The thing was incredible.'

The rest of the tour was an anti-climax. The Corinthians were always forced to squeeze a number of games into just a few days when on the road, and the players quickly tired. Of the remaining six games they won just one. But the victory over Blackburn Rovers meant they would now have no trouble attracting top-class opposition.

The tour also marked the start of a long rivalry with Preston North End. The Corinthians had lost 3–1 at Deepdale five days after the victory over Blackburn Rovers. But over the next seven years the two sides played each other nineteen times, Preston winning twelve and the Corinthians five – a far better record than most clubs achieved against The Invincibles at this time. When Jackson's and Sudell's men met it was always a juddering collision. Hand-picked thoroughbreds, unlike most professional teams Preston yielded nothing to the Corinthians in weight and size. But the Corinthians enjoyed these games. 'Against the Preston North End men, whom we knew well, we had regular butting matches, and they were as happy as kings,' recalled the Corinthian full-back P. M. Walters. The matches were also social events, sometimes followed by a series of contests between the two teams which included shooting, billiards, whist and athletics. And there was always a dinner afterwards – a custom that was common in late Victorian football – at which players would make speeches, sing songs and sometimes even recite poetry. 'Sudell . . . used to do us very well indeed,' wrote Walters.

In 1887 Preston and the Corinthians were chosen to contest a match in front of the Prince of Wales at the Oval celebrating Queen Victoria's Golden Jubilee, drawing 1–1. And on 18 November 1889 the Corinthians gained perhaps their most famous victory, defeating Preston, fresh from the League and Cup double, 5–0 at Richmond. 'The brilliant triumph of the Corinthian gentlemen yesterday will convey to the professional clubs in a most practical manner the fact that University and public school men are still able to hold their own and occasionally to vanquish the paid players, in spite of the training and preparation undergone by the latter,' wrote *The Times*. This, of course, was precisely Jackson's aim.

Jackson was fortunate in being able to draw on a particularly rich crop of players in this period. Up front were Tinsley Lindley and W. N. 'Nuts' Cobbold. Lindley was 'a brilliant dribbler, a sure passer of the ball, and a thrilling shot', according to Jimmy Catton, and a typically eccentric amateur. He turned out occasionally for Nottingham Forest and 'used to drive up to the ground in a dogcart . . . ready dressed for the fray'. Cobbold was regarded as the top amateur forward of his day. 'As a dribbler we have never seen his equal,' wrote C. B. Fry. 'He had a peculiar shuffling run; just a wriggle between the halves, and a wonderful knack of shooting at quite unexpected moments and impossible angles.' Like many early amateurs, Cobbold, a Charterhouse man, attributed his dribbling skill to the peculiarities of the games he'd played at school. 'We played what was known as "run about" on a very hard ground, practically devoid of grass,' he wrote. 'There were often thirty a side, and one was of necessity forced to learn how to hold the ball and keep it close with so small a space to manoeuvre in. It was a great test of one's dribbling powers and made dribbling later in life on a well-grassed pitch quite easy.'

At the back were the famous 'morning and afternoon brothers', A. M. and P. M. Walters. Also Charterhouse men, they were pioneers both in the art of playing men offside and in passing to each other, a skill which until then had been largely confined to forwards. 'A pair of battering rams', they weighed 'thirteen stone a piece and a ton together', according to Jimmy Catton. Most full-backs in this period had to decide between charging or going for the ball; the Walters brothers overcame this dilemma by acting in unison. 'One went for the man, the other for the ball, and between them they achieved a *tour de force*,' wrote John Goodall. On one occasion A. M. deposited an opposing forward into the crowd, prompting the player's irate mother to emerge from the stands brandishing an umbrella at him.

The Corinthians played in the old amateur style, adapted to the age of combination. 'Passing forward on the run' was the defining feature of their game, according to Jackson. 'The whole line of forwards is on the run together and, until it loses the ball or shoots at goal, does not stop,' wrote C. B. Fry. Jackson would stand on the sidelines yelling, 'First time! First time!' The ball was always kept on the ground as heading was still a rarity among amateurs, and forwards like Cobbold would be positively irritated if they received a pass in the air.

Their style contrasted with professional teams who played a far less direct game. 'Much of the scientific and exceedingly clever short passing of professional forwards involves stopping and dodging backwards, a method which often retains the ball but also retards the wave of attack,' wrote Fry. 'Mechanical piffling' he called it on another occasion, and sycophantic journalists often waxed lyrical about the supposed intelligence, spontaneity and flair of the Corinthians' game compared to the more regimented, 'learned' style of professionals. 'Their play has a flash of inspired and spectacular brilliance which the highly trained – perhaps too highly trained – professional teams rarely show,' read one report in *The Times*.

At its best, the Corinthian style was clearly pleasing to the eye. After the Second World War old-timers drew comparisons with the Moscow Dynamo team of 1945 and the Spurs 'push and run' side of 1950–51. But it could easily degenerate into kick and rush. 'Accuracy of passing' was often 'made subservient to dash and pace', wrote John Goodall. And the truth was that the Corinthian game still relied very heavily on brute strength.

Like the amateur sides of the 1870s, the Corinthians benefited from the fact that, Preston aside, they were generally far larger than their professional opponents. 'The Corinthians when they entered the field of play looked like a team of giants opposed to a team of pigmies,' read one match report from 1888. Charging remained a central feature. In his old age, W. N. Cobbold recalled a game in which the Corinthians had a dubious goal awarded against them. Jackson was so furious he stormed on to the pitch and encouraged his team to walk off. 'I thought we could do better by staying on the field and teaching our opponents a lesson,' wrote Cobbold. 'This we did by the simple expedient of using our weight in a perfectly legitimate manner, as was the custom in old time football. We did not pass that day. Our forward with the ball merely dribbled up to the opposing half back and charged him over, then going on to treat the backs and goalkeeper in the same way. We got four goals in twenty minutes by this means.' (The Blackburn Rovers forward Jimmy Brown developed an interesting way of countering tactics like this: when a defender stooped to charge him he would leapfrog over his back. But he seems to have been unique in this.)

Although the press was often caught up with the supposed romance of the Corinthians – the amateur David doing battle with the professional Goliath – evidence suggests that the football-watching public was less enthused. From 1886 the Corinthians played an annual New Year's Day fixture against Queen's Park at Hampden which normally drew crowds of ten to fifteen thousand. Games at Preston attracted similar attendances. But generally in the 1880s and 1890s the Corinthians were playing in front of fewer than ten thousand people and they rarely drew more than a few thousand to their home games at the Oval where the atmosphere was notoriously flat. 'The Corinthians who were not playing viewed the game from the stand, gently clapping their kid-gloved hands when applauding the team, or encouraging their men with a "Well played, old chappie" uttered in a listless drawling style,' wrote a Sunderland newspaper. The working-class spectator who dominated football crowds by the late 1880s wanted to see trained professionals and they wanted to see competitive matches. The Corinthians could provide neither.

Nevertheless, for most of the 1880s Jackson's promise that playing for the Corinthians was a sure step to an international cap often proved true. In 1886, when Blackburn Rovers' J. H. Forrest became the first acknowledged professional to play for England (and was forced to wear that different coloured shirt), nine of his team-mates were Corinthians. By 1892 forty-four Corinthians had played for England. Professionals believed the FA was biased against them, and they were probably right. P. M. Walters shared their view, and since he was on the selection panel he knew what he was talking about. But by the end of the 1880s the balance of power was shifting.

On 12 November 1890 H. M. Walters, the younger brother of A. M. and P. M., received a kick in the abdomen while playing for the Casuals (a feeder team for the Corinthians) against St Bartholomew's Hospital. He was carried off and lay in agony for two weeks before dying of acute peritonitis on the 27th. His parents were distraught and, in deference to their wishes, both

A. M. and P. M. retired from the game. They were just twenty-five and twenty-seven. W. N. Cobbold stopped playing in 1888, and, although Tinsley Lindley made the occasional appearance until 1894, in the early 1890s the Corinthians entered a fallow period, struggling to compete with the top professional teams.

They soon rallied; 1892 saw the emergence of the forward G. O. Smith, yet another Charterhouse man, who would go on to be the greatest of all Corinthians. Smith scored 11 goals in 20 games for England and 132 goals in 137 games for the Corinthians, and with Smith leading the line, between 1894 and 1898 the Corinthians were once more able to compete with the best professional sides. However, they never regained their grip on the national team.

This was a source of enormous bitterness for Jackson. He complained that Charles Clegg, who had become chairman of the FA in 1890, 'like most of the other members of the Selection Committee . . . rarely sees the best amateurs play'. It nevertheless remained the convention that a Corinthian would captain England (on the one occasion a professional was appointed Jackson denounced it as a 'discourtesy' to the amateurs in the team). And these Corinthian captains continued to treat their professional team-mates with extraordinary feudal disdain, as if nothing had changed since the 1860s. In 1892 the *Athletic News* complained 'it hardly seems the right thing to our unsophisticated mind for a captain of an international team not to recognize his men on a long railway journey, not to speak to them in any way, to travel in a separate compartment, to dine away from them at the hotel, to leave them severely alone until driving off to the match, and generally to behave as if he were a superior sort of being'.

The great Derby County striker Steve Bloomer told a revealing story about the 1898 international against Scotland in Glasgow. The Corinthian Charles Wreford-Brown was captain. He wore 'good old-fashioned knickers which had side pockets in them', wrote Bloomer, and when Freddy Wheldon of Aston Villa scored England's first goal Wreford-Brown slipped his hand in his pocket and pressed a gold sovereign into Wheldon's hand. When Bloomer himself scored England's second the same thing happened. Both men gave the money to the ref for safe-keeping, and when Bloomer got another sovereign for scoring England's third the ref remarked, 'If you keep this up, Steve, I shall have to go for my handbag!' England won 3–1, and after the game Wreford-Brown invited the team to his (separate) dressing room for champagne. Bloomer told the story without resentment, but he did not need the money and kept the sovereigns as souvenirs.

By this time the amateurs on international duty were finally having to adapt. They had already begun to travel with the pros and stay at the same hotel. And in 1898, for the first time, they deigned to eat with them. This resulted in an embarrassing incident when the waiter refused to serve the amateurs potatoes, a dietary restriction imposed by the FA which the officials accompanying the team hurriedly made clear applied only to professionals.

Jackson was furious. 'Not content with almost filling the international teams with professionals', the FA 'did all in its power to reduce the one or two amateurs who did play to the level of professionals', he spluttered. For him a hierarchy, with the amateurs at the top and the professionals at the bottom, was built into the system and unquestioned. But the fact was that, in footballing terms, by the turn of the century the amateurs were falling well below the level of the professionals.

G. O. Smith retired in 1901. After that Corinthians rarely made it into the international team and the club entered a period of sharp decline. Professional teams were soon putting out reserve sides against them. The extent of the deterioration became painfully clear in the Sheriff of London Shield game against Sunderland in 1903.

Inaugurated in 1898, the Shield was the forerunner of the Charity (now Community) Shield and was played at the end of each season between the top amateur side and the top professional side, the latter being either the League champions or the FA Cup winners. Other than 1899, when Queen's Park were selected, the Corinthians always represented the amateurs. But, a solitary victory against Aston Villa in 1900 aside, they had never won it, and they had been beaten 5–2 by Spurs in 1902. Against Sunderland they lost 3–0, but the scoreline was flattering to the Corinthians. 'The aimless manoeuvrings of the Corinthian forwards provoked much mirth amongst the spectators, who found themselves sighing for the old days,' wrote one observer. So one-sided was the contest that Sunderland soon lost interest and 'the play never rose above mediocrity. At times it degenerated into a mere kick about,' reported the *Athletic News*. Most of the Corinthians were exhausted long before the end and 'it was really only a question of how many goals the Northerners would win by'.

It was now doubtful the Corinthians were genuinely the strongest amateur team in the country. The Old Boys teams they drew their players from were being eclipsed by working-class amateur sides. The FA had instituted a new Amateur Cup in 1893 but the old boys complained that 'the play of many of the contending elevens was often not quite of the style which is expected in amateur football' – which meant they were lower class and kept beating them. In its first year the Amateur Cup was won by the Old Carthusians, but thereafter teams such as Middlesbrough, Bishop Auckland and Stockton dominated. In response the public school men broke away and in 1902 established the Arthur Dunn Cup, a competition which initially refused to recognize the penalty kick before bowing to pressure from the FA, and from which working-class teams were conveniently excluded.

The Corinthians might have slowed their decline if they had selected the one outstanding amateur of the period, Vivian Woodward. Woodward played as a forward for England twenty-three times between 1903 and 1911, scoring twenty-nine goals, and was a regular first for Spurs and then Chelsea. He appeared to fit the bill of the gentleman amateur perfectly. He never claimed so much as a bus fare (in contrast to the Corinthians, for whom Jackson was always ruthless in exacting the maximum in expenses) and was a man of spotless reputation and gentle demeanour. His game was 'all art and no violence', wrote Jimmy Catton. Fouled repeatedly during one match by the opposing centre-half he ignored the provocation; when he was eventually injured he simply murmured, 'Please don't do that again, you have hurt me.' The centre-half was so astonished he promised the referee 'I'll never touch him again', and he didn't. Woodward would have been the ideal successor to Cobbold and Smith, and, unlike them, he could head the ball. But, although upper middle class, he had not been to public school or university and was never invited to play for the Corinthians.

The Corinthians still had their moments of glory. In 1904 they defeated Bury 10–3 in the Sheriff of London Shield and the following year saw a famous 11–3 victory over Manchester United. In both games the old forward passing game was flowing smoothly once more. But it was a last flickering of the Corinthian flame. The club was about to be plunged into its darkest period.

The crisis that now engulfed them was political rather than sporting. Tensions between the gentleman amateurs and the FA had been growing for some time. Pa Jackson had resigned as vice-president of the FA in 1897 after it attempted to assert control over the scratch teams he still organized for charity games. The Association was concerned some of these teams – which were brought together for single matches – were profiting surreptitiously and wanted all scratch teams to register with them, which Jackson regarded as an insult. A muttered 'I'm tired of all this' had been his parting shot. 'How long the amateurs will rest content under the present state of affairs it is impossible to say,' he wrote, ominously, in 1900.

Jackson felt the FA was dominated by professionals who wanted to exert too tight a control over the amateur game. He was particularly critical of Charles Clegg. 'Throughout the forty or fifty years that I have known him he has always appeared to be hostile to the public school and university element,' he wrote in 1932. This was true, and went right back to Clegg's traumatic experience of public school snobbery in that first international. But the FA chairman was trying to pull off a difficult balancing act. Three groups were vying for control of football: amateurs, professionals, and the owners of the professional clubs. Clegg saw it as his job to hold the ring, and all three groups saw him as an enemy at one time or another. But he was certainly an autocrat. For him the authority of the FA, and his own authority within it, was sacrosanct. It was this that guided his actions in the crisis that followed.

In 1905 Clegg introduced a resolution demanding that all local football associations be compelled to admit professional clubs as members. In most of the country this was already the practice, but the Surrey and Middlesex Associations remained exclusively amateur and they decided this was a line they were not prepared to cross, arguing that it would inevitably lead to professional teams becoming dominant.

In February 1906 the Amateur Football Defence Federation was set up to combat the rule change. It proposed a compromise: all professional clubs in Surrey and Middlesex would be allowed to join the London FA, which did admit professionals, even if they were outside the London area. This was rejected out of hand, the London FA fearful there would be a corresponding flow of its own amateur members to the Surrey and Middlesex Associations, and the FA declared the Defence Federation an outlaw organization. It was an absurd dispute. There were no professional clubs in Surrey or Middlesex outside London. But the issue was now one of power. 'Nothing short of total submission would satisfy the FA,' wrote W. E. Greenland, a leading amateur who later wrote a history of the crisis. 'It had now become obvious that a struggle for freedom was in prospect.'

The whiff of insurrection was in the air. Mass meetings were called at the Holborn Restaurant, and from the crowd a leader emerged, a prominent lawyer called Henry Hughes-Onslow, who was both an Old Etonian and a Corinthian. Rising from the floor at a meeting of the Middlesex Association he urged defiance and spoke with such fervour he quickly found himself catapulted to the position of honorary secretary of the Defence Federation. 'The original cause of the trouble is, of course, the introduction of professionalism ... some twenty years ago,' Hughes-Onslow declared. Amateurs, he said, should 'resist by all legitimate and honourable means the illegal policy of coercion the object of which is to force them ultimately to submit to professional government'. For many the aims were wider. 'What the amateurs desire is the restoration of the real sport of football,' proclaimed another rebel. 'We want the game as played in the eighties. We want neither "gates" nor penalty kicks.'

This was an upper-class rebellion. The rebels, wrote Frederick Wall, who had replaced Charlie Alcock as honorary secretary of the FA in 1895, 'seemed to think that the word "amateur" was solely applicable to "Old Boys" clubs'. Oxford and Cambridge University and the Civil Service team were also heavily involved, and the Defence Federation had very little presence in the North and the Midlands.

In January 1907 the crisis appeared to be defused. H. P. Gregson, secretary of the Lancashire FA, put forward a compromise proposal overturning the original resolution obliging local associations to admit professionals and deferring a decision to a later date. The motion was passed, to the obvious surprise of Charles Clegg, who immediately resigned as chairman of the FA. The rest of the FA Council was aghast and, rallied by Lord Kinnaird, now FA president, they begged Clegg to reconsider. On 14 March he relented, making clear he was resuming his duties on the clear understanding 'that there is no intention to bring about any general change of policy'.

Clegg had flexed his considerable muscle. 'The Napoleon of the Association returned from his self-selected Elba and the war broke out again,' wrote one newspaper.

On 31 May Clegg's original resolution was re-passed at the FA's AGM. In response the rebels called a meeting at the Holborn Restaurant for 8 July. Alfred Lyttelton, the notorious 'bunter' and Kinnaird's team-mate in the Old Etonian and Wanderers teams of the 1870s, was in the chair. 'The alternatives,' it was declared, were 'either to allow their amateur principles to be swamped for ever in the flood of professionalism or pseudo-amateurism, or to withdraw their game from the danger that was encompassing it and manage their own affairs in future.' They opted for the latter and voted to establish a breakaway Amateur Football Association. The FA, which had held together through the crisis of 1885 and the formation of the Football League in 1888, had split.

The roll-call of the new association's leading officials revealed the central role played by the Corinthians: P. M. Walters, W. N. Cobbold, G. O. Smith and C. Wreford-Brown were all vice-presidents and A. M. Walters sat on the platform next to Lyttelton. But the formation of the association proved a disaster for the club. FA members were immediately banned from playing teams belonging to the AFA. And although the new association quickly recruited close to a thousand clubs, its membership was almost entirely confined to southern England. The AFA was amateurish in every sense. Henry Hughes-Onslow, who was honorary secretary, was so averse to any hint of professionalism that he refused to raise funds and the association had no permanent headquarters. The decision of the Army not to join the new organization was also a mortal blow. The AFA limped on and many of the Old Boys sides and other minor amateur teams were happy enough playing games against one another. But for the Corinthians, top-class opposition was their life blood.

The club spent much of the next seven years organizing foreign tours, a practice they had begun when they visited South Africa in 1897 ('Missionaries of Empire' one old Corinthian called them). Brazil was a particularly popular destination and they toured twice, providing the inspiration for the creation of the famous Corinthians club of São Paulo in 1910. But at home they played no more than nine games a season, four of these against Oxford and Cambridge universities. They lost just five matches in England during this period but that was scant consolation for the decline in the quality of opposition, which inevitably began to tell on the Corinthians. By the eve of the First World War they were a shadow of their former selves. 'It is terrible to think what would happen to them . . . in a game with Blackburn Rovers or even with Chelsea,' wrote *The Times* in February 1914.

At the Corinthians' AGM of 1912 a motion was passed urging 'a reconciliation between the Amateur Football Association and the Football Association'. But it took almost two years for a deal to be struck. And when it was there was no disguising the fact that it was a defeat for the AFA. The association was to be admitted to the FA as an affiliate and would retain responsibility for its own members, but the overall authority of the FA was firmly acknowledged and never again was there any suggestion amateurs would be allowed to exclude professionals from local associations.

The deal was unpopular with many AFA members. 'Strong feelings of disapproval were expressed at the severity of the terms and it was urged that the negotiations should be reopened having regard to the fact that the AFA representatives had entered into discussions on equal terms and not as supplicants,' wrote Greenland. But the leadership was only too painfully aware of how weak their position was and, faced with the threat of resignations, the membership narrowly approved the agreement by the required two-thirds majority.

Pa Jackson was bitter. 'Unfortunately many so-called amateur clubs were not loyal to the movement,' he wrote. 'Evidently the evils of professionalism had demoralized some of them, particularly those composed of the type of player who only waits until he is good enough to become professional to change his status.' William Pickford, later president of the FA, was more perceptive. Most amateurs by this time were working class like the professionals, he pointed out, and they 'resented the idea of introducing a "class" element into the game'.

Today, the split of 1907 is entirely forgotten. But it was potentially disastrous and could have led to a permanent schism similar to that between rugby league and rugby union. This was football's counter-revolution, a belated attempt to reverse the events of 1885, but it was always doomed to failure. Uniquely among the sports of Edwardian England, the balance of power in football had long ago shifted against the traditional upper class. The sport was now in the hands of working-class players and spectators and, above all, middle-class club owners. It responded to the dictates of public demand, of the market, rather than the self-serving ethics of public school men. 'If there had ever been any moment at which a division of the sport into sheep and goats was opportune it had passed,' wrote Pickford. 'Football had already become the great national winter game.'

As for the Corinthians, they marked the end of the split with a game against the English Wanderers, a team of top-class amateurs who had remained loyal to the FA, whose attack was led by Vivian Woodward. They lost 4–2. The 'superior training' of the Wanderers was key, wrote *The Sportsman*. 'The Corinthians were more or less a spent force long before the finish.' It noted too that, while the Wanderers had adapted to the style of the professional sides most of them played for, the Corinthians remained wedded to their old kick and rush game. A surprise 4–0 victory over West Bromwich Albion followed, then a 3–2 defeat at West Ham. A few months later the outbreak of World War One cut short the Corinthians' attempts to resurrect their first-class status. But already they were dinosaurs wandering a landscape that had been transformed out of all recognition since the 1880s.

The players of the Rugby Union game are probably
twice as numerous as those of the Association.

The Times, November 1880

9

'The Cleverer Game': Football, Rugby and the Battle for Supremacy

Bradford Park Avenue, 15 April 1907

AS UPPER-CLASS MEN BECAME ALIENATED FROM FOOTBALL, MANY turned to rugby. But by the early decades of the twentieth century the sister code was increasingly under threat from the irresistible rise of football.

On 15 April 1907 some three hundred members of Bradford Rugby Football Club crowded into a meeting room at their Park Avenue ground. One of the premier sporting arenas of the North, Park Avenue contained two pavilions, a grandstand 'in a modified Italian style of architecture' and a sixty-foot-long refreshment bar. The ground had cost the club £13,000 when they bought it back in 1880 and could hold twenty-five thousand people. Those present were divided between 'guinea members', who had voting rights, and 'half-guinea members', who did not. All were drawn from Bradford's middle and upper classes. This was an august, even an elite, institution. But before them was an astonishing proposal: that the club abandon the sport they had first begun playing forty-four years earlier and convert to Association football.

The move had not come out of the blue. Five other clubs from Rugby's Northern Union had made the switch over the previous four years, beginning with Bradford's local rivals Manningham, who had become Bradford City in 1903. But they were all second-rank teams. The defection of Bradford was far more significant. Formed in 1863, they were among the pioneers of rugby in northern England and along with York, Hull, Huddersfield and Leeds had been part of a 'pentarchy' which effectively controlled Yorkshire rugby until the late 1880s. By that time they were probably the richest football club, of either code, in the whole of England with annual profits that consistently topped £1,000 – the sort of return Association clubs of the era drooled over. More recently they had been champions of Yorkshire in 1900 and 1901 and champions of the new Northern League in 1904. In 1906 they had won both the Yorkshire Cup and the Northern Union Challenge Cup.

The season just ending had been a poor one, however: they finished eighteenth in the League and made a loss of over £600. But this was the first time the club had been in the red in more than a decade and to most of the members assembling that day the crisis scarcely seemed terminal. Key members of Bradford's committee thought otherwise.

The club was dominated by its chairman, Arthur Briggs. A woollen manufacturer from Harrogate, Briggs was fabulously wealthy and had business interests that stretched as far as Poland and Russia. A colourful, slightly Toad-of-Toad-Hallish character, he was also on the board of Rolls-Royce and liked to boast he could dismantle and reassemble a motor car single-handed. He was one of the first people ever stopped for speeding by the police after he exchanged nods with the engine driver and attempted to race the Scotch Express. Briggs was a man in a hurry and he had come to a firm, unshakeable conclusion: football was the sport of the future, rugby the sport of the past. 'The only solution,' he told Bradford's members that day, 'was at once to establish the Association game at Park Avenue.'

The meeting in Bradford that night marked the culmination of more than twenty years of decline for rugby. Today we take the dominance of football as Britain's winter sport for granted. But football's triumph was far from inevitable and for two decades following the establishment of the FA in 1863 it was rugby that had the upper hand.

As with football, rugby clubs began to be formed in London in the early 1860s, Blackheath (established in 1860) and Richmond (established in 1861) playing the role of the Forest Club, Crusaders and Dingley Dell. Initially rugby lagged a year or two behind football, which was why the 'dribblers' were able to steamroller the rugby clubs at the inaugural meetings of the FA. But by the middle of the 1860s rugby was forging ahead and in 1873 the *Football Annual* recorded eighty-nine clubs playing the code in the capital compared to just thirty-eight playing the Association game. London would remain a pre-dominantly rugby city until the rise of working-class football there in the 1890s.

The reason for this was simple. In the decades following 1840 there was a massive expansion in the number of public schools as new institutions sprang up to cater for the growing middle class. Among the best known were Cheltenham (1841), Marlborough (1843), Rossall (1844), Wellington (1853), Clifton (1862) and Haileybury (1862). For their winter sport the bulk of these schools chose rugby rather than Association football.

Their choice in part reflected the influence of Thomas Arnold, whose tenure as headmaster at Rugby between 1828 and 1842 marked the start of the great revolution in methods and manners at the public schools. Many of the new schools were run by disciples of Arnold, often former Rugby pupils, and it's no surprise that they adopted Rugby's game as well as its ideals.

But rugby also had a particular appeal to the apostles of muscular Christianity. Some of the earliest schools to adopt the game were in Scotland. In 1862 a twenty-nine-year-old called Hely Hutchinson Almond took over Loretto just outside Edinburgh and it quickly became the most extreme example of the cult of athleticism. Almond developed an extraordinary, ascetic routine that involved students rising at seven o'clock in order to 'have a run or smart walk of about three-quarters of a mile' followed by 'a cold bath and rub down' before breakfast. He placed little stock in academic achievement and saw his methods as sanctioned by the founders of the Christian Church. St Paul, he confidently declared, always preferred 'vigorous manhood, full of courage' over 'the languid, lisping babbler about art and culture'.

Three hours every day were dedicated to sport, and rugby

enjoyed pride of place. Almond had no doubt of its superiority over Association football. 'The defect of the Association game,' he wrote in 1892, 'is that it gives no exercise for the upper limbs, and thereby does not tend to the strengthening of the lungs, and the equal development of both sides of the person, as the Rugby game does.' He also felt that professional clubs had become too powerful in determining the rules of Association football and that they had forgotten the real aim of the game, 'viz. to produce a race of robust men, with active habits, brisk circulations, manly sympathies, and exuberant spirits'. Football clubs regarded the sport merely 'as a means of attracting spectators' – a cardinal sin in his eyes. 'No idle spectators should be allowed to stand looking on at school sides. The very sight of loungers takes the spirit out of players.'

Like so many of his contemporaries, Almond felt that the more robust school sports were, the better. 'On the indirect bearing of all this upon school morality I need scarcely enlarge to all who know anything about schools . . . I have never yet known a genuine Rugby forward who was not distinctively a man,' he wrote. It is again revealing that, far from being a civilizing influence, the majority of public schools, when faced with a choice between the two football codes, instinctively gravitated towards the more violent.

And rugby certainly remained extremely violent. Newspapers regularly carried reports of deaths on the pitch, sparking a flurry of concern from the mothers of public schoolboys and calls for reform. In March 1875 a medical student died from internal injuries after being tackled and falling on the ball during a game in Battersea Park. The following year two deaths were reported: a fifteen-year-old boy in

Manchester, also from internal injuries, following a shoulder charge, and a British student at the High School in Allahabad in India who died from 'concussion of the spine' after charging head first into an opponent's hip.

Defenders of the sport were unsympathetic. 'If the rules were altered in the interests of milk-sops, and the game freed of all risk, I am confident that its value as a physical and moral agent would be vastly lessened,' wrote a correspondent to *The Times* in 1882. 'It is a remarkable fact that the outcry against the Rugby Union game proceeds principally or entirely from nervous women or coroner's juries,' he added. But to the un-initiated the game was bewilderingly savage. 'A detailed account of the play is simply impossible, consisting as it did of wrestling, struggling, running with the ball under the arm and striking opponents in the face with the disengaged hand,' wrote a Sheffield journalist after the Manchester team Free Wanderers visited the city in 1870. Rugby rules 'are quite suitable for schoolboys, who are proverbially impervious to accident, but we should have thought adults would prefer a game with more skill and less roughing', he went on.

As in the dribbling game, the first moves to make rugby slightly less lethal came when adult men, some of whom had not been to public school, began to play the game in London in the 1860s. Blackheath outlawed 'scragging', or throttling, and also introduced the enlightened rule that 'No player may be hacked and held at the same time'. In 1866 Blackheath and Richmond began a movement to ban hacking altogether – although, in the short run, the effect of this was simply to make scrums last even longer.

It was partly to improve the image of the sport, and also to select a team for the first international against Scotland, that the Rugby Football Union was formed in 1871. This drew up fifty-nine laws of the game, the fifty-seventh of which confirmed the abolition of hacking. Other innovations followed. In the mid-1870s the number of players on each side was reduced from twenty to fifteen. This made for a faster, more free-flowing game, and led shortly afterwards to the introduction of passing which, as in football, was almost unheard of in the old public school game (the boys felt it would 'look like funking', H. H. Almond recalled of his first attempts to introduce passing at Loretto). But the game was still horrifically dangerous and the death rate remained the crude calculus by which violence in rugby was measured. In Yorkshire in the late 1880s and early 1890s men were still dying at a rate of three every two seasons.

The RFU had been set up by twenty-one clubs from the South (there would have been twenty-two but the Wasps representative got lost on the way to the venue). But by that time the game was already spreading to the North. As early as 1857 a trial game had been organized by Old Rugbeians in Liverpool. This led to the establishment of the Liverpool club and was followed by a similar match in Manchester three years later, leading to a club being set up there. Both were elite institutions and they would dominate Lancashire rugby for the next two decades. The game spread to Yorkshire almost immediately afterwards. By 1870 Bradford, Hull, Leeds and Huddersfield were all in existence, and York was founded in 1874. As in Lancashire, membership of these early teams was drawn largely from the upper and middle classes.

In the North in the 1860s rules tended to vary from club to

club and the dividing line with Association football remained fuzzy. For the first Roses match between Lancashire and Yorkshire in 1870 five Sheffield men were invited to be part of the Yorkshire twenty, despite the fact no rugby was played in the city. They 'played as if they had never seen a Rugby ball', commented one observer, which they quite possibly hadn't. Irritated by the tackling, at one point 'one of the Sheffield men grabbed the ball by the lace and hammered his opponent about the head with it', recalled one spectator. Sheffield footballers were not invited again, and with the establishment of the RFU and a uniform set of rules in 1871 the two codes diverged more sharply.

By the mid-1870s rugby was beginning to filter down the social scale in the North. A cup competition was introduced in Yorkshire for the 1877–78 season and, as in football, provided a massive stimulus. Cup games were soon attracting crowds of over ten thousand. Spectators were drawn from all social classes but, as with football in East Lancashire, a number of the top teams quickly came to be dominated by working-class players.

By 1880 rugby was without doubt the more popular of the two codes in the country as a whole. Football as a mass sport was still largely confined to Glasgow, Sheffield and Nottingham, the Black Country and the Bolton–Blackburn axis. Throughout the rest of Lancashire and Yorkshire, in the North-East, in Edinburgh and in London, rugby reigned supreme. 'The players of the Rugby Union game are probably twice as numerous as those of the Association,' declared *The Times* in November of that year.

But it was at this point that the tide turned. The decision of the ever far-sighted Billy Sudell to switch Preston North End from rugby to football at the start of the 1880s was the first straw in the wind. Prior to 1880 Association football was almost unknown in the town, which was partly why Sudell was forced to import professionals en masse to build his new team. Preston's top rugby club, the Grasshoppers, had been established in 1869 and was one of the most prestigious and popular in the North. But by the Christmas of 1883 North End were already drawing crowds ten times as large.

In 1882 Burnley's rugby club also switched codes. By 1884 they were attracting attendances of twelve thousand and the town had been firmly won over to the Association game. By the mid-1880s football was pulling ahead in the North-East, and at the start of the 1890s it conquered the Barnsley–Doncaster belt just north of Sheffield.

Liverpool was a latecomer to mass spectator sport, the casual, unskilled labour which dominated the docks winning the Saturday half-holiday later than more skilled workers elsewhere in Lancashire. But by the end of the 1880s Everton were the best-supported football team in the country; with the establishment in 1892 of Liverpool, a football culture was firmly established. In Manchester rugby retained its grip a little longer, but by 1902 the City–United derby was drawing crowds of fifty-three thousand compared to just seventeen thousand for comparable rugby games. By the turn of the century rugby as a working-class game had pretty much shrunk to South Lancashire, the West Riding of Yorkshire and South Wales. What had happened?

In part the answer lies in the stifling conservatism of the rugby establishment. In the 1870s and 1880s rugby sank much deeper roots in the middle class, in both London and the provinces, than football ever did. The transitional phase between the public school and working-class game in football, represented by clubs such as Nottingham Forest, Blackburn Rovers and The Wednesday, was relatively brief and by 1885 football was already an overwhelmingly proletarian sport. In rugby the balance was much less skewed and middle-class clubs were prepared to take a much tougher stand in defence of what they perceived to be their interests.

The attitude of the Southern public schoolboys was also very different in rugby. In football, Alcock, Kinnaird and Marindin, and even Jackson initially, were a force for moderation. Rugby had no such voices and the RFU rarely showed much interest in accommodating and appeasing the new working-class clubs. It may well be that this reflected the newer, lower-status public schools many of the men running rugby had attended. Like the Sheffield and Birmingham representatives at the FA in 1885, they were less secure socially than the Eton and Harrow men who ran football and therefore less comfortable compromising.

Divisions first emerged over the issue of competitive matches. The creation of the FA Cup in 1872 had played a key role in spreading football and spawned countless local imitators, but no equivalent cup was established in rugby. The Yorkshire Cup proved a huge success, but there was not the same proliferation of local cups elsewhere. Crucially Lancashire, held in the deadening grip of the Manchester and Liverpool clubs, refused to establish a county-wide competition. This reflected a fierce hostility on the part of rugby's elite to what was called 'pot hunting'.

'Experience has conclusively shown that whatever be the class of the players, Rugby cup-ties give an opening for ill-feeling and the exhibition of unnecessary roughness,' wrote one observer in 1887. 'The friendly rivalry which used to exist between clubs has . . . given place to unconcealed animosity, and certain players in the cup ties behave in such a brutal manner, that they have not only disgraced the clubs which still tolerate them, but have brought the game itself into disrepute,' wrote another, six years earlier. Both players and spectators cared *too much* about cup ties, and this led to unseemly aggression and partisanship. Similar sentiments existed in football, but they were less widespread. The Corinthians' refusal to take part in cup competitions was only partly driven by the need to avoid clashes with Old Boys fixtures. The club saw the 'no cups' rule as a virtue. 'In these days of cups and medals . . . this "self-denying ordinance" on the part of the Corinths should act as a valuable protest against the growing tendency to play the game only for the prizes it will bring,' wrote one Corinthian.

This upper-class hostility to competitive fixtures is puzzling. Hadn't cup competitions originated in the public schools? And weren't house matches and inter-school games played in a spirit of ferocious competitiveness? In Alec Waugh's 1917 portrait of public school life, *Loom of Youth*, a player is described sitting on an opponent's head, punching him repeatedly and shouting 'Damn you! Damn you! Damn you!', for which he earned a mild rebuke from the ref. In the same story the hero attempts to bribe someone to 'lay out' a player he has a grudge against. Confronted by the headmaster he throws his arms wide and protests, 'Well, sir, it is the sort of thing any fellow might do!' Real-life accounts of public school games contain frequent examples of sharp practice as well, of course, as brutality. What was the late Victorian public school if it wasn't the ultimate Darwinian environment? The journalist Jimmy Catton was alive to the hypocrisy. 'One might as well contend that the giving of prizes at school and the establishment of scholarships and exhibitions at the universities should be discouraged as tending, not to the cultivation of the mind for the pleasures which knowledge gives, but to the greed of personal gain and to "cramming",' he wrote.

What the elite teams really objected to, of course, was not competing, but losing to their social inferiors. Sides such as Manchester and Liverpool, and those that aspired to imitate them, were notorious for refusing to play working-class teams. 'As our club is pretty nearly free from the working-class element, you have nothing to fear about a rough or noisy game,' the secretary of Goole FC had written to York in 1882. For teams like this the key problem with cup competitions was that you were at the mercy of the draw and could not choose your opponents. And by the mid-1880s, more often than not, working-class teams were in the ascendant.

There is no doubt that the lack of cup competitions was catastrophic for the expansion of rugby, meaningless friendlies holding little appeal for a paying public. In Lancashire it left the field open for the rise of football, which received a massive boost from the successful FA Cup runs of Darwen, Blackburn Olympic and Blackburn Rovers in the late 1870s and early 1880s. Having initially dominated rugby in the North, Lancashire was soon eclipsed by Yorkshire, where the Yorkshire Cup provided protection against football in the rugby heart-land of the West Riding. The rugby authorities took a similarly blinkered attitude towards leagues: it was only in the teeth of fierce opposition from the RFU that the top Yorkshire and Lancashire clubs were able to establish league competitions in the early 1890s.

By then these disputes were being overshadowed by an even more contentious issue – professionalism, which began to creep into Yorkshire and Lancashire just a year or two after football. The reaction of the rugby authorities was very different from that of the FA. The 'legitimisation of the bastard' was not an option, declared one RFU official. 'The Associationists sanctioned professionalism because they had no alternative . . . The Rugby Union Committee, finding themselves face to face with the hydra, have determined to throttle it before it is big enough to throttle them . . . No mercy but iron rigour will be dealt out.' In 1886 stringent new rules were passed outlawing payments of any sort to players, even for time lost at work, and making it illegal for club members to employ players in any outside capacity.

This left the deeply conservative owners of clubs like Bradford in a quandary. Instinctively they sympathized with the stance of the Southern teams, but they were heavily dependent on working-class players and knew these men could not play without receiving at least 'broken time' payments. This now became the key issue, and in 1893 Lancashire and Yorkshire delegates introduced a motion at the RFU AGM 'that players be allowed compensation for *bona fide* loss of time'. It was thrown out by 282 votes to 136.

The virulence of some of the anti-professional sentiment in sport at this time is astonishing. Caspar Whitney's 1894 *Sporting Pilgrimage to Oxford and Cambridge and the Shires* is the most extreme example. 'I am more than willing to help my labouring brother of lesser refinement . . . but I do not care to dine or play football with him,' he wrote. 'The labouring class are all right in their way; let them go their way in peace, and have their athletics in whatsoever manner best suits their inclinations . . . Let us have our own sport among the more refined elements, and allow no discordant spirits to enter into it.' Mixing professionals and amateurs, he said, was as absurd as expecting 'the negro, lifted suddenly out of generations of bondage, to fraternize and favourably compare with the race whose individuals have always been the refined and cultured members of the civilised world'.

In rugby, at no stage did the Southern establishment show the least willingness to compromise. In fact, where in football the amateur faction had been caught by surprise by the superb organization of Billy Sudell and his allies, in rugby it was the Southern gents who held meetings beforehand and organized voting caucuses. 'The Rugby game, as its name implies, sprang from our public schools. It has been developed by our leading London clubs and universities; and why should we hand it over without a struggle to the hordes of working men players who would quickly engulf all others?' declared one amateur.

This intransigence in part reflected the changed social atmosphere of the 1890s. The FA had tackled professionalism at the end of a long period of social calm. But with the rise of militant new trade unions in the late 1880s Britain entered a phase of industrial strife and class conflict which harked back to the tense years of the 1830s and 1840s. In 1890–91 there was a five-month strike at Manningham Mills in Bradford, and this was followed in 1892 by a lengthy cotton strike in Lancashire. At Featherstone near Wakefield in 1893 troops opened fire on striking miners, killing two and wounding sixteen. The long golden afternoon of the Victorian era was over. The shadows of renewed class conflict were closing in, and it was against this backdrop that the negotiations over professionalism in rugby took place.

The atmosphere made the inherently conservative RFU even more uncomfortable with retreat and compromise. Some, at least, within the rugby establishment seemed almost to be willing a split as a way of segregating the sport and freeing themselves of the unpleasant obligation of wrestling and writhing in the mud with their social inferiors. 'The loss of followers to the grand old game is regrettable, yet looking at the present state of all professional sports, we cannot but think that this possible loss is far preferable to legalizing professionalism,' wrote an 'Old Player' in the *Football Annual* of 1889. A split was precisely what they achieved.

Faced with even tougher anti-professionalism legislation, in 1895 the leading Yorkshire and Lancashire clubs finally broke away to form the Northern Union, which, over the next eleven years, developed the modern, professional game of rugby league. Had the FA not compromised in 1885, it's likely the still-born British Football Association of 1884 would have evolved in much the same way. Rugby was now split down the middle. But the schism provided an opportunity. Freed from the constraints of the Southern establishment the big Northern clubs could confront football head on. Numerous leagues and cup competitions were set up and changes were introduced to make the game more free-flowing and attractive, culminating in the reduction to thirteen players in 1906.

Initially the Northern Union was a success. Crowds were up,

clubs were making profits and attempts to infiltrate football in the West Riding proved a failure. A series of new Association clubs were set up in the wake of the split but almost all had folded by 1900. 'There seems little likelihood that the dribbling game will ever prove a formidable rival here to Rugby as it has done in Lancashire,' wrote the *Yorkshire Observer* in 1894, and this was still the general opinion five years later. It looked as if the forward march of football had finally been halted.

But it was an illusion. There was a subterranean process eating away at the foundations of rugby in northern England. During the 1895–96 season the Bradford Schools Athletic Association switched from rugby to football after a boy suffered a serious leg injury. State schools all around the country at this time were making the same decision. By 1897 schools football associations had been set up in Birmingham, South London, Sheffield, Manchester, Liverpool, Nottingham, Brighton, Sunderland, Leicester, Leeds and Blackburn. As the cult of athleticism seeped down the social scale, football, it seemed, was the team game of choice in the state sector. And the widespread adoption of football by elementary schools would do more than anything to make it the great working-class sport of the twentieth century.

The reasons local school boards opted for football over rugby go to the very core of its ultimate victory in the war between the two codes. First and foremost it could be played on a hard surface – in the street or in a school playground – whereas rugby was only really practical on grass. For boys living in the densely built-up cities of late Victorian Britain, this was key. Birmingham in 1886 had just ten green spaces comprising 222 acres. Most public schools, by contrast, were surrounded by oceans of playing fields. By 1900 Harrow alone had 146 acres.

Football was also a far simpler game. At its inauguration the RFU had drawn up fifty-nine rules; the FA in 1863 had made do with just thirteen. In the years that followed the rugby authorities endlessly tinkered with the game in a bid to make it more attractive – a process continued by the Northern Union – while the essentials of football were already in place by the early 1870s. 'The rules this season had puzzled even the referees,' declared Bradford chairman Arthur Briggs in 1907. 'The result of this was a transference of the affections of the spectators from Rugby to the Association code, under which they could see a good game and keep acquainted with the rules.'

The threat of injury was also a factor, as the decision by the Bradford Schools Athletic Association indicated. Not only was football less dangerous than rugby, but success was less dependent on physical size – a key factor for schools attended by undernourished working-class boys. This was something the journalist William Pickford had observed in Lancashire back in the late 1870s. Pickford had been brought up playing rugby, and when he was posted to work on the *Bolton Evening News* in 1878 he tried to join a local team. Pickford was middle class, but he was small and slight of build and was told by the team secretary that he 'might grow a bit bigger and come again in a year or two. He was a big chap and towered over me, and I went,' Pickford recalled. It was an experience of rejection that must have been shared by countless working-class men.

Soon afterwards Pickford went to see Bolton Wanderers play. 'I fell in love with "soccer" at once,' he wrote. 'The players were not bunched together half the time in struggling heaps, but each man in his place, like chessmen, and the footcraft, passing and speed fascinated me . . . I was a convert on the spot.' This account flags up the most fundamental reason of all why thousands of working men opted for football over rugby: they simply regarded it as a better game.

The top rugby clubs were soon looking nervously over their shoulders. 'Many of our important Rugger teams belonging to the Northern Union ranks look with uneasiness on the general adoption of the socker [*sic*] game by the rising generation,' wrote *Yorkshire Sports* in September 1900. 'Soon they will begin to wonder where their recruits for the future will be coming from.' By 1902 there were nine junior football leagues in West Yorkshire, and by 1904 there were 436 football clubs affiliated to the West Yorkshire FA.

In 1901 the leading Northern Union clubs responded to the challenge of soccer (a piece of public school slang derived from the word 'association' that began to be used at the end of the 1880s) by setting up a new top division covering the whole of the Northern Union area; previously Lancashire and Yorkshire clubs had played in separate leagues. It bolstered the revenues of the elite teams, but those consigned to the new Second Division found themselves travelling long distances to meet second-rate opposition. Many second-tier clubs were quickly in serious financial trouble.

The FA – which, in stark contrast to the lethargic RFU, always showed great vigour in attempting to spread the game – sensed an opportunity. 'Nothing would please the football authorities more than to extend their influence to the densely populated West Riding,' wrote the *Bradford Daily Telegraph* in January 1903. The FA, it said, 'will do all in its power to assist the club who will take the first step. Shall it be Bradford or Leeds?'

In fact it was Bradford's city rivals, Manningham, who were the first to switch codes. Established in 1880, Manningham had always been a far more working-class outfit than Bradford (during the great mill strike of 1891 Manningham had played matches to raise money for the workers, while three of Bradford's players had enlisted as special constables, to help break up demonstrations). Manningham were league champions in the Northern Union's first year. But since 1898 they had been in decline and were now a Second Division side. They made losses of £660 in the 1902–03 season, and when representatives of Bradford and District FA approached them early in 1903 they were receptive. At an Extraordinary General Meeting on 26 March the club treasurer declared bluntly that 'Rugby was a dismal failure, and as businessmen they must look to something better.'

Initially it was decided the club would run two teams and play football and rugby on alternate weekends. Then, on 24 May, the Football League took the extraordinary decision to admit Bradford City, as Manningham were now known – a club that had never played a game of football and didn't even have a team – to the Second Division. The members needed no further encouragement. At an AGM five days later they ratified the decision to adopt football and the idea of playing rugby on alternate weeks was quietly dropped. Bradford City was now a football club, pure and simple.

A squad was quickly assembled for the following season and the club performed respectably, finishing tenth. Revenues rose sharply – they made as much from a single Cup tie against Wolves as they had in the whole of their last season as a rugby side. And although costs rose equally steeply they made steady progress and at the end of the 1907–08 season won promotion to the First Division. Three years later they defeated Newcastle United in the FA Cup Final, at the same time finishing fifth in the League. For other struggling professional rugby clubs in the North, Bradford City appeared to be a successful model to follow.

Over the next few seasons Birkenhead, South Shields, Stockport and Holbeck all made the switch, Holbeck ultimately morphing into Leeds United. By the end of 1906 the mighty Bradford Rugby Club was wavering. Their average gate receipts were down to £57 a game from £134 four years earlier and crowds had fallen to four or five thousand, compared to an average of more than eleven thousand for Bradford City's home games in the Football League.

Initially the suggestion was put forward that Bradford should merge with Bradford City to form one football team which would play at the rugby club's larger Park Avenue ground. However, when Bradford's members assembled for the meeting on 15 April 1907 the committee found they did not share their enthusiasm for a switch to what *Yorkshire Sports* called 'the cleverer game'. 'If [we] had cohesion and enthusiasm on the Committee, the results would have been much better than they were,' said one, voicing a widespread suspicion that the board, having decided to switch to football, was deliberately running the club down.

The proposal to switch to football was thrown out by an overwhelming majority. Instead the middle-class membership, who were innately conservative and had always been un-comfortable with the defection to the Northern Union in 1895, decided to revert to the rugby union game, to become an amateur club once more and to rejoin the RFU.

Chairman Arthur Briggs, who had missed the meeting through ill health and been forced to communicate by letter, was horrified. Within twenty-four hours he was manoeuvring to have the vote declared invalid on the grounds that the meeting, although called to discuss this specific issue and chaired by the town's Lord Mayor, had no decision-making powers. The club's solicitor accepted this somewhat spurious argument and a few weeks later Briggs steamrollered the club's Finance and Property Committee – which he had now decided was its sovereign body – into approving the change to football. He then accelerated the negotiations with Bradford City, and at the start of May the two committees announced that an agreement had been reached for a merger. With the members of the rugby club sidelined, all that remained now was for the City membership to give their approval.

But here Bradford's fierce class antagonisms raised their head. A mass meeting of City's members was called for 27 May, and more than 1,500 attended. There were clearly strong arguments in favour of a merger. Promotion to the First Division was looming and City would need a larger ground; and if a second football club were formed in the city it would draw off support. Against this was the traditional rivalry between the two clubs, sharpened by the fear that the rugby club's wealthier membership would dominate the new club. 'There was no need for amalgamation. It was confiscation pure and simple,' argued one member. Above all they feared being swallowed whole by Arthur Briggs. 'The Association egg was floating about Bradford long ago. City was the hen which took it up and hatched it. Now they were going to keep it,' declared another member, tangling his metaphors. When the vote came, the merger was thrown out by 1,031 to 487.

This was a body blow to Briggs, and worse was to follow. A few days later the Football League rejected Bradford's application to join the Second Division. One Bradford club, it seemed, was enough for the time being. Briggs now made an extraordinary decision: to enrol Bradford in the Southern League. It made no financial sense at all, but it did show Bradford were serious (containing many professional sides, the Southern League was the strongest in the country after the Football League), and the move helped them win election to the Football League the following year.

But Bradford Park Avenue, as the new football club was known, struggled to compete with Bradford City. Over the next few years they were kept afloat only by Arthur Briggs's generosity. And although they won promotion in 1914, the First World War intervened and they were relegated again almost immediately afterwards. They would spend the rest of their history bouncing between the lower divisions, and eventually went bankrupt in 1974.

Like Nottingham and Sheffield, Bradford simply wasn't big enough to support two consistently top-class football teams, and the decision not to merge in 1907 proved fatal. Bradford City never repeated the success of their Cup-winning year in 1911 and struggled on at their inadequate Valley Parade ground, the main stand of which, built in 1908, was burned down in the tragedy of 1985, with the loss of fifty-six lives. The problems of the two football clubs were compounded by the fact that die-hards from the old Bradford Rugby Club got together and established a new club, Bradford Northern, which competed professionally in rugby league. Although rugby never again seriously challenged football in the city, this further drew off support.

But for the sport of rugby generally, 1907 proved to be the low point. Thereafter both forms, league and union, bounced back. Rugby league had shrunk to what proved to be an irreducible core in towns such as Wigan, St Helens, Warrington, Wakefield, Featherstone and Castleford. After the defection of the Bradford club in 1907 the football tide was halted and a rugby league micro-culture was consolidated in the West Riding and South Lancashire which has survived to this day.

As for rugby union, the years following the split of 1895 were torrid ones. Membership of the Rugby Football Union shrank from 432 clubs in 1893 to 244 ten years later, and, deprived of Northern players, England won just ten out of forty-two internationals between 1895 and 1909. But there was a subterranean process going on that mirrored that in football. Just as state schools, en masse, were adopting soccer in this period, so the schools of the middle and upper classes, both public and grammar, were switching en masse to rugby – in part because football was coming to be seen as such a working-class sport. It was this that lay behind the sharp decline in the quality of football clubs like the Corinthians, deprived, as they were, of fresh recruits.

It was a process the RFU was aware of and keen to exploit. In 1906 it launched a campaign to consolidate the grip of rugby on the public schools, issuing a circular which warned 'of the danger of young men being driven to look on at games between paid-for men ... The game of Rugby football has always been at its best when good players were available from our Public

Schools, and the more Public School men get to play our game, the better we are certain it is for it.'

It worked. By the immediate pre-war period the England side, now shorn of any working-class presence, had bounced back, winning sixteen games between 1910 and 1914 and losing just three. Football may have become the sport of the masses, as the defeat of the elitist Amateur Football Association between 1907 and 1914 showed. But rugby was becoming equally firmly established as the winter sport of the middle and upper classes. A class divide was solidifying that would persist for the rest of the century.

Before you can get to the football to kick it you must
run . . . Has anyone seen a woman run gracefully or fast?
Pall Mall Gazette, February 1895

10

A Most Unfeminine Exhibition

**British Ladies' Football Club, North London v. South London,
Crouch End Athletic Ground, 23 March 1895**

AND SO FOOTBALL WAS TO BE THE SPORT OF THE WORKING CLASS.
But what of women? Was football to be exclusively male? It
might seem self-evident that late Victorian football was a
masculine sport. But there were those who thought otherwise.

On 27 January 1895 the readers of *Lloyd's Weekly* in London
opened their papers to a startling announcement. ' "A British
Ladies' Football Club" has been started,' it read. 'The President
of the club is Lady Florence Dixie and there is at present a
membership of twenty-six . . . There is a vacancy for two more
ladies and those wishing to join the club should apply to the
energetic secretary, Miss Nettie J. Honeyball, 27 Weston-Park,
Crouch End.' The women, apparently, were training twice a

week at the Crouch End Athletic Ground in Alexandra Park and planned to play an exhibition game. 'The dress,' *Lloyd's* added, 'is of the "rational" kind and consists of blue serge knickers of the divided skirt pattern.'

If it had been almost any sport other than football the announcement might not have been so surprising. The 1890s was a period when women were just beginning to break free from the straitjacket of taboo and convention that had cruelly confined them for much of the Victorian era. Driven by the dramatic expansion since the 1870s of schools and colleges for girls of the upper and middle classes, the movement for female emancipation was taking flight. And as women took their first tentative steps out of the home a surprising number were stepping straight on to the sports field.

By the early 1890s physical education was a central part of the curriculum at most girls' schools. Where once gentle strolls and the occasional game of croquet had been considered sufficient exercise for young ladies, now they were actively encouraged to take part in a range of sports, hockey and tennis being the most popular. Cycling, a craze which took off in the mid-1890s with the invention of the safety bicycle and the pneumatic tyre, particularly captured the imagination of young women. For fearful conservatives and radical feminists alike the bicycle was a symbol of the new age – a taste, in the words of one female cyclist, of 'the intoxication which comes with unfettered liberty'.

But if there was one sport almost all educationalists, male and female, agreed was entirely unsuitable for women, it was football. There were three reasons for this: it was a rough, contact sport; it was increasingly a working-class sport (at a time when organized sport for women was confined to the middle and upper classes); and it was impossible to play in a long dress. This last objection might seem absurd, but it was central.

In other sports women had carved a space for themselves through a policy of caution and compromise. The deal, essentially, was this: they could become sportswomen so long as they didn't stop being ladies. And that meant three things. Firstly, they were expected to play sports with restraint, without being too vigorous or rough (preferably badly). In hockey, women were described, approvingly, as tackling 'gently and fairly'. Secondly, they would not make an exhibition of themselves. For the most part women's sports took place in private. At Newnham College in Cambridge men were actually banned from watching the hockey team. Thirdly, they would continue to dress as ladies. This meant ankle-length skirts, corsets, hats and gloves, even in sports as physically demanding as mountain climbing and skiing. This just wasn't going to work for football, and the organizers of the new club knew it. So who were 'Lady Florence Dixie' and 'Miss Nettie J. Honeyball'? And what were they playing at?

Lady Florence Dixie, the club's president, was well known to the readers of *Lloyd's Weekly*. Thirty-seven years old, she was the sister of the Marquis of Queensberry, who was at the time being sued for libel by Oscar Wilde after accusing him of sodomy with his son, Lord Alfred Douglas. Wilde lost the case, which would lead later that spring to Wilde himself being successfully prosecuted for 'gross indecency' and sentenced to two years' hard labour. Queensberry, also famous for sponsoring the first boxing rules in 1867, had two years earlier attempted to attack the Foreign Secretary, Lord Rosebery, with a dog-whip because he believed he was having an affair with another of his sons. In April 1895 the Marquis's youngest son, Sholto, was arrested in California after he attempted to marry an underage waitress. And on 21 May the Marquis and Lord Alfred fought a prolonged fist fight in Piccadilly on the first day of Wilde's trial, leading to them both being arrested and frogmarched off to the local police station, to the delight of the large crowd that had gathered. It was the sort of aristocratic family today's tabloids drool over.

'The Queensberry family enjoy an almost unique reputation for eccentricity. Every member of it is distinguished by some startling singularity,' wrote the *Echo*. And Florence Dixie was no exception. Twelve years earlier she had hit the headlines after claiming to have been attacked in Windsor by two knife-wielding Irish assassins who were for some reason dressed as women. She said she had been saved by her St Bernard dog, but doubts were cast on the story when it was revealed she had no injuries.

But Lady Florence was also a remarkable woman in many ways. A poet and a novelist, she served as war correspondent for the *Morning Post* during the First Boer War (1880–81). She later became an advocate of the rights of the Zulus and went on to be involved in a whole range of radical political causes, from animal rights to the campaign for Home Rule in Ireland (she was nevertheless a fierce critic of the violent Irish Land League, which was supposedly behind the assassination attempt). Above all, she was a passionate feminist, and it was this that led her to accept the presidency of the British Ladies' Football Club.

'Football is *the* sport for women, *the* pastime of all others which will ensure health, and assist in destroying that hydra-headed monster, the present dress of women,' she told the *Pall Mall Gazette*. It was this last point that was key for her. Florence Dixie was a supporter of the 'rational dress' movement, which sought to liberate women from the corsets and petticoats in which Victorian society had always been determined to imprison them. She saw football as a weapon of subversion, a means of pushing at the boundaries. 'The members of the club do not play in fashion's dress, but in knickers and blouses,' she said. 'There is no reason why football should not be played by women, and played well, too, provided they dress rationally and relegate to limbo the straitjacket attire in which fashion delights to clothe them.'

Staring boldly at the camera, Nettie Honeyball modelled the club's kit for *The Sketch* on 6 February 1895. It is scarcely risqué: the 'knickers' come to the knee and below that she is wearing stockings covered by shin guards. ('They actually allow the calves of their legs to be seen . . . Terrible! Is it not?' wrote Florence Dixie, mockingly.) The top half is just as voluminous and shapeless. But to many this was scandalous. It forced spectators to confront the dreadful reality that women had legs, and for most men before the First World War this was a step too far.

Cyclists had already been down this road. They had come up with a similar 'bifurcated garment' or 'divided dress' (anything to avoid using the word 'trousers'), but few were brave enough to wear it. 'One wants nerves of iron,' wrote a female cyclist, describing the ordeal of cycling through the London suburbs in her 'rationals'. 'The shouts and yells of the children deafen me, the women shriek with laughter or groan and hiss and all sorts of remarks are shouted at one, occasionally some not fit for publication.' Most continued to wear long dresses and crack their teeth on the ground as they became tangled up in wheels and chains rather than submit themselves to this ridicule.

But Nettie Honeyball was as determined as Lady Florence not to compromise. 'I will have nothing to do with balloon-sleeves and trained skirts,' she declared. 'Women are not the "ornamental and useless" creatures men have pictured . . . We don't want any la-di-da members. We play the game in the proper spirit.'

Honeyball was a more obscure figure than Lady Florence. Beyond her involvement in the British Ladies' Football Club we know nothing about her, and her name may be a pseudonym. But she was the driving force behind the project. As the announcement in *Lloyd's* revealed, she lived in Crouch End in North London and she described herself and the other members of the team sometimes as 'middle class', other times as 'upper middle class' ('How else could they spare the time and expense to indulge in practice?' she asked). A journalist from *The Sketch* went along to interview her 'in her pretty little study' at the start of February 1895 and found 'a thoughtful-looking young lady, with a strong personality'. She told him her 'convictions on all matters . . . are all on the side of emanci-pation' and assured him there was nothing 'farcical' about an attempt to set up a women's football team.

Most of the members, she said, were in their late teens or early twenties. 'None of them, of course, had previously played, but, like myself, had gained all their experience and love of football from frequent on-looking.' They came, she told another reporter, from all over the London area. 'One girl came over the other day from Ewell [near Epsom] on her bicycle, played football vigorously for a couple of hours, and then went back home again on her machine . . . At first, some of the girls wore high-heeled and pointed boots, but these have been abandoned.' The women now wore 'proper football boots, with the corrugated toe and heel'. They were being trained by the Spurs half-back John William Julian.

Honeyball took the reporter from *The Sketch* along to a practice and he was impressed, and surprised, 'at the amount of ability already attained . . . The ladies went about their various duties pluckily and energetically, skill and shooting power making up for any lack of speed or force.' The visit, he confessed, had 'dispelled the suspicion of burlesque that came into my mind'.

Others were less sympathetic. 'Before you can get to the football to kick it you must run . . . Has anyone seen a woman run gracefully or fast?' asked the *Pall Mall Gazette*. 'A woman sometimes waddles like a duck and sometimes like a chicken – it all depends on her weight. She is physically incapable of stretching her legs sufficiently to enable her to take the stride masculine. Dame Nature never intended her to do anything of the sort,' wrote a correspondent to the same paper.

The club had originally applied to play at the Oval but Charlie Alcock had turned them down – a decision enthusiastically supported in the sporting press. 'There is a good deal of difference between a lot of schoolgirls romping after a ball in their own field in their own way, and a promiscuously selected set trying to make money,' wrote one paper, after it became clear the club intended to charge admittance for their games.

But this was not the first time women had played football, and played it in public. It has always been thought the Crouch

End ladies was the first serious attempt to get a women's football club off the ground. But a careful trawl of the press reveals a previously unknown team in Glasgow fourteen years earlier, in 1881. It's not clear if Nettie Honeyball and Florence Dixie were aware of this earlier experiment. If they were, it won't have encouraged them.

The background of these Glasgow women is not known but, as with Nettie Honeyball's team, it's likely they were from the respectable classes. They staged their first match at Hibernian Park in Edinburgh, the home of Hibs, on 7 May 1881; they had hoped to play in Glasgow but struggled to find anyone prepared to lease them a ground. It was styled an international, Scotland v. England, but all the players belonged to the same club and it's likely most of the 'English' players were Glasgow-based. As with the British Ladies' Football Club, they wore knickerbockers, and close to two thousand people turned out to witness the spectacle.

'So it has come at last! What next? Two teams of young women have just played a game under Association Rules in Edinburgh,' snorted *Bell's Life* on 14 May. 'The football shown was of the most primitive order,' it said, comparing the women to novice schoolboys and dismissing the match, which Scotland won 3–0, as a 'farce'. *The Scotsman* reported that the crowd, almost entirely male, treated 'the various episodes and accidents of the game with sarcastic or personal remarks, and with loud guffaws'. Most, 'having satisfied their curiosity with a look at the players, left the ground and before the match was concluded more than half the spectators had gone. The general feeling seemed to be that the whole affair was a most unfeminine exhibition.'

The following week the women managed to persuade the owners of the Shawfield Ground on the outskirts of Glasgow to allow them to stage a match there. The result was a disaster. Around five hundred people paid a shilling to get in, but early in the game a couple of thousand people of 'the rougher element' broke through the feeble fences surrounding the ground. 'They laughed, cheered, and occasionally hooted, the most shocking imprecations and vulgarities being audible in all quarters above the general din,' wrote the *Glasgow Herald*. After fifty-five minutes the mob cut the ropes and invaded the pitch, forcing the game to be abandoned. The women were trapped and the police were forced to baton-charge the crowd to rescue them, but not before some had been 'badly treated' and one had fainted. Later they were hissed as they drove away from the ground. The *Herald* said it hoped 'such an exhibition will not be repeated in the neighbourhood of the city'.

There were similar scenes when the women staged a match in Manchester a month later. Once more a mob broke into the ground, and then on to the pitch. The women, after their experience in Glasgow, ran straight to their waiting wagonette and fled the scene 'amid the jeers of the multitude and much disorder', according to the *Manchester Guardian*. A couple more games in Liverpool followed but the club folded shortly afterwards. It was hardly an inspiring example. The sight of women playing football clearly touched a raw nerve among late Victorian males.

In the years since 1881 women's sport had made great strides. The mid-1880s saw the establishment of the All-England Ladies' Championship in tennis and the Ladies' Amateur Golf Championship. And in 1887 Lottie Dod won the

Women's Singles Championship at Wimbledon at the age of just fifteen to become the first female sports superstar. She went on to claim four more singles titles and also represented England at both golf and hockey. But women's involvement in football had gone backwards. In amateur days newspapers had frequently commented on the large numbers of the 'fairer sex' present at football games. Matches involving teams such as Wanderers, Royal Engineers and Old Etonians were social events, and opportunities for flirtation and courtship. A female presence was also noted at early professional games, encouraged by the fact women got in free. Preston North End abandoned this policy in April 1885 after two thousand turned up for a game. Most other clubs soon followed suit, and as football became more exclusively working class and grounds became more packed the proportion of women in the crowd declined. Younger women might still turn out for big FA Cup games, particularly the final, but for the most part photos from the Edwardian era show a sea of flat caps and male faces.

But the ladies of Crouch End were undaunted. The first game, after a number of delays caused by the weather, was scheduled for the Crouch End Athletic Ground on Saturday, 23 March 1895. Admission was a shilling (two shillings for the covered grandstand) and a crowd of around five hundred was expected. In fact, ten thousand turned up.

'All through the afternoon train-loads of excited people journeyed over from all parts, and the respectable array of carriages, cabs, and other vehicles marked a record in the history of football,' wrote the man from *The Sketch*. (For comparison, Woolwich Arsenal, London's only Football League side at this time, had an average home League gate of 6,400.) The

Crouch End ground had a single turnstile and was hopelessly inadequate for such numbers. The vast majority simply climbed the fence, and many more took up positions, perched like rooks, in the trees around the ground. There was no banking and it's unlikely more than a fraction of those present could see anything.

There was a men's game first, between Crouch End and the Third Grenadier Guards. But these were both very minor sides and the huge crowd certainly hadn't turned out to watch them. It was curiosity that drew them, fuelled by the controversy (ably stoked by Honeyball and Dixie) that had raged in the press since the announcement of the new club.

Four thirty, the scheduled time for the kick-off, came and went without any sign of the women. The proud, feminist rhetoric and the bold costumes had all seemed well and good when they were practising alone, or talking to individual journalists. Now, peeking through the pavilion windows at this vast mass of sceptical, potentially hostile manhood, nerves set in. It was almost five o'clock when the two teams finally emerged into the pale spring sunlight.

'There was a roar of laughter,' wrote the *Pall Mall Gazette*. 'Hundreds fell off the fence. Tears rolled down the cheeks of men who had never been known to weep in public. Other men … fell upon each other's necks and shoulders for mutual support. Small boys fell into paroxysms. Women smiled and blushed.' Such was the effect of the sight of women in trousers in 1895.

It was a daunting reception and, not surprisingly, nerves showed in the ladies' play. 'The first few minutes were sufficient to show that football by women … is totally out of the question,' wrote the man from *The Sketch*, who had been so sympathetic when he'd visited Nettie Honeyball six weeks earlier. 'A footballer requires speed, judgement, skill, and pluck. Not one of these four qualities was apparent on Saturday. For the most part, the ladies wandered aimlessly over the field at an ungraceful jog-trot.' 'Few of the girls seemed even to know the rudiments of the game,' the *Pall Mall Gazette* informed its readers. Even the 'Lady Correspondent' of the *Manchester Guardian*, who tried hard to be sympathetic, was forced to admit, 'Only two of the girls were able to kick with any freedom and not many ran well, the habit of wearing long skirts and tight waists showing plainly in the violent elbow action of the majority.'

Nettie Honeyball had divided the club arbitrarily into North and South London teams for the match, and North London quickly took the lead. They were helped by the fact that they possessed by far the two best players: their goalkeeper, 'Mrs Graham', and their left-winger, Nellie Gilbert.

'Mrs Graham' was a pseudonym for Miss Helen Graham Matthews, and she was from Glasgow. It was clear she was one of the few members to have played regularly before and she drew 'hearty applause' for 'her neat punts and cool punches', according to *The Sketch*. She was also a decent outfield player and regularly came out of goal to help the defence. Nellie Gilbert was tiny and ran with such freedom and displayed such touch that it was assumed by many she was a boy. 'Her appearance created shrieks of laughter,' wrote the *Pall Mall Gazette*. The crowd quickly nicknamed her 'Tommy' and her true gender remained a source of speculation for the remainder of the life of the British Ladies' Football Club.

By half-time North London were 2–1 in the lead, all of the scoring, according to some reports, coming from own goals, which rather suggests the women hadn't quite got the hang of things yet. Exhausted, they sat down on the touchline to suck some lemons, subjected to the taunts and abuse of the crowd. There was a raucous element and some had been drinking; the police had to intervene during the interval to break up fights. In the second half North London added five more goals to finish 7–1 winners. But by then much of the crowd, weary of the novelty, had drifted away.

Lady Florence had planned to present copies of her book *Gloriana; or the Revolution of 1900* – in which the heroine, disguised as a man, becomes prime minister, grants women the vote and creates a utopia of sexual equality – to the winning team. But this didn't happen. The temperature was dropping rapidly, a storm was threatening and the two teams were only too happy to get out of Alexandra Park and make their way home.

The press, for the most part, was hostile. 'Let not the British Ladies misconstrue the enormous attendance into a sign of public approval,' wrote *The Sketch*. 'It must be clear to everybody that girls are totally unfitted for the rough work of the football-field. As a means of exercise in a back-garden it is not to be commended. As a public entertainment it is to be deplored.' 'The match was little more than a burlesque,' the *Standard* opined, while the *Pall Mall Gazette* described the women as 'misguided females' who 'knew nothing about football'.

But Nettie Honeyball and her colleagues were not to be discouraged, and they now took their show on the road. Over the next three months they played at least twenty-three matches around the country, drawing crowds of between five hundred and eight thousand and taking a share of the gate that was sometimes as much as £50. Their reception varied. In Belfast on 19 June they were 'enthusiastically cheered' as they passed through the streets; the crowd removed the horses from their wagonette and pulled it themselves to show their admiration 'of the New Women'. But in Newcastle on 20 May, where they'd drawn eight thousand to St James's Park, the reporter from the *Northern Gossip* was 'disgusted' by the abuse they received. 'The big majority of the men seemed to visit this novel contest merely to pass unseemly remarks about the persons of the players, and to gloat over their own imbecilities,' he wrote. Honeyball also complained that in Maidenhead on 15 May 'the remarks passed by some of the crowd were not all that could be desired'. Sometimes the local press managed simultaneously to generate publicity and stir up hostility. The *Grantham Times* invited working men to come along to see 'twenty-two specimens of liberated womanhood, dressed in real rational costumes, making pantomime of the Association game'.

Nevertheless, the standard of play seems to have steadily improved. 'The fair exponents of the game played with a considerable amount of combination and with no little dash,' wrote the *Newark Advertiser* at the end of May. 'Mrs Graham' and 'Tommy' (Nellie Gilbert's nickname had stuck) were singled out again and again for special praise. In Newark the diminutive Tommy particularly 'delighted the crowd by charging opponents and knocking them down'. But in the main the press was contemptuous of the standard of the football, and it's clear most spectators watched games more in the spirit of a circus act than a sporting occasion.

More matches were organized the following season. In early November the ladies drew between seven and eight thousand to the Harlequins Athletic Ground in Cardiff where the female correspondent of the *Western Mail* criticized them for being a 'frowsy, untidy lot' with 'blouses all crumpled up, as if they had been crammed into a carpet bag and left there for weeks'. A week later they were at Loakes Park in Wycombe where the first ever photos of a women's football match were taken. And at the end of November they played in Rochdale, upsetting the Bishop of Manchester who denounced the match as 'a disgrace to the town'. But by now the press was losing interest and the number of games was dwindling.

In the spring of 1896 there was a tour of Scotland. This was undertaken by a team that was an offshoot of the London club, organized by Mrs Graham. It proved the death-knell of the experiment. One of the first games was against a junior men's side at Irvine at the end of May. Their opponents had a mocking attitude, according to the *Irvine Herald*, and would run up to the women with the ball at their feet and laugh in their faces. Whether intentionally or not, Mrs Graham was given a black eye; then, in scenes reminiscent of Glasgow and Manchester in 1881, there was a pitch invasion. The women were 'hustled' and they had to 'kick their way' to the clubhouse, according to press reports.

Worse was to follow a few days later at Saracen Park in Glasgow. Here the women were attacked by a large stone-throwing mob as they made their way back to their hotel after the game. The windows of their cab were smashed and poor

Mrs Graham, attempting to shelter one of her team-mates, received nasty cuts to the hands and was stunned by a blow to the head. In a letter to the *Glasgow Evening Citizen* on 1 June one of the women blamed the groundsman for opening the gates shortly before the end of the game, 'letting in the rabble – gathered presumably from the slums ... I may mention that Eastern [Scotland] crowds are no disgrace to civilisation like the Glasgow half-breeds, Scottish as they are.'

A handful more matches were played, but after that the British Ladies' Football Club faded from view. We hear nothing more of Nettie Honeyball, and if women's football did continue to be played, it failed to spark any interest in the newspapers. In 1902 the FA banned its members from playing against 'lady teams'. It was a gratuitous gesture. Women's football was already dead, and would remain so until the First World War.

It's easy to see the mistakes Nettie Honeyball and Florence Dixie made. Where other sportswomen had proceeded cautiously, taking care not to ruffle feathers, they went out of their way to turn football into a political statement. The presence of Lady Florence as president – 'the recognized leader of the Advanced Women's Brigade', according to the *Pall Mall Gazette* – was provocation enough for many. Like the Glasgow women of 1881, they played in public and charged admission. But then, there's not much point in making a political statement in private. And once they had gone on the road they had to cover costs. The truth is, British society in 1895 simply wasn't ready for women playing football, and there wasn't really a great deal the ladies could have done to overcome this.

Twenty years later, during the First World War, there was a sudden, dramatic revival of women's football, this time led by

Right: The 1889 FA Cup final, as seen by the *Illustrated Sporting and Dramatic News*. Having been defeated in the semi-final and final in previous years, Preston finally defeated Wolves 3–0.

Left: The West Bromwich Albion team that defeated Preston in the FA Cup Final of 1888. The picture neatly captures the power structures of late-Victorian football – the working class players to the fore, the middle class owners controlling from the background.

West Bromwich Albion out for a 'brisk walk', the standard method of training among early professional teams. It was thought best to limit the time players spent with a football, so as to make them all the hungrier for it come Saturday.

Above left: Jimmy Catton, editor of the *Athletic News* and the leading football journalist of the era. 'Jimmy was a little tubby fellow, not five feet in height. He was, however, the greatest writer of his day, knowledgeable, benevolent and respected by all the soccer authorities,' wrote Sunderland's Charles Buchan.

Above right: Jimmy Catton interviewing the great Derby County and England striker, Steve Bloomer.

CORINTHIANS

The Corinthians line-up before a game against Sheffield Wednesday in 1905. For some reason only gentlemen amateurs ever posed with their hands in their pockets. *Left to right*: Vassall, Day, Hewitt, G. S. Harris, Craig, Simpson, Rowlandson, Morgan, Owen, Timmis, Vickers, S. S. Harris, Wright.

Left: Nicholas Lane 'Pa' Jackson, the founder of the Corinthians. He believed the 'democratization of the game' led to a lowering of standards and looked back to a golden age when the game was 'confined to old public school boys [and] the laws were strictly observed'.

Below: The Corinthians on tour in Budapest, 1904.

THE PARTING OF THE WAYS.

Left: In 1907 the Corinthians led a breakaway Amateur Football Association, comprised almost entirely of middle- and upper-class Southern teams. It was quickly crushed by the FA.

WOMEN

Lady Florence Dixie, President of the British Ladies and leader of the 'advanced women's brigade'.

Nettie Honeyball, founder of the British Ladies Football Team in 1895. Their dress was considered very risqué by the standards of the time.

Below: The British Ladies in action at Crouch End, March 1895. 'Few of the girls seemed even to know the rudiments of the game,' sneered the *Pall Mall Gazette*. Their matches provoked violent scenes in some places.

Left: The British Ladies at Loakes Park in Wycombe in 1896 – the first ever women's football match to be photographed. The club folded shortly afterwards and in 1902 the FA banned members from playing against women's teams.

EDWARDIAN FOOTBALL

Right: The FA Selection Committee casts its expert eye over a trial game at the start of the twentieth century.

Newcastle schoolboys line up – minus a player – to play London at White Hart Lane in 1914. The adoption of football by state elementary schools did more than anything else to make it the mass sport of the working class.

Crystal Palace, scene of FA Cup Finals from 1895 to 1914. 'It was utterly unlike any other place where football was ordinarily played. It was just a space – sylvan, verdant, luscious – God's work,' wrote Jimmy Catton. Crowds in excess of 100,000 watched the Cup Final in 1901, 1905 and 1913.

The folk festival of football reborn – sailors dance with their girls before an FA Cup Final at Crystal Palace.

Above: Manchester City's Billy Meredith flies down the wing against Bolton Wanderers at Crystal Palace during the FA Cup Final of 1904. Meredith scored the only goal of the game.

Right: Billy Meredith after his move to Manchester United in 1907. The greatest player of the pre-First World War period, Meredith was also the driving force behind the formation of the Players' Union.

Below: Meredith's Manchester United team mate and fellow unionist Charlie Roberts. The shortness of his shorts upset the FA.

THIS IS *NOT* THE WAY THE TRANSFER OF A PLAYER IS ARRANGED.

Left: The Players' Union campaigned – unsuccessfully – against both the retain and transfer system, which effectively reduced players to the status of chattels, and the maximum wage, set at £4 in 1901.

Right: 'No-one gets lost on a straight road.' Charles Clegg, Chairman of the FA from 1890 and the dominant figure in the second generation of men to run the game. He crushed both the Amateur Football Association and the Players' Union.

Above: The Outcasts FC – Manchester United players suspended by the FA in the summer of 1909 for refusing to resign from the Players' Union. *Back row, left to right*: Moger, Picken, Corbett, Holden, Burgess, Clough, Meredith, Boswell. *Front row*: Wall, Turnbull, Roberts, Coleman, Duckworth.

THE GREATER GAME.

Right: When war broke out in August 1914 the football season continued, to the fury of the right-wing press who saw it as another example of the mercenary nature of football.

working-class ladies drafted in to work in munitions and other factories. The most famous of the new teams was Dick Kerr Ladies from Preston. They played charity matches, initially to raise money for the war effort, and on Boxing Day 1920 drew a crowd of more than fifty thousand to Goodison Park for a game against St Helen's Ladies. During 1921 Dick Kerr Ladies played a total of sixty-seven games, drawing almost a million spectators in total.

But the football establishment was still deeply uncomfortable with the sight of women kicking a ball. On 5 December 1921 the FA issued an infamous decree: 'Complaints having been made as to football being played by women, the Council feel impelled to express their strong opinion that the game of football is quite unsuitable for females and ought not to be encouraged ... The Council request clubs belonging to the Association to refuse use of their grounds for such matches.' Incredibly, it was not until 1971 that this was rescinded. The brief liberty women had enjoyed under conditions of war was crushed and they were herded back into the home. It was a fatal blow. Dick Kerr Ladies continued until the mid-1960s, but the number of women's football teams in Britain slumped from 150 in 1921 to just seventeen in 1947. Only in recent decades has the women's sport recovered.

Today, it is hard to conceive the degree to which society in the late nineteenth century was dominated by middle- and upper-class men. They organized society economically for their own benefit; they also set the emotional, intellectual and cultural framework within which issues were discussed. By the 1890s the working-class movement was challenging this control, putting forward an alternative view both of itself and the world it lived in. But women lagged far behind.

'When I first opened my eyes as a girl ... and realized that my sex was the barrier that hid from my yearning gaze the bright fields of activity, usefulness, and reform, the bitterness and pain that entered into my soul can never be obliterated in my lifetime,' declared Florence Dixie in 1891. Lower-class women lived lives of grinding toil, exploited both in the workplace and the home. And women of Lady Florence's class were often trapped in lives of unspeakable tedium, sitting around waiting for husbands to appear. For any woman wishing to break free society had to hand a whole range of taboos and conventions with which to strip her of her self-belief and whip her back into line. The demands of sexual modesty in particular were crippling. Generally the process was subtle, even unstated – women did their own policing. But at times it could be horrifyingly crude, and the male urge to control and confine was seen at its most brutal in the violence that accompanied the women's football matches in Glasgow and Manchester in 1881 and at Irvine and Saracen Park in 1896. Bold spirits such as Nettie Honeyball and Mrs Graham were attempting to kick their way out of a box men had constructed for them. But they were ahead of their time and they paid the price.

As football became more working class it became increasingly male. For supporters and players alike it was an exercise in male bonding, an escape to an all-male world. For the most part wives and girlfriends would have no place either on the terraces or on the pitch. Football had become the people's game, but it would belong to only half of the people.

It would be vanity for me to pretend that
I was unaware of the fact that I am a great footballer.

Billy Meredith, 1919

11

Billy Meredith: Professional

Bolton Wanderers v. Manchester City, FA Cup Final
Crystal Palace, 23 April 1904

DAWN ON SATURDAY, 23 APRIL 1904 REVEALED AN EXTRAORDINARY
sight at Euston station: thousands upon thousands of bleary-
eyed Lancastrians squeezed on to the platforms, packed into
the waiting rooms, milling around the ticket halls, some
sprawled on benches, others propped up against walls or
against each other, trying to get a little sleep. All through the
night train after train had rumbled in from the North disgorg-
ing legions of cloth-capped football fans, down in London for
the Cup Final. But they had been greeted by torrential rain, and
most opted to stay under shelter until it eased off, or at least
until dawn broke. There were similar scenes at King's Cross, St
Pancras and Marylebone.

Eighty years later it would have been a nightmare scenario for the Metropolitan Police. But, although late Victorian and Edwardian football crowds were often rowdy, violence was normally sparked by a specific incident – a poor refereeing decision, a particularly bad foul, the cancellation of a game. It was not ritualized, tribalized, in the way it would be later. Supporters of the two sides that morning mingled happily, exchanging good-natured banter and sharing the beer and pork pies they had brought down with them. For many this was the experience of a lifetime. Most had been saving all year through the 'Cup Final Clubs' and they hadn't travelled five hours to pick a fight with men who lived ten miles down the road.

The finalists that year were Manchester City and Bolton Wanderers. Oddly it was the first time two Lancashire sides had met, although a Lancashire team had been present in fourteen of the twenty-two FA Cup Finals since 1882. The annual invasion of the Northern hordes had swelled dramatically since 1895 when the final was switched to Crystal Palace, which had a far larger capacity than the Oval. A crowd of 42,560 had watched the first Palace final and after that numbers rose steadily, to 65,891 in 1897, 73,833 in 1899, culminating in the astonishing crowd of 110,820 that watched Spurs draw with Sheffield United in 1901. Spurs won the replay, becoming the first professional Southern team to lift the Cup and this huge attendance marked football's arrival as a truly national sport.

With no London side involved, the turn-out for the City–Wanderers game was a mere 61,374. But when the clouds finally parted shortly after dawn that morning a deluge of humanity poured forth from the stations and flooded the streets of central London. Many had never visited the metropolis before (this was City's first final and Bolton had not been there since 1894) and the torrent flowed first towards Westminster Abbey, the Houses of Parliament, Trafalgar Square – the great sights of London. Sporting their club colours in hats, button holes and in their umbrellas, fans wandered, blinking, around the historic monuments. Then, as midday drew near, they made for Ludgate Hill, London Bridge and St Paul's, the terminals from which they would make the six-mile journey down to Sydenham.

Crystal Palace was a sporting arena like no other. It was located in the grounds of the enormous glass palace that had been built for Prince Albert's Great Exhibition of 1851 and then transported, lock, stock and barrel, from Hyde Park and rebuilt in South London to become the centrepiece of the world's first mass entertainment theme park. The palace itself contained permanent displays on the history of art, as well as a vast 4,500-pipe organ. Outside, life-sized (laughably inaccurate) statues of dinosaurs roamed through landscaped gardens and along the shores of ornamental lakes, and a spectacular series of fountains containing twelve thousand jets of water and requiring seven million gallons for each display sparkled in the sunlight. There was also a maze and a roller-coaster, and the site hosted numerous temporary exhibitions on topics from flower arranging to aeronautics.

It was one of the great attractions of Victorian London, and from its opening in 1854 through to the mid-1880s Crystal Palace drew two million visitors a year. But by the end of the century it was struggling financially. The fountains proved costly to operate and maintain and in 1894 the two largest lakes were filled in and grassed over. This occurred just as the FA was casting around for a new location for the Cup Final and it was decided to convert one of these, in the south of the park, into a sports arena. Charlie Alcock, in his final year as honorary secretary of the FA, inspected the site and gave the go-ahead, and Cup Finals were played there every year from 1895 to 1914. The same space is now occupied by the National Athletics Stadium.

The pitch ran, more or less, from north to south, and on the western side was a small pavilion flanked by two low stands. These provided seating for a few thousand; other than that the ground was a natural amphitheatre and spectators simply gathered on the grass banks, swaying, according to one observer, like 'a cornfield shaken by the wind'. 'The great charm of the Crystal Palace was that it was so utterly unlike any other place where football was ordinarily played,' wrote Jimmy Catton, who loved the venue. 'It was just a space – sylvan, verdant, luscious – God's work.'

Admission to the Cup Final also bought admission to the palace and theme park, and many fans arrived early to take in the sights. They then sprawled on the grass to get some much-needed sleep, or unpacked the picnics they had brought with them from home, while the more athletic shinned up the trees that fringed the ground to get the best vantage points. The amphitheatre was considerably larger than the football pitch, and in the flat space behind the goals bands played and, according to Catton, 'sailors danced with their lasses'. The sun always seemed to be shining and for men of Catton's generation the Crystal Palace finals would become a golden memory of the pre-war era. With their colourful crowds and holiday atmosphere they were in many ways a throwback to an earlier age, the great Shrove Tuesday folk festival of football reborn – but in more structured, ordered form, shorn of the violence and mayhem, safe within the confines and restraints of the new industrial society.

'The conduct of these vast masses was, considering that it composed a football crowd, wonderfully good,' wrote one newspaper after the 1901 final, and it was an event the upper class was happy to patronize in more ways than one. Present in 1904 were the Conservative Prime Minister Arthur Balfour, who also happened to be a patron of Manchester City, Kinnaird's old team-mate and now Colonial Secretary Alfred Lyttelton, who would present the Cup, and the Postmaster General, Lord Stanley. Numerous other Members of Parliament, particularly those with seats in the North-West, were keen for their faces to be seen. And the first stirrings of the alliance between football and showbiz were visible in the presence of leading music hall stars George Robey and Harry Lauder. A good seat in the pavilions or stands was a sign you were part of the Edwardian A-list. And there to greet them all were Kinnaird, Alcock, Clegg and the rest of the FA hierarchy, resplendent in top hat and tails.

From the great and the good supping tea in the palace to the masses sprawled on the lawns outside, the Cup Final was now a national institution. Football was unquestionably the national sport, and this was its showpiece. Here on display was a whole new world, a new culture, one that had scarcely existed twenty years before, of fans, players, officials, trainers, journalists and patrons, which no national figure could afford to ignore. It was a culture in the process of creating its own traditions and myths and one which was already throwing up its own heroes and icons. And it was one such figure the majority of the crowd at Crystal Palace that day had turned out to see: Billy Meredith, Manchester City's captain and outside-right, and football's first superstar.

In central Manchester it was Meredith's image, firing the ball past the Bolton goalkeeper, that adorned the huge poster advertising the Grand Central Railway Company's Cup Final excursions. Singing was already common at football matches (often music hall songs) and it was Meredith's name that was on the lips of the Manchester lads standing on the grass slopes:

> Oh I wish I was you Billy Meredith,
> I wish I was you, I envy you, indeed I do!
> It ain't that you're tricky with your feet,
> But it's those centres that you send in
> Which Turnbull then heads in,
> Oh, I wish I was you,
> Indeed I do,
> Indeed I do . . .

And when the players emerged on to the pitch late in the morning it was Meredith the journalists crowded around, hopeful of squeezing a few words from the notoriously taciturn Welshman. They were in luck. 'We ought to win,' he told them. 'If we play anything like our normal game, the Cup is ours. All the boys are going for all they are worth. If today's game had been a League match, it would have been a pretty certain couple of points, but this is the Cup Final and, well, anything might happen.'

*

Billy Meredith was the greatest player of the pre-war era. In fact, as late as 1960 the journalist Percy Young was seriously arguing he was the greatest footballer of all time. But he also embodied his age, and the rhythms and patterns of his career capture what life was like for this, the first generation of full-time professional footballers. He also found himself at the heart of the struggle that was the central feature of football in the twenty years before the First World War, that between the professional players and the clubs that employed them.

Meredith was born in 1874 in the picturesque village of Chirk in North Wales, just a few hundred yards from the English border. His background was typical both of early footballers and of many of the men who watched them. Like the early Labour Party, football drew its support from the skilled and semi-skilled sections of the working class. The very poor had neither the time nor money, nor it seems the inclination, to devote themselves to either politics or sport until after the First World War. Meredith was the youngest of ten children and his parents were Primitive Methodists and teetotallers. His father was an engineer in the local coal mine, and when Billy left school and went down the pit at the age of twelve it was with ambitions to follow him. But football intervened.

Meredith was taught at school by T. E. Thomas, a football fanatic who, largely single-handedly, turned Chirk into the powerhouse of early Welsh football. Including Meredith, he coached thirteen Welsh internationals and later went on to be president of the Football Association of Wales. Under his guidance Chirk won the Welsh Cup five times between 1887 and 1894, an extraordinary achievement for a village of little more than two thousand people. The teenage Meredith appeared in the finals of 1893 and 1894.

By then bigger clubs had their eye on him. With Chirk crippled by a strike in the local mines at the start of the 1893–94 season he turned out a number of times for the Second Division side Northwich Victoria. Then, in the autumn of 1894, Manchester City came courting. Initially Meredith had no desire to become a full-time footballer, and in this too he was typical of many of his contemporaries.

Until the emergence of players like Meredith himself there was little mystique attached to professional footballers. By the early 1890s top players were earning £3 a week during the season, an excellent salary by working-class standards: very few skilled workers could expect to earn much more than £2 a week. But their playing careers were short and could be ended at any moment by injury. It was also a dead-end job. There were few openings within the game for ex-pros and most had either to return to their old trade or, if they had none, find some other way of earning a living. Many became publicans, but the former professional hanging around the dressing-room door cadging money from old team-mates was a tragically common sight.

By this time club bosses were steadily tightening the screws on players, restricting their freedom to sell their services to the highest bidder in ways that totally contravened the laissez-faire principles of the age and were unique in late Victorian Britain. In 1890, on the initiative of Billy Sudell at Preston, the Football League had introduced the retain and transfer system. This effectively reduced players to the status of chattels. Once a club had bought them they could hold on to them as long as they liked, so long as they continued to pay them a reasonable wage. And if they decided not to retain a player at the end of the season they could demand a transfer fee for him, regardless of the fact they were no longer paying him. 'Slavery pure and simple' Meredith later called the system, and many others shared his instinctive revulsion at the buying and selling of human beings, including Charles Clegg at the FA. But the smaller clubs were determined to keep a system which prevented the richer teams poaching their best players. And the Football League was the one body the all-powerful Clegg was never able to impose his will on.

Professional football drew young men away from their homes and families, as well as their local teams, and club representatives often had to run a gauntlet of angry locals. Legend has it that the two Manchester City representatives who first approached Meredith were chased by an angry crowd and ducked in the village pond. The story is probably apocryphal but Meredith's parents were certainly hostile. 'It is all very well for you gentlemen to leave your big cities and come to our villages to steal our boys away,' his mother told them, 'but a mother thinks of other things besides money. Our boys are happy and healthy, satisfied with their work and their innocent amusements . . . If Billy takes my advice he will stick to his work and play football for his own amusement when his work is finished.' Both parents remained bemused by the concept of playing a game for a living and never showed the slightest interest in Meredith's subsequent career, even when he was a big international star and a Welsh hero.

Meredith had inherited their austere work ethic and, like many others, always believed it was better for players to have a job outside football. It kept them occupied and meant they had a skill when they finished playing, and he felt evening training was quite sufficient to keep a man fit. Initially he signed as an amateur for Manchester City and commuted from Chirk, where he continued to work in the mine. But in January 1895 he was pressured into signing on as a full-time professional and the following year City made this compulsory for all their players. For Meredith, football was now a job, and having been forced to abandon his dream of becoming an engineer he would treat it as such, taking a hard-headed approach and always ensuring he got the best possible terms. 'Money must be everything to the professional footballer – even if his enthusiasm for the game is as great as that of any amateur in the land – because he cannot live without it,' he later said.

The move to Manchester was a wrench for a country boy like Meredith. Little more than a village in the mid-eighteenth century, Manchester's population had soared to 338,000 by 1851. The beating heart of Lancashire's cotton industry, it was the phenomenon of the age, a source of awe and wonder, and sometimes horror, to contemporaries. The town centre was ringed with what the political philosopher Friedrich Engels called a 'girdle of squalor', and Ardwick, the home of Manchester City, was typical of this unplanned industrial sprawl. Crowded with cotton mills, limeworks, ironworks, sawmills and grimy, jerry-built, back-to-back housing, it was sliced apart by railway viaducts. Manchester City's Hyde Road ground lay at the heart of this and was just a scrap of waste ground hemmed in by railway lines, factories and housing with one small stand. Players changed at a local pub, the Hyde Road Hotel, and then walked under a railway arch and along a muddy path to get to the pitch. In later life Meredith recalled having to run across a plank to take corners. From match reports it seems it was eternally raining on Saturday afternoons, and the ground epitomized the new industrial face of professional football. It wasn't the sort of place the Corinthians visited if they could help it.

But Billy Meredith quickly settled there. Although a Second Division team, Manchester City attracted decent crowds for the time, generally averaging between five and ten thousand, and there was a carnival atmosphere at home games. Supporters blew bugles and banged drums when City attacked and for big matches they wore fancy dress. Meredith soon became a local hero.

Five feet nine inches in his boots and weighing eleven stone, Meredith was a showman, a classic tricky winger. He would hypnotize full-backs, shifting the ball from foot to foot, then suddenly poke it past them and beat them for pace. For such a consummate professional, there was something very Corinthian about him, a studied nonchalance. He always played with a toothpick in his mouth – a replacement for the tobacco he had chewed as a teenager – and this, combined with his bandy legs, was a godsend to the cartoonists. He was soon the most recognizable footballer in the country.

His ball skills were the key to his success. 'A player,' he wrote in 1906, 'is always fairly master of the situation so long as he feels that he has the ball completely under his control.' In his old age he would instruct youngsters to practise dribbling with the ball attached to their boot by a two-foot piece of string, making sure the string never became taut. He liked to hug the touchline, and sometimes even ran outside it, keeping the ball just in play with his toe. His trademark move was a dash to the corner flag from where he would whip back a cross between the penalty spot and the six-yard line. This was unusual. Most training manuals at this time instructed wingers to cross early, before beating the last back; they were also encouraged to cross low since it was still assumed defenders were better headers of the ball than forwards. But Meredith would put in crosses at varying heights and the centre-forwards who played with him needed to be good in the air – a style that became the norm after the First World War.

He was also a prolific goalscorer himself, particularly in his early years. For Manchester City between 1894 and 1905 he scored 146 goals in 339 League games, his speciality being a cross-shot from a spot just ten yards from the corner flag. He had the technique to volley crosses from the opposite wing first time, and he was also an excellent passer of the ball. At times he could be selfish, and he tended to fade out of games if man-marked. His right-half and inside-right were crucial to him and had to work as fetchers and carriers to feed the great man. But he was always generous in his praise of them.

He'd arrived at Manchester City at a pivotal moment in the club's history. Formed in 1880 from the Working Men's Club at the local St Mark's Church, they were known initially as Gorton, then Ardwick, and by the early 1890s they were Manchester's second team, behind Newton Heath (later Manchester United). But in the summer of 1894 they came close to bankruptcy and had to be restructured as a limited company. The modern name was adopted and it was then that they were elected to the Second Division of the Football League for the first time.

It was an odd club for Meredith, with his teetotal, Methodist background, to have chosen. City was kept afloat on a sea of alcohol, its ownership dominated by local brewing interests. The journey from chapel to pub was common among early professional football teams. Early church connections were usually quickly severed and brewers and publicans owned stakes in many clubs. But at City the control was almost total. The Hyde Road ground was rented from Chester's Brewery, whose managing director, Stephen Chester Thompson, was the club's honorary president. The chairman, John Chapman, owned several local pubs. And the club secretary, Joshua Parlby, who had persuaded Meredith to make the move from Chirk, was also a publican. FA rules restricted directors' dividends to just 5 per cent and football club owners were forever protesting they were involved in the sport for love rather than money. But there could be lucrative spin-offs, and the owners of Manchester City made large profits from their control of the pubs and bars in and around the ground.

The alcohol-soaked atmosphere that surrounded the club grated on Meredith, who, although not a teetotaller himself, rarely drank. He just had to look around him in the pub changing rooms to see its effects. City's centre-forward William Gillespie had a particular problem and frequently had to be dropped from games because he was drunk. Meredith took it upon himself to look after Gillespie, rooming with him and at times even holding his money for him so he wouldn't spend it on binge drinking.

An article at this time in a sporting magazine captured the ambience at many football clubs. Like some of the descriptions of Preston in their heyday it has a disturbingly modern ring. The journalist visited a large hotel in a manufacturing district in the North where football clubs often stayed. 'Drunkenness, distinct drunkenness, was very common,' he wrote. 'The members of the two teams were often the core of a welter of riot. The players themselves were treated by their admirers until they became intoxicated. Quarrels of all sorts were of almost momentary occurrence.' He interviewed the barmaid, who told him, 'I hate all big sporting days. You've no idea what we girls have to put up with. They all seem to go mad. But there, the takings are enormous, so I suppose sport's for the good of trade!' What was true of football in general was doubly true of Manchester City.

But if he disliked the brewing connection, Meredith appreciated his employers' generosity. The club's owners were as ambitious as he was, and having signed Meredith, they were determined to keep him. Within a year he was earning £3 a week and £2 out of season, and by the end of the decade these figures had doubled. He also received large amounts in bonuses, placing him among the best-paid footballers in the country.

In return he was expected to take on a workload that was far from onerous. Professional footballers of the late 1890s began their working week on Tuesday and trained for just a couple of hours each day, starting at ten o'clock. Pre-season training could be intense, but after that it was fairly relaxed, many trainers terrified that their men would break down or become 'stale and listless' if overworked – an attitude that appears neurotic but probably reflected the more fragile constitutions of men raised on late nineteenth-century working-class diets. Players spent much of their time out for 'brisk walks', fully dressed in jackets, waistcoats and caps. They then changed to jog round the pitch and do sprinting work. Meredith himself believed there was too much emphasis on strength and speed and not enough on the twisting and turning required in a real game, and he blamed this, perceptively, for the large number of knee and ankle injuries players suffered. Most clubs had gyms and, according to Meredith, at City the players worked with 'heavy clubs and dumb bells' and did a lot of 'skipping and ball punching'. At Newton Heath in the early 1890s hammer throwing was part of the routine for a time until the centre-forward, Donaldson, was laid out by a misdirected throw. Training generally concluded, somewhat exotically, with a vapour bath and a massage.

Players rarely saw a football. It was the general view that this would make them all the hungrier for it come Saturday, an attitude that persisted well into the twentieth century. Most trainers, in any case, were either boxing or athletics coaches or military men and had little to contribute in the way of tactics or skills. But, fortunately for Meredith, Manchester City in the mid-1890s were an exception. 'We used to train very largely with a football. We were out on the ground every day dribbling and shooting and kicking,' he later wrote.

It was still common practice for teams to retire to some seaside resort or health spa for a few days before a big match. There they would follow much the same routine, but with the difference that the club was able to keep a closer eye on their diets and social habits. Meredith disliked these trips. 'I always thought it was a waste of time,' he said later. 'Had to go for long walks to stop stiffening up in armchairs.' He understood perfectly well the main purpose was to keep players out of the pub and, since he didn't drink, he resented being dragged away from his home and family. He always kept himself superbly fit, often putting in extra training, alone, in the afternoons, and he remained miraculously free of injury throughout his career.

The money Chester's Brewery was pouring into Manchester City soon paid off and at the end of the 1895–96 season they were second in the Second Division, qualifying them for the play-offs which were then the method for deciding promotion. But they performed bizarrely badly, losing 6–1 to West Bromwich Albion and 8–0 to Small Heath (later Birmingham City). There were hints of corruption and Meredith himself believed some players were concerned their contracts would not be renewed if the club gained promotion. He was bitter at the missed opportunity. It wasn't until 1899 that City finally reached the First Division. Even then they made little impact in the top flight.

The club's lack of success during this early part of Meredith's career is puzzling. By the turn of the century they were among the best-supported teams in the country with home League gates averaging fifteen to nineteen thousand. And the generosity of the club's owners to their star players was legendary. This may have been part of the problem. After the failure to gain promotion in 1896 the *Athletic News* hinted at 'little jealousies' within the team and there was a general feeling that the club lacked discipline. The board had little experience in running a football team and appeared too concerned to curry favour with their men. The chairman, John Chapman, it was said, was 'too kind-hearted to run a football club'. In more ways than one City had the feel of a pub team.

Meredith himself was not always the asset he might have

been. He was the best player in the country but, as so often when a club contains one big star, it skewed the team. He was fussy about who he would accept as his partner at inside-right. And, with Meredith monopolizing the ball at outside-right, the outside-left position was a particular problem. The club needed to find a competent player who was nevertheless prepared to spend most Saturday afternoons standing, hands on hips, as a spectator while Meredith weaved his magic on the opposite flank. The club used thirteen different men in this position during Meredith's first five seasons at Hyde Road.

'Meredith evidently thinks that when he gets the ball there is only one player on the field and that is himself,' read one early match report. City's play inevitably flowed through him, and if he wasn't sparking the whole team ground to a halt. 'On his day Meredith, well-fed and nursed, is the most dangerous and brilliant player,' read a report from the 1900–01 season, 'but he doesn't like donkey-work and if his partner is off, Meredith is off too ... With Meredith off-colour there doesn't seem to be much stuffing left in the City attack.'

He wasn't always the easiest man to get on with either. 'Meredith had a countenance that made a man think that life had not been too happy for him,' wrote Frederick Wall, honorary secretary of the FA after 1895. When the team gathered for sing-songs he would sit quietly in the corner, not contributing. And at home in later years his daughter recalled him being tense and sullen on match days. He had a strict routine which involved a glass of port before the game and a boiled chicken afterwards and he expected his wife (he married a girl from Chirk in 1901) to be waiting silently by the door ready to hand him his leather kit bag, embossed with the letters 'WM', when the time came to leave for the ground.

In part this reflected his quiet, reserved nature. He was not anti-social and his taciturn personality concealed a wry sense of humour. He had a twinkle in his blue eyes and in old age would delight in slipping his nephew a penny to poke his head round the door and shout 'Bugger!' to scandalize his maiden aunts. But he could be truculent and had a rebellious streak in his character. 'I am told that I had not been introduced to the world very long before I began to kick and I've been kicking ever since,' he wrote in 1919. 'When I haven't a football to kick I can generally find something to kick against and I guess I shall give a mighty kick when the time comes for me to leave the world behind.'

His relationship with the board at City was not always easy. He was made captain aged just twenty-one, partly as a sop to his vanity, partly to justify the fact that he was already the club's best-paid player. But he came close to leaving on a number of occasions. Spurs and Celtic in particular tried to lure him away. In the end he generally got what he wanted, both on and off the pitch, and the weak, inexperienced City directors had little success persuading him that what was good for Billy Meredith was not necessarily good for Manchester City.

By the spring of 1902 the club was in crisis. It had lost thirteen of its first twenty League games and was plunging back towards the Second Division. John Chapman and the other genial buffers running the club now came under pressure from a faction on the board led by a local businessman called John Allison. A Conservative councillor (he'd dragooned the City team into campaigning for him although Meredith, at least, was a Liberal), Allison owned Matlock House, a pioneering establishment for the treatment of sports injuries which stood opposite the City ground on Hyde Road. He wanted to stream-line the management of the club and put its finances on a more businesslike footing. After a brief struggle the Allison faction took control, and in the early months of 1902 a series of key signings were made from Celtic. Most important, though, was the acquisition of former Celtic player Tom Maley as club secretary.

At this time clubs did not have managers in the modern sense. Trainers, generally pictured in team photos in shirt-sleeves and waistcoats with a towel over their arm, were responsible only for fitness. The secretary, a more middle-class figure, took responsibility for organizing fixtures and the day-to-day running of the club. It was from this secretary figure that the modern manager was just beginning to evolve.

Billy Sudell, of course, had in many ways fulfilled the role of manager at Preston, but he was chairman of the club rather than a paid employee, which made him unique. Tom Watson, secretary at Sunderland then Liverpool in the 1890s, was the first to stray beyond purely bureaucratic functions into team management. He had football acumen and saw it as part of his job to take a hand in the buying and selling of players, and even team selection, both of which were normally the exclusive responsibility of the directors. At Manchester City, Tom Maley operated in the same way and, like Watson, he was often referred to as a manager.

Maley was a product of the old Scottish short-passing school. He was also a tough character who generally got what he wanted. For the first time City's resources were channelled towards building a coherent team rather than a machine for servicing Billy Meredith. A key acquisition was the nineteen-year-old Sandy Turnbull from Hurlford Thistle, a village team close to Kilmarnock. He was initially tried as a partner for Meredith at inside-right but proved a failure. The club was on the point of selling him when Maley tried him at inside-left. It was an inspiration. Maley knew Turnbull was too good a player to serve as Meredith's bag-man and he instantly began to score goals. He and the centre-forward Gillespie were now the target men for Meredith's crosses.

Maley also tightened up discipline and began to take the team on regular two- to three-day trips to various health spas for special training. As ever, this grated on Meredith, who also resented his diminished role in the team. But he could appreciate Maley's professionalism and the fact was the new balance in the side made him less the focus of attention for defenders and gave him greater space and freedom.

It was all too late to prevent relegation, but the following season City stormed straight to the top of Division Two and between 26 November 1902 and 14 April 1903 they lost just one game, scoring seventy goals. 'They move with a smartness and precision which could not fail to evoke admiration, the forwards sweeping along like one man brooking no resistance,' wrote one journalist. 'Now a feint, now a pass, now a short dribble, maybe a shot or a wide pass to the wings, to be followed by a true, insidious centre – all these moves were executed with a perfect understanding and with clockwork precision.' They finished as champions, and it was this rejuvenated Manchester City that Meredith led out to face Bolton Wanderers at Crystal Palace in April 1904 at the end of their first season back in Division One.

*

City were also challenging strongly for the championship that season, and the one anxiety Maley and his men had as they prepared for the match was that they had to face Everton at Goodison Park in a key League match just two days later. Just before the game there was a row in the City dressing room. Centre-half William 'Doc' Holmes, who had been with the club since 1896, had been dropped in favour of the amateur S. B. Ashworth. Disgusted, he threw his boots through the window. Despite this, they were in confident mood – as Meredith's comments to journalists that morning indicated – and most pundits shared their optimism. Bolton were a Second Division side and were not even challenging for promotion. They were workmanlike, but had none of City's class.

The pitch they trotted out on to would have been familiar to us. Modern markings (minus the 'D' on the edge of the penalty area, which would not appear until 1937) had been introduced in 1902 and goal nets had first appeared in 1891. The players too looked more or less as we expect them to. Shorts had replaced knickerbockers in the 1880s and studs began to be used around the same time. At the turn of the century players had begun to tuck their shin pads inside their socks.

But play was still a lot rougher than today. In 1892 it had finally been made illegal to charge the goalkeeper when he was not in possession of the ball (the so-called 'Goalkeeper's Protection Act'), but it was still perfectly legal to bundle him into the back of the net if he had the ball in his hands. In the outfield it was illegal to charge from behind and referees were becoming less tolerant of violent play, but a winger like Meredith still spent much of his career being sent crashing into the hoardings, whether he had the ball or not. It's a miracle he never did himself serious injury since he frequently swallowed his toothpick. Many wingers took advantage of the wide open spaces at Crystal Palace to run several yards beyond the touchline when advancing up the pitch without the ball so as to avoid being charged, re-emerging on to the field of play as they neared the penalty area.

There was a novelty at the 1904 Cup Final, which was the inspiration of Jimmy Catton, now editor of the *Athletic News*. He decided to send a reporter up in a hot-air balloon to cover the game from above. The idea proved impractical. Tethered to the ground with a rope, the balloon swirled round and round in the wind. 'I retained my place in the basket only by holding on hard to the ropes,' wrote 'Balloonatic', the unfortunate young journalist assigned the job. 'I saw the glittering Crystal Palace float past, and then I got a glimpse at the footballers, and then a tree tried to scratch my face off.' Finally the balloon sank to earth with 'a terrific bump'. 'While we climbed out,' Balloonatic continued, 'a sky splitting roar told me that I had just missed seeing the winning goal.'

The scorer was Billy Meredith. Standing close to the touchline he'd received a swinging cross-field pass from Livingstone, the City inside-right. Struthers, the Bolton left-back, stopped to appeal for offside. This left Meredith 'just that vital necessary second to place the ball where he wanted for the shot', Bolton's keeper Di Davies later recalled. 'The shot came and whizzed past me into the corner well out of my reach though, of course, I made a desperate dive for it.' Most observers felt Struthers had been right and Meredith was offside, but the goal stood.

It came at the end of twenty minutes of steady City pressure and City remained on top for the rest of the first half. But after the interval (which was now spent off the pitch) they eased off. Catton felt they were saving themselves for the Everton game on Monday, in which case they were taking a risk. Bolton dominated the first thirty minutes of the second half and hit the bar twice. Meredith took to repeatedly straying offside in order to waste time. But City held on and reasserted control for the last quarter of an hour, emerging winners by Meredith's solitary goal.

It was generally felt to have been a drab game – Cup Finals often were, the players apparently overcome by the excitement and tension of the occasion. But the FA Cup was coming to Manchester for the first time. Meredith – 'the lion of the hour' according to Catton – went up to receive the Cup from Alfred Lyttelton. Called on to make a speech, the tongue-tied Welshman said simply, 'I am sure it has given me great pleasure to win the Cup,' then covered his embarrassment by calling for three cheers for the Bolton team. He could be forgiven for being overwhelmed. After ten years, at the age of almost thirty, the boy from Chirk had finally achieved the success he felt his talents merited.

At the final whistle the grounded *Athletic News* balloon quietly slipped its mooring ropes and took off. 'Our balloon rose and swung across the scattering throng, while the band played "Rule Britannia",' wrote Balloonatic.

I caught a glimpse of their glittering instruments and then, so rapidly did we soar, the grounds were spread out beneath us like a massive map. The stands were but half-peopled and thousands of tiny atoms were rushing across the ground and down the slopes to the grandstand where the coveted trophy was to be handed to the victors; it looked like flies swarming round a honey-pot, and other flies crawling up the broad path to the Palace . . . When we were three thousand feet and two miles away from the Palace, I could still see that mass of folk in front of the grandstand, but we were beyond the sphere of excitement, for below us was open country, and above the glorious sky, too beautiful for words . . . Gradually the haze and the clouds shut out the view, and the great glass house on Sydenham Hill became but a huge diamond sparkling in the sun.

The player refuses any longer to be treated
as though he were both child and slave.

Billy Meredith, 1909

12

Billy Meredith: Radical

The Association Football Players' Union, 1907–14

MANCHESTER CITY LOST THEIR GAME AT EVERTON THE MONDAY after the Cup Final and narrowly missed out on the double. The following season, although knocked out in the early rounds of the Cup, they were once more challenging strongly for the championship. But, out of a clear blue sky, disaster was about to strike.

Billy Meredith's and Manchester City's fortunes began to unravel in an away game at Aston Villa on 29 April 1905, almost exactly a year after the Cup Final victory. It was City's last match of the season and they were level on points with Newcastle United at the top of the table. Newcastle's goal average was better but they had a tough derby game away at

Middlesbrough and City knew if they could collect both points they might snatch the title. Villa themselves were out of contention and the City players rather hoped they would roll over for them. They were disappointed.

Villa, who had won the FA Cup the week before, were fired up and the match quickly got bad-tempered and physical. Early in the second half, with Villa leading 3–1, Sandy Turnbull went in for a heavy challenge on the Villa captain, Alec Leake. Leake responded by throwing mud at Turnbull and Turnbull stuck two fingers up at Leake. Just who threw the first punch was disputed, but the two men were soon involved in a fist fight and had to be separated. At the end of the game, which City lost 3–2, they needed a police escort as they left the pitch. Then, as Turnbull walked down the tunnel someone leapt out on him from the urinal and dragged him into the Villa dressing room from where he emerged a few moments later with bruised ribs, a cut face and howling in pain.

Even by the robust standards of Edwardian football this was a little over the top. City had been involved in a similarly violent encounter at Everton a couple of weeks earlier and the FA, concerned for the image of the game, set up an inquiry. By now the players were scattering for the summer break and the general assumption was that there would be a few slapped wrists, a fine or two and some short suspensions, to be served out at the start of the next season. But then something odd happened. The FA inquiry dragged on, and it soon became clear they were probing into something deeper.

City had a sense that the FA did not like them as a club, and they were probably right. They were a classic nouveau riche team with none of the history or pedigree of Everton and Aston

Villa, both founder members of the Football League. And they had a reputation for bending the rules where the payment of players was concerned.

In 1901 the FA had introduced the infamous maximum wage. Like the retain and transfer system, this was the initiative of small- to medium-sized clubs such as Preston and Wolves and was justified by the need to stop the top teams monopolizing the best players. The ceiling on earnings was set at £4 a week and the FA also abolished bonuses, although players were to be allowed a benefit match if they remained at the same club for five years. For a man like Meredith, who had effectively been earning around £7 a week, it was a gross restriction on the freedom of trade. Many of the richer clubs quickly found ways to get round the new rule. At Liverpool the centre-half, Alex Raisbeck, was supposedly appointed 'bill-inspector', receiving extra pay for checking that match posters had been put up correctly. Another man was said to have sold his dog to a director for an inordinate fee. Edwardian football finances became a world of smoke and mirrors, and Manchester City were among the worst offenders.

In October 1904 the FA had fined City £250 and closed the Hyde Road ground for two weeks after they discovered irregularities in the transfer of two players from Glossop. Five directors were suspended but the FA was fairly sure they were just scraping the surface at City and that there was plenty more dirt to be discovered. The inquiry into the Everton and Villa games provided them with an opportunity to do more digging.

'The nature of the allegations could not be indicated at this stage,' declared Charles Clegg early on, instantly sparking rumours there was more to the investigation than met the eye.

The FA was conducting a 'fishing inquiry', the Northern press complained, and as the hearings stretched into the summer speculation mounted. Finally, on 5 August, the report was released. It was a sensation. Billy Meredith was found guilty of attempted bribery.

'Bombshell in the City Camp', 'The Football World Shocked' declared the headlines. The violence at Goodison and Villa Park was largely forgotten (although here too City had cause to be unhappy: while Turnbull was suspended for a month, the Villa and Everton players involved got off scot-free); Meredith was now the story. He had supposedly offered Leake, the Villa captain, £10 to throw the match. The information came not from Leake but from a 'gentleman' from Birmingham who had overheard 'a most interesting conversation'. The FA had instantly called Leake for a second interview, at which point he was 'forced to admit' Meredith had said something along those lines, but that he had dismissed it as a 'joke'. Meredith was suspended from football for a year without pay and he was also denied the benefit he was due.

From his wife's home in Chirk, where he always spent the summers, he denied the charges. 'I am entirely innocent and am suffering for others. Such an allegation as that of bribery is preposterous! I could never risk my reputation and future by such an action.' He felt he was being victimized. 'Manchester has not many friends among the Association officials ... Had I been anyone but a Welshman I would have been better dealt with.'

Much of the press was sympathetic to him. The FA hearings had been held in secret, the principal witness against him was anonymous, and there was no right of appeal. 'The method seems un-English, most autocratic and arbitrary,' wrote the

Athletic News, while the *Daily Dispatch* muttered about 'Russian darkness, the air of which is alien to English lungs'.

Meredith, though, appeared resigned to his fate. 'I suppose I must have twelve months' rest,' he said. He had recently become partner in a sports shop in St Peter's Square in Manchester and this would take up his time for the next year. The one problem was money. Meredith, it seems, was not resigned to losing out financially, and City had indicated to him that they would see he was all right. 'My Dear Billy,' the City manager, Tom Maley, wrote privately to him; 'The unexpected has, I am sorry to say, happened and we are to be denied the pleasure of giving to you a well earned benefit . . . We have determined to see that all that is reasonable and just in this matter is done on your behalf . . . I don't think . . . that you will be the loser.'

If, as seems very likely, City were hoping to slip him some money under the table, they had a problem. The FA had forced them to accept Tom Hindle, the Association's auditor, as their accountant for the year. He would be keeping a hawk-like eye on the club's books so it was going to be impossible to make any illegal payments until he was ushered out the door, which would not be until the following season. Meredith quickly became impatient and took to hanging around Hyde Road badgering the directors for money. The FA became aware of this and forced City to report Meredith. This they did, with great reluctance, on 14 February 1906.

Clegg and the FA were playing a canny game. Convinced there was more to be uncovered at City, they were using Meredith as a wedge to prise open the club's murky finances. 'It is evident that the all powerful Association is anxious to give Meredith a further opportunity of unburdening his mind in reference to the past,' wrote Catton's *Athletic News*, perceptively, on 26 February. Clegg had judged the Welshman's complex psychology well. Resentful at his treatment, Meredith now took the extraordinary decision to bring the whole house of cards crashing down around him.

Meredith was speaking 'with a frankness that amounts to fearlessness', reported the *Athletic News*, which clearly had an inside track on the story, on 19 March. 'Meredith has made many extraordinary statements,' it wrote a month later. By the time the inquiry into Meredith's behaviour concluded at the start of June he had laid bare the entire system of illegal payments City had been operating ever since the introduction of the maximum wage five years earlier.

The secret of City's success, he wrote later, was very simple. 'The club put aside the rule that no player should receive more than £4 a week. From 1902 I had been paid £6 a week and Livingstone was paid ten shillings more than that in wages ... The season we carried off the Cup, I also received £53 in bonuses for games won and drawn ... Altogether, the club paid in bonuses £654 12s. 6d. The team delivered the goods and the club paid for the goods delivered and both sides were satisfied.' A portion of the gate receipts was put into a secret bank account from which the illegal payments were made.

Never before had the FA received such chapter and verse on a club's hidden finances. City's players and officials had no option but to throw themselves on the mercy of Clegg and his colleagues, and the history of Manchester City might have come to an end there and then – the FA came very close to disbanding the club. In the end they simply threw the book at them.

'Enormous Offences; Overwhelming Sentences' wrote the

Athletic News on 4 June. The entire board was removed and suspended from football and Tom Maley was banned from the sport for life (although this was later lifted). A total of seventeen players were suspended for the rest of the year, including Meredith, receiving fines totalling £900, and the club was ordered to sell them (Meredith later hinted that his own fine of £100 was paid by Frederick Wall, the FA's secretary, presumably in gratitude for the information he had provided). By the start of the following season City had just eleven players on their books. They limped gamely on but were relegated in 1909 and would not be a major power in English football again until the 1930s.

It is extraordinary that Meredith ever found any club or group of players prepared to work with him again. He'd shown remarkable ingratitude to a club that had paid him well for eleven years and had cost his team-mates hundreds of pounds in fines and lost wages. But he clearly felt a deep sense of injustice. He now admitted to having attempted to bribe Leake, but said he'd done it at the instigation of Maley and with the knowledge of the rest of the team. The FA do not seem to have doubted this. 'He said he had allowed himself to be a scapegoat for others, and he expected they would see that he did not suffer monetary loss,' reported the *Athletic News*. Instead he felt he'd been hung out to dry.

Everyone knew the abuses Meredith had exposed were widespread, and the hypocrisy of the system was revealed when top clubs – many equally guilty of illegal payments – moved to snap up the suspended players. Bury, Bolton, Arsenal, Millwall and Glasgow Rangers all swooped, vulture-like, on the carcass of Manchester City. The main beneficiaries, however, were their neighbours Manchester United, newly promoted to the First

Division. It was there that Meredith himself moved in January 1907, saving himself the trouble of uprooting. Three other City players moved with him, including Sandy Turnbull, and the first great Manchester United side would be built from the ashes of the first great Manchester City side.

Meredith's new employers were originally a factory team, set up in 1878 by the Dining Room Committee at the Carriage and Wagon Works of the Lancashire and Yorkshire Railway Company in north-east Manchester. The city's top club by the end of the 1880s, they were elected direct to Division One of the Football League in 1892 but were relegated after a couple of seasons and spent the next twelve years in Division Two. In 1902 they came close to bankruptcy, at which point they changed their name from Newton Heath to Manchester United and, like City, fell under the control of local brewing interests.

In the seasons after Meredith's arrival United won the championship in 1908, the FA Cup in 1909 and the championship again in 1911. In 1910 they made the move to their plush new state-of-the-art Old Trafford ground where Meredith could enjoy sunken baths, a gym, a massage room and a recreation room complete with billiards table. It had covered seating for thirteen thousand and could hold eighty thousand – a far cry from the primitive state of Hyde Road in Meredith's early years. Although thirty-two when he arrived at United, Meredith was a regular in the side during their glory years and quickly regained his iconic status, despite his apparent disgrace. 'Meredith's advent in Manchester United's forward line has worked wonders,' wrote the *Football Field* shortly after his arrival. 'Meredith undeniably is the greatest forward of all time and he looks like going on for a long time yet in first-class football.' Only the goals would dry up. In his first five seasons at United he scored just twenty-five in League games, a far lower strike rate than during his City days.

Meredith's departure from Manchester City was a turning point for him in more ways than one. He had now become, in footballing terms, a political radical. In the autumn of 1907 he sent round a circular to his fellow professionals proposing the establishment of a footballers' trade union. Previous attempts to set up a union had been made in 1893 and 1897 but neither had much success either in removing the retain and transfer system or preventing the introduction of the maximum wage – the two chief bones of contention for professional footballers. But Meredith's was a more serious attempt.

Meredith was motivated partly by bitterness at his treatment over the last couple of years. Like most professional footballers he regarded the contractual restraints footballers operated under as self-evidently unjust, and he was angry at the illegal position he'd been placed in at Manchester City. A proud man, he chafed at the control club directors – 'those little shop-keepers who govern our destinies' – had over his life. He was also resentful of the FA. He'd brought with him from the Welsh mines an innate class antagonism and found the various grillings he'd received at the hands of FA officials humiliating. 'Personally I really don't think that the gentlemen who sit on the FA Council have ever at all realised how absurdly auto-cratic, unfair and unjust has been their attitude towards the players,' he wrote.

Ask any man who has had to attend an FA Commission to tell you what he thinks about it. They have always treated the player as though he were a mere boy, or a sensible machine or a trained animal. When they were displeased they just cracked the whip or gave him a slap. They had never dreamed that the man might be able to explain things if he were given a fair chance and that if he did give a good explanation he might be man enough to resent his treatment if that explanation were merely pushed aside with a contemptuous laugh.

Aware that his own behaviour had hardly been honourable, he may also have been looking to redeem himself in the eyes of his fellow professionals.

Meredith's circular was well received. 'We cannot conceive of any player with a grain of sense refusing to support the establishment of a body for the protection of his own interests,' wrote the *Athletic News*. On 2 December 1907, in a meeting at the Imperial Hotel, Manchester, the Association Football Players' Union was formally established. Meredith was in the chair and was elected to the Management Committee while Manchester United's reserve goalkeeper, Herbert Broomfield, was made full-time secretary. The union quickly claimed seven hundred members, a figure which had risen to 1,300 by the time of its first AGM in December 1908.

Initially it presented a moderate face, claiming to be a defensive organization concerned primarily with the welfare of players; Meredith originally wanted it to be called the Players' Union and Benefit Society. The Manchester United chairman, John Davies, was invited to be president and Jimmy Catton, in his capacity as editor of the *Athletic News*, was invited to be vice-president. The union quickly gained FA recognition, and when a fund-raising game between Manchester United and Newcastle was organized in April 1908 the Manchester United board actually paid their players' expenses.

Sooner or later the issues of the retain and transfer system and the maximum wage would have to be tackled. But here too the union had powerful allies. Clegg and other senior officials at the FA still disliked the transfer system and were ambivalent about the maximum wage, although determined to enforce it so long as it remained on the rule book. The wealthier clubs were also keen to have freedom to reward their top players more generously. Only the small- and medium-sized clubs, which felt threatened by the rise of the union, were firmly in favour of the restrictions.

'Who shall be masters – players or clubs?' wrote C. E. Sutcliffe, a director of Burnley and the spokesman for the smaller sides, in the *Athletic News* in January 1909. He accused the union of 'greed', of being 'immoderate and unreasonable', and of spouting 'contemptible clap-trap'. His outburst was a response to the union's AGM of December 1908 at which they had finally nailed their colours to the mast, calling for the abolition of both the maximum wage and the transfer system. This radical stance alarmed many clubs, but Sutcliffe was still out on a limb in his extreme hostility to the union. Events, however, were about to move in his direction.

The clash between the union and the football authorities initially arose over an issue entirely separate from that of wages and transfers. The union was keen to ensure clubs paid compensation to players incapacitated through injury. There was an appeals process at the FA if clubs refused, but this was slow and cumbersome and the union wanted to make use of the 1906

Workmen's Compensation Act. This instantly brought them into conflict with Charles Clegg.

Rule 48 of the FA constitution stated that members could not go to court without prior consent of the FA. The union argued that this was absurd, that recourse to the law of the land was the basic right of every British citizen. But for Clegg the issue was control and the authority of the FA. As the Amateur Football Association had discovered two years earlier, these were always bad grounds on which to pick a fight with the FA chairman.

In mid-February 1909 the union was ordered not to take cases to court. It refused, and on 8 March the FA withdrew its recognition of the union. Tensions quickly mounted and wild rumours began to circulate of a strike at the England v. Scotland game on 3 April at Crystal Palace. This idea backfired when key England players declared themselves firmly opposed, making the union look unpatriotic. On 3 May the FA ordered all of the union's officials to resign or face suspension. All did so, with the exception of the secretary, Herbert Broomfield, and the chairman, H. L. Mainman, both of whom had by then finished their playing careers. On 17 May both men were suspended anyway, and on 9 June all union members were told to resign by 1 July.

The union was now fighting for its life. How had it come to this? Many observers were bewildered. 'The players have been fighting for a shadow,' declared the Burnley director C. E. Sutcliffe, who was nevertheless delighted at the course events had taken. As with the dispute between the FA and the AFA, it was now a struggle over power, pure and simple – 'Who shall be masters?' as Sutcliffe himself had written back in January.

But the union was far from beaten, and it was the Manchester United side – Cup winners that year – who now became the focus of resistance. Besides Meredith, it also contained Charlie Roberts, club captain and lynchpin of one of the greatest half-back lines in United's history. Roberts had already been in trouble with the FA for pioneering 1970s-style short shorts, which upset the sensibilities of Clegg and his colleagues. He'd been earmarked a troublemaker following an argument with FA secretary Frederick Wall at half-time in the Cup Final that year, and many felt his meagre haul of just three international caps was punishment for his union activities. He was a passionate and articulate advocate of players' rights and, like Meredith, was part of the union's Management Committee.

Rallied by Meredith and Roberts, the United players voted to defy the FA and remain in the union. They were immediately suspended and their pay was stopped. This was a particular blow to the two ring-leaders. In June that year Meredith's sports shop had been badly damaged by fire, leaving him with few assets, and Roberts stood to lose out on a lucrative benefit match. But both were determined to stand firm. To keep fit, the suspended players organized training sessions at the Fallowfield ground in south Manchester. During one of these a photographer came along to take a team picture. On an impulse, Roberts picked up a bit of wood and wrote 'The Outcasts FC' on it. The picture was taken with the sign between Roberts' legs, immortalizing the moment when Manchester United were the rebels of the football world.

The situation at other clubs was confused. Most members had resigned from the union but many were telling union leaders that they had done this purely so they could collect summer pay and would rejoin once the season started in September. The union, in any case, did not collect dues during the summer. Support for the union varied around the country. It was weak in the Midlands and the South but much stronger in the North-West and North-East. The League champions, Newcastle, led by their captain, Colin Veitch, were known to be particularly militant.

With talk of a strike once more in the air, by the start of August the FA was beginning to get nervous. On 1 July the Players' Union had affiliated to the General Federation of Trade Unions (GFTU), an organization set up by the Trades Union Congress in 1899 to lend assistance to smaller unions in conflict with their employers. This provided them with access, for the first time, to professional trade union leadership, and Meredith, with his mining background, was well aware of the value of this. The union's inexperienced leaders had been placed on the 'mighty shoulders' of a 'great big warrior', he wrote.

They were also forging an unlikely alliance with the outlawed Amateur Football Association. This amused the union's critics. 'If my memory serves me right the last time the amateurs played [in the Sheriff of London Shield] the match was with Newcastle United, and they would not sit at the same table with them when they had dinner,' wrote a correspondent to the *Athletic News*. The upper-class AFA was hardly known for its sympathy towards the professional foot-baller. But it was quite happy to make mischief for the FA and plans were soon being laid for a fund-raising game between a Union XI and the Corinthians.

The FA now backtracked. Having withdrawn recognition for

the union in March, it agreed to a series of meetings with union leaders and GFTU officials through August. At these, most of the key issues were resolved. It was agreed the union would have the right to take compensation cases to the courts, provided the FA was given a chance to resolve them first. The FA would recognize the union and withdraw the suspension of union members, while the union would acknowledge the authority of the FA. There was just one sticking point: the question of back pay for the Manchester United rebels. They had been without wages since their suspension by the FA and each was owed £38. Here the FA point-blank refused to budge, and on 24 August the talks broke down.

With the season due to start on 1 September the union was now at its moment of maximum strength. At least 150 top players had rejoined and a strike would be crippling for League clubs. Meredith was the most belligerent of the union's leaders. 'The FA have been ruling us just as the bad barons of old ruled their people, and it is only just being brought home to them that it won't do any longer . . . The player refuses any longer to be treated as though he were both child and slave,' he wrote in his column in the *Weekly News*.

But Meredith and his colleagues were amateurs in the art of class struggle compared to Charles Clegg and the other businessmen and factory owners who ran football. Clegg now once more showed his class as a political operator. First, he moved to shore up his alliances. Back in March the FA had granted an amnesty to League clubs for past misdemeanours if they agreed to abide by FA rules on wages and bonuses in future. This freed the clubs from the fear of players 'doing a Meredith' and betraying them to the FA and so strengthened their hand in dealing with the union. Clegg now arranged talks with leaders both of the Football League and the Southern League to agree a common front. 'There was a wonderful ring of sincerity and unanimity at the meeting,' wrote the *Athletic News*. 'If the Players' Union anticipated a divided opposition they now surely realise what to expect.'

Clegg then called a mass meeting of professional footballers to be held at the Grand Hotel in Birmingham at two o'clock on 31 August – the day before the season was due to start. The Manchester United men and the GFTU representatives were not invited; Charlie Roberts was actually turned back at the door. The GFTU instantly sensed a trap and urged union members not to attend. But a number ignored this, including the Newcastle captain Colin Veitch.

Clegg opened the meeting with a long defence of the FA's position, attacking the union for its 'spirit of persistent and unremitting hostility'. Other FA officials took a similar line. Then Veitch stood up to speak on behalf of the players.

Veitch was an intelligent, educated man and, unlike Meredith and Roberts, an avowed socialist. In practice, though, he was more conciliatory, and he now took it upon himself to start negotiating on the union's behalf. It was a fatal mistake. Veitch identified the issue of back pay as the one stumbling block in the way of a deal. If the FA would concede that, they could have an agreement that night, he said. Clegg asked him if he could deliver the rest of the union leadership, and Veitch left the room to try to make contact with them. He failed, but on the basis of this exchange a truce was agreed. The threat of strike action was lifted. And it was understood that a formal agreement, including the payment of back pay, would be concluded within the next few weeks.

'Peace with honour' Veitch called it, and he was hailed as the great conciliator. 'The players have never had a man of such vision and suave power,' wrote Jimmy Catton, who had become a fierce critic of the union over the previous few months. Meredith was less sure. The obvious question arising from the Birmingham meeting was why Clegg hadn't agreed to the payment of back pay at the talks a week earlier. Meredith felt the FA chairman was playing power games, and he was probably right. A cut-and-dried deal on 24 August would have been a victory for the union, and this Clegg could not allow. The situation was now fuzzier, and the moment of greatest danger for the FA had passed. With the season underway and a mood of reconciliation in the air, Clegg knew it would now be far harder for the union to call out its men. He moved fast to exploit his new position of strength.

Rather than quickly firming up a formal deal, he dragged his feet. At the start of October the FA suddenly introduced a new demand, that the union disaffiliate from the GFTU. Like Meredith, Clegg knew just how much the advice and support of the GFTU strengthened the Players' Union. He'd seen it first hand during the talks in August and was much more comfortable dealing with the union's own callow leadership. The union was forced to call a ballot on the issue and the membership, weary of conflict, agreed by 470 votes to 172 to cut its links. Meredith was furious at what he saw as an act of gross ingratitude. 'The FA have got their little revenge,' he wrote, adding bitterly, 'the players have not the pluck of the miners.'

On the face of it the deal that was now finally agreed was a compromise. The union had lost over the issue of the GFTU but gained the substance of their demands in all other areas. But the real issue was power – 'Who shall be masters?' – and here there had been a fundamental shift since the summer. In February 1910 the union distributed badges to be worn by all members during games. The Football League moved swiftly to ban them, and the union meekly backed down. 'The Day Will Come when the players will wear the badge whether the League likes it or not!' wrote Meredith. But this was mere bravado. The union was also dependent on charity games to raise funds. To stage these games it needed approval from the FA and the Football League, and over the next few years both bodies shamelessly used this power to control the union. When, in 1910, the union finally turned its attention to the maximum wage it was soon clear it was in a far weaker position than a year previously.

The middle- and upper-class men who ran the game were bemused by the players' discontent over wages, pointing out how favourably they compared with those of skilled workers. But for the players a more valid comparison was the music hall stars they mixed with, some of whom earned more than £100 a week. Weren't footballers also entertainers, fêted and famous wherever they went? Why should they always be compared to carpenters and engineers? The club bosses could not conceive of footballers as anything other than working-class employees, ultimately no different from the men they employed in their factories and mills. It was this the players were challenging.

In February 1910 the Players' Union called for the removal of all restrictions; failing this, it wanted to see the maximum wage increased to £6 a week and the introduction of win and draw bonuses. Its proposals were dismissed out of hand. Instead, the Football League adopted a much more modest reform proposed by C. E. Sutcliffe which rewarded players for long service at the same club by increasing the maximum to £4 10s after two years and to £5 after four years. It also permitted the FA Cup winners and teams finishing in the top five of the First and Second Division to pay limited bonuses at the end of the season. For the players it was an improvement, but the fundamentals of the system remained in place.

In March 1912 the union challenged the legality of the retain and transfer system in the courts. The case was badly handled by the union's lawyers and they were defeated, leaving the union with large debts and forcing it into the humiliating position of having to borrow from the Football League. Ten months later the union's new chairman, Syd Owen, was forced to resign after the FA refused to communicate with him in retaliation for what it considered an impertinent letter. The union had been effectively neutered without achieving any of its core demands.

Meredith always remained enormously proud of his achievement in setting up the Players' Union. Now known as the Professional Footballers' Association, it is the oldest continuously existing sporting trade union in the world. But it would be almost half a century before it fully recovered from the defeats of 1909–12. Charles Clegg had now faced down twin revolts from opposite ends of football's social spectrum, the Amateur Football Association and the Players' Union. Their defeat meant that in the three-way struggle for power within football that had been raging since the mid-1880s, it was the club owners who had emerged triumphant.

Both Roberts and Meredith blamed the defeat of the union on the spinelessness of their colleagues. 'I know no class of working people who are less able to look after themselves than footballers. They are like a lot of sheep,' wrote Roberts, bitterly, in 1914. 'The unfortunate thing is that so many players refuse to take things seriously but are content to live a kind of school-boy life and to do just what they are told,' remarked Meredith. The professional footballer, he said, seemed incapable 'of think-ing and acting for himself and his class'.

By this time Meredith's powers as a player were finally diminishing. He was approaching forty, and in the 1912–13 season, for the first time, he was not an automatic choice in United's first team, although he continued to turn out regularly for Wales. But he was unable to tear himself away from the game. Too old for military service, he continued to play throughout the First World War, and when peace came the men returned from the trenches to the familiar sight of Billy Meredith trotting out at Old Trafford for Manchester United. In 1921 he fell out with the club over money and made an emotional return to Manchester City where, incredibly, he played for a further three seasons. He made a handful of appearances at City's new Maine Road ground, which the club moved to in 1923, and it was not until the end of the 1923–24 season that he finally retired, just a few months short of his fiftieth birthday.

For all his hard-headedness and occasional cynicism, the one constant in Meredith's life was his genuine love of football. 'My heart was always full of it,' he told Jimmy Catton. His longevity as a player also reflected his extraordinary fitness. But there was one other factor that compelled him to play on and on – fear.

It was a fear he would share with generations of footballers to come and which resulted in large part from the defeat of the Players' Union in 1909–12 – fear of financial insecurity and an impoverished old age.

13

Football at War

Fritz 3 Tommy 2, Pont Rouge, Western Front, 25 December 1914

LATE ON CHRISTMAS EVE 1914 SCOTTISH TROOPS STATIONED CLOSE TO the village of Pont Rouge in northern France became aware of lights appearing in the enemy trenches opposite. Initially mystified, they soon realized that, amid the carnage, the Germans were decorating their parapet with Christmas trees illuminated by candles. They watched as the lights slowly spread along the line, in both directions, as far as the eye could see. Then the sound of singing began to drift through the clear, frosty air – *Silent Night,* a carol most British troops had never heard before. 'I shall never forget it, it was one of the highlights of my life. I thought, what a beautiful tune,' wrote one man. Astonished, the Scots responded with applause and cheering and songs of their own.

The merriment continued late into the night and Christmas Day dawned to an eerie silence, the guns temporarily quiet. The sky was bright and clear and there was a thick hoar frost, leaving the corpses in No Man's Land shrouded in white. The Scots began to poke their heads above the parapet. The Germans held their fire. Then a German non-commissioned officer advanced towards the Scottish trenches carrying a Christmas tree. A Scot went to meet him, ignoring shouts of warning from his own side, and the two men shook hands to wild applause. Soon the troops were eagerly fraternizing, exchanging gifts and working together to bury the dead.

It was the Scots who first produced a football. Lt Johannes Niemann of the 133rd Saxon Regiment later recalled seeing a 'Tommy' emerge from the trench with one at his feet, 'kicking already and making fun'. It was agreed to organize an impromptu international there and then, in the hell of No Man's Land. 'We marked the goals with our caps. Teams were quickly established for a match on the frozen mud,' wrote Niemann.

It can't have been easy, amid the shell craters and the barbed wire. But what made the strongest impression on the Germans were the kilts of the Scots. 'Our privates soon discovered that the Scots wore no underpants under their kilts so that their behinds became clearly visible any time their skirts moved in the wind,' Niemann recalled. 'We had a lot of fun with that, and in the beginning we just couldn't believe it.'

No detailed description of the action survives. But we do know the score – the Germans won 3–2 – and the match has gone down in folklore as the ultimate example of sport transcending boundaries.

The informal truce at Pont Rouge was not an isolated incident. There was fraternization up and down the line, and by lunchtime on Christmas Day 1914 the guns had fallen silent in two-thirds of the British sector (the French, defending their own territory, were less inclined to halt hostilities). Football was played in a number of places, although the problems of the terrain and the lack of footballs in some units meant few games were as structured and organized as the one at Pont Rouge. The Lancashire Fusiliers played the Germans using a bully beef tin (also losing 3–2). And at Loos, Private William Dawkins of the East Kents recalled having 'great fun' using a German ball until a lieutenant colonel threatened the men with a machine gun to stop them fraternizing. 'Had just one of these Big Mouths gathered together ten thousand footballs, what a happy solution that would have been, without bloodshed!' he wrote.

The fact that at this highly emotive moment so many troops instinctively turned to football as a means of socializing and reaching across the divide captures the extraordinary grip the sport had on the British working class by 1914. And although some officers disapproved of the Christmas Day matches, this was something they were more than happy to exploit. At Loos in the spring of 1915 officers of the 1st Battalion of the 18th London Regiment led an attack by kicking footballs into No Man's Land for the men to pursue. This soon became a commonplace act of bravado. The most famous example was on the first day of the Battle of the Somme, 1 July 1916, when Captain W. P. Nevill of the 8th East Surreys offered a prize for the first platoon to kick a football up to the enemy trenches. The event was immortalized in verse:

*

> On through the hail of slaughter
> Where gallant comrades fell
> Where blood is poured like water
> They drive the trickling ball.
> The fear of death before them
> Is but an empty name.
> True to the land that bore them –
> The SURREYS play the game!

Captain Nevill himself led the attack, kicking a ball high into the air towards the German lines as he emerged from the trench, and was mown down almost instantly, like thousands of others on that dreadful first day at the Somme, which remains the most costly in the history of the British Army.

The Somme falls like a shadow across British history, dividing the bright, sunny optimism of the Victorian and Edwardian eras from the darker, more wary age in which we still live. The war cut a swathe through all sectors of British society, but none suffered proportionally as much as the upper class. The world which first spawned modern football died in the mud and the blood of 1 July 1916.

For the traditional upper class, on the retreat politically in the thirty years before the war, the outbreak of hostilities provided an opportunity to prove their value to society, to show they were still the warrior caste. Public schoolboys flocked to the colours, eager to do their duty. But the war destroyed them. Serving as junior officers, they were the first over the top, leading their men through the barbed wire into the hail of machine-gun fire, and they died like cattle. Of the 5,650 Old

Etonians who served in the war, 1,157 were killed – a ratio of one in five, compared to one in eight for the lower ranks. This was typical of the public schools and the major universities. The Corinthians were en route for their third tour of Brazil when war broke out and immediately turned round and enlisted to a man. Three of the touring party died, and a total of twenty-two Corinthians, past and present, gave their lives in the conflict. Lord Kinnaird, now well into his sixties, lost two of his four sons. The 'flower of British aristocracy . . . perished', wrote the former cabinet minister C. F. G. Masterman; 'The Feudal System vanished in blood and fire, and the landed classes were consumed.' The old elite never recovered, and when peace finally returned in 1918 their grip on British society was broken for ever.

In football this had already happened thirty years earlier with the eclipsing of the gentleman amateurs by the rising middle-class club owners. Socially and politically the sport was ahead of the curve. The war completed the process that had been gathering pace ever since then – the flight of the wealthier classes from the game.

Their final alienation from the sport began in the early months of the war when the FA issued a call for all players and spectators who were single to join up. But the clubs had a problem: they had signed contracts with their players to the end of the season and these contracts had to be honoured. The League season therefore continued, although many professionals voluntarily enlisted and crowds slumped. This provoked fury in the right-wing press. 'Every club that employs a professional football player is bribing a needed recruit to refrain from enlistment, and every spectator who pays his gate money is contributing so much towards a German victory!' raged the historian A. F. Pollard in a letter to *The Times* on 7 November 1914. *The Times* itself echoed these views in an editorial a few weeks later, claiming that the selfish and mercenary approach of football reflected the fact that, uniquely among national sports, it was now a 'business' rather than a 'pastime'. It was soon advertising 'petticoats for footballers'.

Clubs tried to compensate by allowing matches to be used as recruiting rallies. Local worthies made speeches at half-time, and the idea was that a military band would lead a large portion of the crowd straight off to the recruitment centres at the end of the game. Unfortunately this aroused little response. At Arsenal just one man stepped forward, at Chelsea none at all. The Arsenal chairman pointed out it was unreasonable to expect young men to go straight from a football match into the Army without at least going home to consult with friends and family first. It was also pointed out that news of football was avidly devoured in the trenches and did much to raise morale. But it did little good. Professional football finally closed down for the duration at the end of the 1914–15 season. But by then a perception that it was an unpatriotic sport had gained a firm hold on sections of the upper and middle classes. 'The sooner the army as a whole takes up "Rugger" . . . the better for Tommy. Let "Soccer" . . . remain the exercise of the munitions workers who suffer so much from varicose veins, weak knees, cod-eyed toes, fowl's livers and a general dislike for a man's duty,' wrote a correspondent to the *Sheffield Star Sports Special.*

All this was grossly unfair. Large numbers of footballers died in the war, including Billy Meredith's old strike partner, Sandy Turnbull. The burly Scot, beaten up in the dressing room at Aston Villa in 1905, was killed at Arras on 3 May 1917. But when the officer class finally staggered from the trenches, bloodied and traumatized, in November 1918, it no longer had much appetite for a game it felt was tainted and which, more importantly, it now associated with the lower ranks. When Henry Hughes-Onslow was asked in March 1919 if he was going to resurrect the Amateur Football Association he said he saw little point. 'I hear that many of the big public schools are giving up the Association game for Rugby and that Oxford and Cambridge Universities cannot get fixture lists for next season,' he wrote. He later changed his mind and football did continue at the ancient public schools. But, these aside, by the 1920s it had been pretty much abandoned by the social elite.

The Corinthians limped on. In 1919 they overturned the rule which prevented them entering competitions and began to take part in the FA Cup. But, starved of a steady supply of fresh recruits from the public schools, they made little impact and in 1933 were involved in an unseemly dispute with the FA when their exemption until the third round was withdrawn. They spent much of the late 1930s touring Nazi Germany (C. B. Fry was a great admirer of Hitler, and when the Trades Union Congress objected to Germany playing in England in 1935 Pa Jackson declared it was proof of 'how dangerous it would be to trust the government of this country to the Labour Party'). In 1939 they merged with the Casuals and today they can still be seen, labouring in the lower reaches of the Isthmian League in front of perhaps a hundred spectators at their Tolworth ground in south-west London.

In the end, upper-class football was a culture that never really became established – a historical dead-end. And it was the rise of working-class football that killed it. For most public school men, playing sport with their social inferiors involved navigating your way around just too many complex social taboos. Did you undress with the working-class professionals before the game? Did you bathe together afterwards? How did you relate on the pitch? (As late as 1923 the England captain, Charles Buchan, was reprimanded by the FA for the apparently disrespectful gesture of shaking the hand of an amateur during a post-goal celebration.) Far easier to take refuge in rugby.

The upper class also found the working-class game un-palatable. They had promoted football in a spirit of muscular Christianity, to instil the public school virtues of sportsman-ship and fair play in the masses. But the workers had seized hold of it and made it their own, recreating it in their own image, and gentleman amateurs recoiled from the raucous passion and partisanship they brought to it. Oddly, their distaste was shared by many socialists. 'There cannot be much doubt that the whole thing is bound up with the rise of Nationalism – that is, with the lunatic modern habit of identifying oneself with large power units and seeing everything in terms of competitive prestige,' wrote George Orwell, himself, of course, an Old Etonian. Both groups felt the workers had rather let them down.

Others were more imaginative and sympathetic. J. B. Priestley's description of the fictional Bruddersford United in his novel *The Good Companions* best captures what football meant to working men:

> For a shilling the Bruddersford United AFC offered you
> Conflict and Art ... It turned you into a member of a new
> community, all brothers together for an hour and a half, for not
> only had you escaped the clanking machinery of this lesser life,
> from work, wages, rent, doles, sick pay, insurance-cards,
> nagging wives, ailing children, bad bosses, idle work-men, but
> you had escaped with most of your mates and your neighbours,
> with half the town, and there you were, cheering together,
> thumping one another on the shoulders, swapping judgments
> like lords of the earth, having pushed your way through a
> turnstile into another and altogether more splendid kind of life,
> hurtling with Conflict and yet passionate and beautiful in its
> Art.

This was what football gave working people: passion, excitement
and beauty in lives that were otherwise drab and monotonous. It
was this, combined with the ease and cheapness with which
it could be played, that explains its extraordinary spread, first
through Britain and then around the world.

But if the workers had captured football's soul, the gentleman amateurs left an indelible imprint. Strangely, one legacy
which has lingered to this day is the historiography of the sport.
Charlie Alcock and other early historians believed straight-
forwardly and uncomplicatedly that the modern game was
created in the public schools. For them the old folk game was
no more than a rustic free-for-all which was civilized on the
playing fields of Eton, Harrow, Westminster, Charterhouse,
Shrewsbury and Winchester. And they credited ex-public
schoolboys at Cambridge with providing the impetus for the
development of a common code.

It's not surprising that public schoolboys placed themselves at the centre of the narrative. What is surprising is that this version of events has been accepted, largely unquestioned, ever since – a reflection of the fact that, as a working-class game, football attracted little serious journalism until the 1960s and no academic study until the mid-1970s. Its depiction of the folk game is a crude caricature, resting on the assumption that Shrove Tuesday games were representative of all early football. And it ignores the blindingly obvious fact that the various public school games, with their roots in the ritual humiliation of fags and in sexual sublimation, were staggeringly violent.

It was only when adult men in London and Sheffield, many of them not from public schools, began to play the game in the 1860s that the process of civilizing the sport and devising a common code began. And it was only with the development of passing by Queen's Park and, to a lesser extent, Royal Engineers that any sort of sophistication entered the game. This passing style was adopted and then refined by working-class professionals – men who depended for their livelihoods on remaining free of injury – and it was they who turned football into the mass sport we recognize today. In short, it was not the upper class who civilized the people's game, it was the common people who civilized the upper-class game.

The city of Glasgow, and surrounding areas, deserves a far more prominent place in the story than it's been given. It was here that passing first evolved. It was here, in the mid-1870s, that a mass, working-class football culture first developed. And it was from here that the vast bulk of the early professionals emerged. Everywhere you turn in the early history of football you bump into a Scot, from William McGregor, who set up the

Football League in 1888, to Archibald Leitch, who designed most of the early stadiums, to men such as Alexander Watson Hutton and William Leslie Poole who pioneered football in Argentina and Paraguay. Glasgow even had the first women's team, in 1881.

As late as 1910 almost a quarter of all English First Division players were Scottish. And England struggled in matches against Scotland well into the twentieth century. Between the wars Scotland claimed eleven victories to England's six, and it wasn't until 1980, more than a century after the first international at the West of Scotland Cricket Ground, that England finally caught up in terms of wins. In the 1950s English professionals still referred to the short-passing game as 'the Scottish style'. It was in the mines and mill towns of Renfrewshire, Lanarkshire and Ayrshire that football acquired refinement, rather than on the playing fields of Eton and Harrow. The game that was adopted with such passion, and then refined further, in continental Europe and Latin America owed far more to the 'Scottish professor' than to the English public schoolboy.

But the gentleman amateurs still left their mark. British football has never entirely escaped what C. B. Fry called the 'cheerful ruthlessness' of the public school game. The early professionals may have passed the ball to one another, but they were hard men who had inherited many of the attitudes of their upper-class predecessors. Football was not for the 'namby pamby', wrote the great Sheffield United half-back Ernest Needham in 1900; 'What Englishman with an ounce of pluck will not brave danger?' An emphasis on guts and manliness over subtlety and artistry has been a constant in British football ever since. Where for Brazilians it is Pelé dummying the Uruguayan goalkeeper and for Argentinians Maradona weaving his way through the English defence that are the iconic images, for us it is a toothless Nobby Stiles and a blood-stained Terry Butcher. It's a style and a set of attitudes that goes right back to the very dawn of the game. And in the more artless performances of the English national team you can hear the distant echo of the boots of Charlie Alcock, Arthur Kinnaird and Alfred Lyttelton thundering up and down the playing fields of Eton and Harrow.

But if their playing style was crude, the contribution of the gentleman amateurs as administrators and custodians of the game should not be ignored. It's easy to mock the stuffiness and pomposity of men such as Alcock and Kinnaird. But by the standards of their time and their class they were liberal, enlightened men and the history of football would have been very different without them.

Alcock died in 1907 at the age of just sixty-four, still vice-president of the FA. 'His love of football was the love of a lifetime,' commented his wife, slightly sadly, at his death. Kinnaird lived on until 1923, dying at the age of seventy-five. He had been president of the FA since 1890, bringing much-needed social prestige, a touch of class, to the organization. But in later years he was primarily a figurehead and it was Alcock's contribution, particularly as secretary of the FA between 1870 and 1895, that was more important.

With his 'keen, kindly eyes' and gentle demeanour, Alcock represented all that was best in the Victorian ruling class. Largely free of personal snobbery, he possessed an instinctive feel for when to give ground gracefully at just the right moment. It was this instinct that saved Britain from social revolution through the nineteenth century. And Alcock's achievement in the 1880s in freeing football from the grip of the public schoolboys *without* causing a split should never be underestimated. You only have to look at the examples of cricket, where the upper class retained control, and rugby, which did split, to realize just how unique it was. Without his soothing presence football might well have torn itself apart. The peaceful revolution of 1885 paved the way for football to become the great national sport of the twentieth century. It had tapped into the enormous, unleashed energy of the working class, and it was the wisdom of men like Alcock that enabled it to absorb this energy without rupturing.

It was in the years after Alcock's retirement as secretary in 1895 that many of the structures and attitudes that would do football such harm in the twentieth century became ossified. Charles Clegg, who succeeded Alcock as the dominant figure at the FA, struggled hard to balance the various forces within football. But ultimately he was a product of his class. Resentful of those above him in the social scale and fearful of those below, he crushed both the Amateur Football Association and the Players' Union. But he knew better than to take on the power of the League clubs. And it was during his interminable reign (he was still president of the FA when he died in 1937) that the tyrannical power of club chairmen became firmly established. They proved a stultifyingly conservative force.

The FA entirely failed to adapt to the spread of football as a world game. Before the First World War England tended to put out amateur sides against continental opposition. This was abandoned after 1918 but the FA continued to take a patronizing view of all football outside the home countries. 'I don't care a brass farthing about the improvement of the game in France, Belgium, Austria or Germany,' declared Charles Sutcliffe, the Burnley director and FA official who had been the scourge of the Players' Union in 1909. 'The FIFA does not appeal to me. An organisation where such football associations as Uruguay and Paraguay, Brazil and Egypt, Bohemia and Pan Russia, are co-equal with England, Scotland, Wales and Ireland seems to me to be a case of magnifying the midgets.' The FA had joined FIFA in 1906, two years after its formation. It left again in 1920, rejoined in 1924, then left again in 1928, not rejoining until after the Second World War. When England did start competing in World Cups in the 1950s the crudeness and lack of sophistication of its football was cruelly exposed.

The defeat of Billy Meredith's union meant the feudal social structures of Edwardian football were also set in stone. In the brief boom which followed the First World War the maximum wage shot up to £9, but the clubs quickly clawed this back to £8. Players received an additional £2 for a win and £1 for a draw, but these bonuses remained unchanged for thirty years. As late as 1948 a player as great as Stanley Matthews could find himself carpeted by the FA, addressed by his surname and barked at to explain a sixpenny discrepancy in his expenses (he'd treated himself to a scone and a cup of tea at Carlisle station on his way up to Scotland for an international). 'Players were treated as second-class citizens,' wrote Matthews. 'Football was a skill of the working class, but those who ran our game were anything but.' At that time men like Matthews and Tom Finney were still plying their trade in front of vast crowds for just £12 a week.

The fate of Billy Meredith in retirement was typical, not just of his own generation but of generations of footballers to come. As a player he had achieved a lifestyle of lower-middle-class gentility. He lived in a comfortable semi-detached house with an indoor toilet and a garden. There was a piano in the front room and his daughters attended private dance classes. But after he retired his fortunes slowly declined. He'd been involved in various business ventures over the years, but most ended in failure. Ironically, given his dislike of alcohol, it was only in the licensing trade that he found any success. He'd taken over a pub on the Stockport Road, close to the City ground, in 1915. Then, in 1930, he became landlord of the Stretford Road Hotel, close to Old Trafford. Locals knew the pub simply as 'Billy Meredith's' and he would stand behind the bar holding forth to anyone who would listen on the decline of football since he'd stopped playing ('I wonder how Stanley Matthews would get on if he were suddenly transported into soccer in the early 1900s? He would be given no time to stand still and entertain the crowds as he does today,' was a typical outburst). When he finally retired from work in 1945 he faced an old age of increasing hardship.

Shortly before his death Cliff Lloyd, the secretary of the Players' Union, went to visit him. 'Billy was ill and destitute,' he recalled. As they chatted, Meredith reached under his bed and pulled out a box containing his forty-eight Welsh caps, his two championship medals and his two FA Cup winners' medals. 'Always remind your members that those caps and medals didn't look after me in my old age,' he said.

Meredith died on 19 April 1958, his death passing almost unnoticed in the aftermath of the Munich air crash. Three years later his beloved union finally achieved his dream – the abolition of the maximum wage. The pay of England captain Johnny Haynes instantly soared from £20 to £100 a week. Football, the kicking, screaming child born of mixed upper- and lower-class parentage almost a century before, was finally coming of age. A new era was dawning, one of which Meredith and his fellow unionists could only dream – an era of player power.

Appendix 1

Football Association Laws, 1863

1. The maximum length of the ground shall be 200 yards, the maximum breadth shall be 100 yards, the length and breadth shall be marked off with flags; and the goal shall be defined by two upright posts, eight yards apart, without any tape or bar across them.

2. The winner of the toss shall have the choice of goals. The game shall be commenced by a place kick from the centre of the ground by the side losing the toss for goals; the other side shall not approach within 10 yards of the ball until it is kicked off.

3. After a goal is won, the losing side shall kick off, and goals shall be changed.

4. A goal shall be won when the ball passes between the goal-posts or over the space between the goal-posts (at whatever height), not being thrown, knocked on, or carried.

5. When the ball is in touch, the first player who touches it shall throw it from the point on the boundary line where it left the ground in a direction at right angles with the boundary line.

6. When a player has kicked the ball, any one of the same side who is nearer to the opponent's goal line is out of play and may not touch the ball himself, nor in any way whatever prevent any other player from doing so, until he is in play; but no player is out of play when the ball is kicked off from behind the goal line.

7. In case the ball goes behind the goal line, if a player on the side to whom the goal belongs first touches the ball, one of his side shall be entitled to a free kick from the goal line at the point opposite the place where the ball shall be touched. If a player of the opposite side first touches the ball, one of his side shall be entitled to a free kick (but at the goal only) from a point 15 yards outside the goal line, opposite the place where the ball is touched. The opposing side shall stand behind their goal line until he has had his kick.

8. If a player makes a fair catch, he shall be entitled to a free kick, providing he claims it by making a mark with his heel at once; and in order to take such a kick he may go back as far as he pleases, and no player on the opposite side shall advance beyond his mark until he has kicked.

9. No player shall carry the ball.

10. Neither tripping nor hacking shall be allowed, and no player shall use his hands to hold or push his adversary.

11. A player shall not throw the ball or pass it to another.

12. No player shall be allowed to take the ball from the ground with his hands while it is in play under any pretext whatever.

13. No player shall be allowed to wear projecting nails, iron plates, or gutta percha on the soles or heels of his boots.

Appendix 2

FA Cup Finals, 1872–1915

Year	Winner	Runner-up	Venue	Attendance
1872	Wanderers 1	Royal Engineers 0	Oval	2,000
1873	Wanderers 2	Oxford University 0	Lillie Bridge (London)	3,000
1874	Oxford University 2	Royal Engineers 0	Oval	2,500
1875	Royal Engineers 1	Old Etonians 1	Oval	1,500
(replay)	Royal Engineers 2	Old Etonians 0	Oval	1,500
1876	Wanderers 1	Old Etonians 1	Oval	4,000
(replay)	Wanderers 3	Old Etonians 0	Oval	3,600
1877	Wanderers 2	Oxford University 1	Oval	3,000
1878	Wanderers 3	Royal Engineers 1	Oval	3,000
1879	Old Etonians 1	Clapham Rovers 0	Oval	3,000
1880	Clapham Rovers 1	Oxford University 0	Oval	5,000
1881	Old Carthusians 3	Old Etonians 0	Oval	3,000
1882	Old Etonians 1	Blackburn Rovers 0	Oval	7,000
1883	Blackburn Olympic 2	Old Etonians 1	Oval	8,000
1884	Blackburn Rovers 2	Queen's Park 1	Oval	4,000
1885	Blackburn Rovers 2	Queen's Park 0	Oval	12,500
1886	Blackburn Rovers 0	West Bromwich Albion 0	Oval	16,000
(replay)	Blackburn Rovers 2	West Bromwich Albion 0	Racecourse Ground (Derby)	12,000
1887	Aston Villa 2	West Bromwich Albion 0	Oval	16,000
1888	West Bromwich Albion 2	Preston North End 1	Oval	19,000
1889	Preston North End 3	Wolverhampton Wanderers 0	Oval	25,000
1890	Blackburn Rovers 6	The Wednesday 1	Oval	20,000
1891	Blackburn Rovers 3	Notts County 1	Oval	23,000
1892	West Bromwich Albion 3	Aston Villa 0	Oval	25,000
1893	Wolverhampton Wanderers 1	Everton 0	Fallowfield (Manchester)	45,000
1894	Notts County 4	Bolton Wanderers 1	Goodison Park (Liverpool)	37,000

1895	Aston Villa 1	West Bromwich Albion 0	Crystal Palace	42,560
1896	The Wednesday 2	Wolverhampton Wanderers 1	Crystal Palace	48,836
1897	Aston Villa 3	Everton 2	Crystal Palace	65,891
1898	Nottingham Forest 3	Derby County 1	Crystal Palace	62,017
1899	Sheffield United 4	Derby County 1	Crystal Palace	73,833
1900	Bury 4	Southampton 0	Crystal Palace	68,945
1901	Tottenham Hotspur 2	Sheffield United 2	Crystal Palace	110,820
(replay)	Tottenham Hotspur 3	Sheffield United 1	Burnden Park (Bolton)	30,000
1902	Sheffield United 1	Southampton 1	Crystal Palace	76,914
(replay)	Sheffield United 2	Southampton 1	Crystal Palace	33,068
1903	Bury 6	Derby County 0	Crystal Palace	63,102
1904	Manchester City 1	Bolton Wanderers 0	Crystal Palace	61,374
1905	Aston Villa 2	Newcastle United 0	Crystal Palace	101,117
1906	Everton 1	Newcastle United 0	Crystal Palace	75,609
1907	The Wednesday 2	Everton 1	Crystal Palace	85,584
1908	Wolverhampton Wanderers 3	Newcastle United 1	Crystal Palace	74,967
1909	Manchester United 1	Bristol City 0	Crystal Palace	67,651
1910	Newcastle United 1	Barnsley 1	Crystal Palace	77,747
(replay)	Newcastle United 2	Barnsley 0	Goodison Park (Liverpool)	69,000
1911	Bradford City 0	Newcastle United 0	Crystal Palace	69,098
(replay)	Bradford City 1	Newcastle United 0	Old Trafford (Manchester)	58,000
1912	Barnsley 0	West Bromwich Albion 0	Crystal Palace	54,556
(replay)	Barnsley 1	West Bromwich Albion 0	Bramall Lane (Sheffield)	38,555
1913	Aston Villa 1	Sunderland 0	CrystalPalace	120,081
1914	Burnley 1	Liverpool 0	Crystal Palace	72,778
1915	Sheffield United 3	Chelsea 0	Old Trafford (Manchester)	50,000

Sources: Green (*History of the FA Cup*), Wall, press reports.

Appendix 3

League Champions, 1889–1915
(Average home league attendances)

Season	Champions	Runners-up	Third Place
1888–89	Preston North End (6,275)	Aston Villa (4,700)	Wolverhampton Wanderers (3,725)
1889–90	Preston North End (7,600)	Everton (10,100)	Blackburn Rovers (6,550)
1890–91	Everton (11,275)	Preston North End (6,800)	Notts County (7,000)
1891–92	Sunderland (8,300)	Preston North End (5,625)	Bolton Wanderers (7,625)
1892–93	Sunderland (8,075)	Preston North End (6,450)	Everton (13,100)
1893–94	Aston Villa (10,700)	Sunderland (6,300)	Derby County (5,675)
1894–95	Sunderland (8,325)	Everton (16,225)	Aston Villa (8,900)
1895–96	Aston Villa (11,875)	Derby County (8,375)	Everton (16,000)
1896–97	Aston Villa (12,925)	Sheffield United (8,200)	Derby County (8,300)
1897–98	Sheffield United (11,800)	Sunderland (10,925)	Wolverhampton Wanderers (6,925)
1898–99	Aston Villa (20,675)	Liverpool (13,975)	Burnley (6,125)
1899–1900	Aston Villa (19,825)	Sheffield United (11,175)	Sunderland (10,475)
1900–01	Liverpool (15,000)	Sunderland (11,525)	Notts County (9,450)

1901–02	Sunderland (12,825)	Everton (17,225)	Newcastle United (14,575)
1902–03	The Wednesday (13,875)	Aston Villa (19,650)	Sunderland (15,300)
1903–04	The Wednesday (12,525)	Manchester City (19,125)	Everton (18,250)
1904–05	Newcastle United (21,250)	Everton (19,300)	Manchester City (19,400)
1905–06	Liverpool (19,425)	Preston North End (8,925)	The Wednesday (11,475)
1906–07	Newcastle United (33,650)	Bristol City (14,325)	Everton (19,100)
1907–08	Manchester United (20,050)	Aston Villa (17,425)	Manchester City (22,725)
1908–09	Newcastle United (28,425)	Everton (22,475)	Sunderland (15,750)
1909–10	Aston Villa (20,125)	Liverpool (19,475)	Blackburn Rovers (13,775)
1910–11	Manchester United (19,950)	Aston Villa (21,650)	Sunderland (16,200)
1911–12	Blackburn Rovers (18,500)	Everton (20,050)	Newcastle United (23,625)
1912–13	Sunderland (17,675)	Aston Villa (23,925)	The Wednesday (18,875)
1913–14	Blackburn Rovers (22,950)	Aston Villa (25,175)	Middlesbrough (14,375)
1914–15	Everton (18,575)	Oldham Athletic (9,450)	Blackburn Rovers (12,550)

Source: Tabner.

Bibliography

Books & Articles

Addington Symonds, John, *The Memoirs of John Addington Symonds*, Hutchinson, London, 2007

Ainger, Arthur Campbell, *Memories of Eton Sixty Years Ago*, John Murray, London, 1917

Alcock, Charles, *The Association Game*, George Bell and Sons, London, 1890

——*Football Annual, 1871, 1876–1882, 1886, 1889, 1890*

Arnold, A. J., 'The Belated Entry of Professional Soccer into the West Riding Textile District of Northern England' in *International Journal of the History of Sport*, vol. 6, no. 3, December 1989

——*A Game That Would Pay: A Business History of Professional Football in Bradford*, Duckworth, London, 1988

Best, Geoffrey, *Mid-Victorian Britain 1851–76*, Panther Books, St Albans, 1973

Bevan, I., S. Hibberd and M. Gilbert, *To the Palace for the Cup: An Affectionate History of Football at the Crystal Palace*, Replay Publishing, Beckenham, Kent, 1999

Bienefeld, M. A., *Working Hours in British Industry: An Economic History*, Weidenfeld and Nicolson, 1972

Blythe Smart, John, *The Wow Factor: How Soccer Evolved Within the Social Web*, Blythe Smart Publications, Isle of Wight, 2003

Bone, D. D., *Scottish Football Reminiscences and Sketches*, John Menzies and Co., Glasgow, 1890

The Book of Football, Amalgamated Press, London, 1906

Booth, Keith, *The Father of Modern Sport: The Life and Times of Charles W. Alcock*, Parrs Wood Press, Manchester, 2002

Brennan, Patrick, *Women's Football*, www.donmouth.co.uk

Brinsley-Richards, James, *Seven Years at Eton, 1857–1864*, Richard Bentley and Son, London, 1883

Bristow, Edward J., *Vice and Vigilance: Purity Movements in Britain Since 1700*, Gill and MacMillan, Dublin, 1977

Brown, M. and S. Seaton, *Christmas Truce*, Leo Cooper, New York, 1984

Butler, Bryon, *The Official History of the Football Association*, Macdonald, London, 1991

Cannadine, David, *The Decline and Fall of the British Aristocracy*, Yale University Press, New Haven and London, 1990

Carter, Neil, *The Football Manager: A History*, Routledge, London, 2006

Catton, James, *The Real Football*, Sands and Co., London, 1900

——*The Story of Association Football*, Soccer Books, Cleethorpes, 2006

Cavallini, Rob, *Play Up Corinth: A History of the Corinthian Football Club*, Stadia, Stroud, 2007

Collins, Tony, *Rugby's Great Split: Class, Culture and the Origins of Rugby League Football*, Routledge, Abingdon, 1998

Corbett, B. O., *The Annals of the Corinthian Football Club*, Longmans, Green and Co., London, 1906

Corrigan, Gordon, *Mud, Blood and Poppycock: Britain and the First World War*, Cassell, London, 2003

Crampsey, Bob, *The Scottish Footballer*, William Blackwood, Edinburgh, 1978

Creek, F. N. S., *A History of the Corinthian Football Club*, Longmans, London, 1933

Crystal Palace History, www.crystalpalacefoundation.org.uk

Curry, Graham, 'Playing for Money: James J. Lang and Emergent Soccer Professionalism in Sheffield' in *Soccer and Society,* Autumn 2004

Dabscheck, Braham, 'Defensive Manchester: A History of the Professional Footballers' Association' in R. Cashman and M. McKernan (eds), *Sport in History,* University of Queensland Press, Australia, 1979

Delaney, Terence (ed), *The Footballer's Fireside Book,* Heinemann, London, 1961

Delves, Anthony, 'Popular Recreation and Social Conflict in Derby, 1800–1850' in Eileen and Stephen Yeo (eds), *Popular Culture and Class Conflict 1590–1914,* Harvester Press, Brighton, 1981

Dunning, Eric and Kenneth Sheard, *Barbarians, Gentlemen and Players: A Sociological Study of the Development of Rugby Football,* Routledge, Abingdon, Oxon, 2005

Farnsworth, Keith, *Sheffield Football, A History: Volume 1, 1857–1961,* The Hallamshire Press, 1995

Football and How to Play It by Champions of the Game, John Leng and Co., London, 1904

Football Calendar, 1877–78, Virtue and Co., London, 1877

Fry, C. B., *Life Worth Living: Some Phases of an Englishman,* Eyre and Spottiswoode, London, 1939

——'The Story of the Corinthians' in *Fry's Magazine,* vol. 2, 1904–05

Fry, C. B., A. Budd, B. F. Robinson and T. A. Cook, *Football,* Lawrence and Bullen, London, 1897

Fussell, Paul, *The Great War and Modern Memory*, Oxford University Press, 1975

Garland, Ian, *The History of the Welsh Cup, 1877–1993*, Bridge Books, Wrexham, 1993

Goldblatt, David, *The Ball is Round: A Global History of Football*, Penguin, London, 2007

Golesworthy, Maurice, *We Are the Champions: A History of the Football League Champions, 1888–1972*, Pelham Books, London, 1972

Goodall, John, *Association Football*, William Blackwood and Sons, London, 1898

Goulstone, John, *Football's Secret History*, 3-2 Books, Upminster, 2001

——*The Working Class Origins of Modern Football*, J. Goulstone, 1997

Graham, R. G., 'The Early History of Association Football' in *Badminton Magazine of Sports and Pastimes*, January 1899

Grayson, Edward, *Corinthians and Cricketers*, The Naldrett Press, London, 1955

Green, Geoffrey, *The History of the Football Association*, The Naldrett Press, London, 1953

——*The Official History of the FA Cup*, Heinemann, London, 1960

Green, Geoffrey and A. H. Fabian, *Association Football*, Knight and Forster, Leeds, 1960

Greenland, W. E., *The History of the Amateur Football Alliance*, Standard Printing and Publishing Company, Harwich, 1965

Harding, John, *Football Wizard: The Story of Billy Meredith*, Breedon Books, Derby, 1985

——*For the Good of the Game: The Official History of the Professional Footballers' Association*, Robson Books, London, 1991

——*Living to Play: From Soccer Slaves to Soccerati – A Social History of the Professionals*, Robson Books, London, 2003

Harvey, Adrian, *Football: The First Hundred Years, The Untold Story*, Routledge, London, 2005

Hill, B. J. W., *A History of Eton College*, Alden & Blackwell (Eton) Ltd, 1953

Holt, R. J., 'Football and the Urban Way of Life in Nineteenth-Century Britain' in J. A. Mangan (ed), *Pleasure, Profit and Proselytism*, Frank Cass, London, 1988

——*Sport and the British: A Modern History*, Clarendon Press, Oxford, 1989

Huggins, M., 'The Spread of Association Football in North-East England, 1876–90: The Pattern of Diffusion' in *International Journal of the History of Sport*, vol. 6, no. 3, December 1989

Hughes-Onslow, H., 'The Association Football Crisis' in *Badminton Magazine*, vol. 24, January 1907

Hunt, David, *The History of Preston North End Football Club*, PNE Publications, Preston, 2000

Hutchison, John, 'Football in Edinburgh from 1800' in *Soccer History*, issue 15, Spring 2007

Hutton, W., *The History of Derby, From the Remote Ages of Antiquity to the Year 1791*, Nichols, Son and Bentley, London, 1817

Inglis, Simon, *League Football and the Men Who Made It*, Willow Books, London, 1988

——*Soccer in the Dock: A History of British Football Scandals 1900–1965*, Willow Books, London, 1985

Jackson, N. L., *Association Football*, George Newnes, London, 1899

——*Sporting Days and Sporting Ways*, Hurst & Blackett Ltd, London, 1932

Jacobs, Norman, *Vivian Woodward: Football's Gentleman*, Tempus, Stroud, Gloucestershire, 2005

James, Gary, *Manchester: The Greatest City – The Complete History of Manchester City Football Club*, Polar Publishing, 1997

Kerrigan, Colm, *Teachers and Football: Schoolboy Association Football in England, 1885–1915*, Routledge Falmer, London, 2005

Knight, Charles, 'On the Discipline of Schools' in *Quarterly Journal of Education*, July 1835

Lee, James F., *The Lady Footballers: Struggling to Play in Victorian Britain*, Routledge, London, 2008

Lewis, Robert William, 'The Development of Professional Football in Lancashire 1880–1914', Ph.D. thesis, Lancaster University, 1993

Lillywhite's Guide to Cricketers, 1859, Piper, Stephenson and Co., London, 1859

Lubbock, Alfred, *Memories of Eton and Etonians*, John Murray, London, 1899

Lyte, Sir H. C. Maxwell, *A History of Eton College, 1440–1898*, MacMillan and Co., London, 1899

Lyttelton, Edith, *Alfred Lyttelton, An Account of his Life*, Longmans, Green and Co., London, 1917

Lyttelton, Edward, *The Causes and Prevention of Immorality in Schools*, G. T. Purnell, Croydon, 1883

Magoun, Francis Peabody, *History of Football, From the*

Beginnings to 1871, Bochum-Langendreer, 1938

Malcolmson, Robert W., *Popular Recreations in English Society, 1700–1850*, Cambridge University Press, 1973

Mangan, J. A., *Athleticism in the Victorian and Edwardian Public School*, Frank Cass, London, 2000

Marples, Morris, *The History of Football*, Secker & Warburg, London, 1954

Marshall, Rev. F., *Football: The Rugby Union Game*, Cassell and Company Ltd, London, 1892

Mason, Tony, *Association Football and English Society, 1863–1915*, Harvester Press, Brighton, 1981

Matthews, Stanley, *The Way It Was: My Autobiography*, Headline, London, 2000

Needham, Ernest, *Association Football*, Skeffington and Son, London, 1900–1901

Owen, O. L., *The History of the Rugby Football Union*, Playfair Books Ltd, London, 1955

Pember, Arthur, 'The Coming Revolution in England' in *Lippincott's Magazine*, vol. 5, March 1870

Phythian, Graham, *Shooting Stars: The Brief and Glorious History of Blackburn Olympic FC, 1878–1889*, Tony Brown, Nottingham, 2007

Pickford, William, *A Few Recollections of Sport*, Bournemouth, 1939

Pickford, William and Alfred Gibson, *Association Football and the Men Who Made It*, Caxton Publishing Co., London, 1906 (four vols)

Priestley, J. B., *The Good Companions*, Heinemann, London, 1929

Robinson, Richard, *History of the Queen's Park Football Club*,

1867–1917, Hay, Nisbet and Co. Ltd, Glasgow, 1920

Routledge, George, *Routledge's Handbook of Football*, George Routledge and Son, London, 1867

Rubinstein, David, *Before the Suffragettes: Women's Emancipation in the 1890s*, Harvester Press, Brighton, 1986

Ruck, Major General Sir Richard M., 'Royal Engineers Football in the Early Seventies' in *Royal Engineers Journal*, December 1928

Russell, Dave, *Football and the English: A Social History of Association Football in England, 1863–1995*, Carnegie Publishing, Preston, 1997

——'Sporadic and Curious: The Emergence of Rugby and Soccer Zones in Yorkshire and Lancashire, c. 1860–1914' in *International Journal of the History of Sport*, vol. 5, no. 2, September 1988

Scotland – The Birthplace of the Modern Game, Scottish Football Museum, 2008

Seddon, Peter, *Steve Bloomer*, Breedon Books Publishing Company, Derby, 1999

Shearman, Montague, *Football*, Longmans, Green and Co., London, 1904

The Silver Wedding of Lord and Lady Kinnaird . . ., Rossie Priory, Perthshire, 1900

Sparling, Richard Arthur, *The Romance of The Wednesday*, Sir W. C. Leng and Co., Sheffield, 1926

Spence, Jeoffry, *Victorian and Edwardian Railway Travel*, B. T. Batsford Ltd, London, 1977

Strutt, Joseph, *The Sports and Pastimes of the People of England*, Methuen and Co., London, 1903

Sutcliffe, C. E. and F. Hargreaves, *History of the Lancashire Football Association, 1878–1928*, Geo. Toulmin and Sons, Blackburn, 1928

Tabner, Brian, *Football Through the Turnstiles . . . Again*, Yore Publications, Harefield, 2002

Taylor, D. J., *On the Corinthian Spirit: The Decline of Amateurism in Sport*, Yellow Jersey Press, London, 2006

Taylor, Matthew, 'Beyond the Maximum Wage: The Earnings of Football Professionals in England 1900–39' in *Soccer and Society*, Autumn 2001

Thorne, Guy, 'Sport and Drink' in *Fry's Magazine*, vol. 5, no. 27, June 1906

Tischler, Steven, *Footballers and Businessmen: The Origins of Professional Soccer in England*, Holmes and Meier, New York, 1981

Tod, A. H., *Charterhouse*, George Bell and Sons, London, 1900

Trudgill, Eric, *Madonnas and Magdalens: The Origins and Development of Victorian Sexual Attitudes*, Heinemann, London, 1976

Twydell, Dave, *Rejected FC: Histories of the ex-Football League Clubs, Vol. 2*, Yore Publications, Harefield, 1995

Tyler, Martin, *Cup Final Extra*, Hamlyn, London, 1981

Vamplew, Wray, *Pay Up and Play the Game: Professional Sport in Britain, 1875–1914*, Cambridge University Press, 1988

Vasili, Phil, *The First Black Footballer: Arthur Wharton 1865–1930*, Frank Cass, London, 1998

Wall, Sir Frederick, *Fifty Years of Football*, Cassell, London, 1935

Walvin, James, *The People's Game: The History of Football Revisited*, Mainstream Publishing, London and Edinburgh, 1994

Warsop, Keith, *The Early FA Cup Final and the Southern Amateurs*, Tony Brown, Nottingham, 2004

Weintraub, Stanley, *Silent Night: The Remarkable Christmas Truce of 1914*, Simon and Schuster, London, 2001

Whitney, Casper W., *A Sporting Pilgrimage to Oxford and Cambridge and the Shires*, Osgood, McIlvaine and Co., London, 1894

Who Was Who, 1897–1915, Adam and Charles Black, London, 1953

Wilkinson, Rev. C. Allix, *Reminiscences of Eton*, Hurst and Blackett, London, 1888

Williams, Graham, *The Code War*, Yore Publications, 1995

Williams, Jean, *A Game for Rough Girls? A History of Women's Football in Britain*, Routledge, London, 2003

Williams, Nigel, *Bradford Northern: The History, 1863–1989*, MQ Printing Ltd, Bradford, 1989

Wilton, Iain, *C. B. Fry: An English Hero*, Richard Cohen Books, London, 1999

Winner, David, *Those Feet: A Sensual History of English Football*, Bloomsbury, London, 2005

Wood, Frederick, *Beeton's Football*, Frederick Warne and Co., London, 1866

Young, Percy M., *Bolton Wanderers*, Stanley Paul, London, 1961

——*Football in Sheffield*, Stanley Paul, London, 1962

——*The History of British Football*, Arrow Books, London, 1973

——*Manchester United*, Heinemann, London, 1960

Newspapers

Aberdeen Weekly Journal (AWJ)
Athletic News (AN)
Belfast Newsletter (BN)
Bell's Life in London and Sporting Chronicle (BL)
Birmingham Daily Post (BDP)
Blackburn Standard (BS)
Bradford Daily Telegraph (BDT)
Derby and Chesterfield Reporter (DCR)
Derby Mercury (DM)
Derbyshire Advertiser and Journal (DAJ)
Edinburgh Review (ER)
Eton College Chronicle (ECC)
Football Field (FF)
The Field (F)
Glasgow Herald (GH)
The Graphic (G)
Hull Packet and East Riding Times (HP)
Ipswich Journal (IJ)
Leeds Mercury (LMerc)
Liverpool Mercury (LivM)
Morning Chronicle (MC)
Pall Mall Gazette (PMG)
Penny Magazine (PM)
The Pioneer or Trades Union Magazine (PTUM)
Preston Chronicle (PC)
Reynold's Newspaper (RN)
Scotsman (Sc)
Sheffield Daily Telegraph (SDT)
Sheffield and Rotherham Independent (SRI)

The Sketch (Sk)
Sporting Gazette (SG)
Sporting Magazine (SM)
Sportsman (S)
Thomson's Weekly News (TWN)
The Times (T)
Topical Times (TT)
Yorkshire Sports (YS)

Other Sources
FA Minute Book, 1863–75
HO 140/161 (National Archives)
James Catton Archives (JCA)

Chapter 1
Delaney, Delves, Goulstone (*Secret History* and *Working Class Origins*), Harvey, Hutton, Magoun, Malcolmson; *DAJ* (25/2/1846, 4/3/1846), *DCR* (27/12/1844, 24/1/1845, 7/2/1845, 27/2/1846), *DM* (27/2/1747, 9/2/1815, 28/2/1827, 15/7/1840, 7/10/1840, 28/2/1844, 5/2/1845, 25/2/1846, 17/9/1851, 12/1/1853, 18/2/1885), *PM* (6/4/1839), *PTUM* (1+22/2/1834), *SM* (July 1830)

Chapter 2
Ainger, Brinsley-Richards, Dunning and Sheard, Green (*History of the FA*), Green and Fabian, Harvey, Hill, Jackson (*Association Football*), *Lillywhite's*, Lubbock, Lyte, Marples, Shearman, *Who Was Who*, Wilkinson, Wood, Young (*History of British Football*); *BL* (3/12/1864), *ECC* (8/10/1832, 10/12/1863), *ER* (April 1830), *F* (4/1/1862, 12/12/1862,

31/10/1863, 7+14+28/11/1863, 5/12/1863), *IJ* (3/12/1863), *MC* (28/10/1857), *SG* (5/12/1863)

Chapter 3

Alcock (*Association Game, Annual 1871*), Blythe Smart, *Book of Football*, Booth, Butler (*History of the FA*), Catton (*Real Football*), FA Minute Book, Farnsworth, Goulstone (*Secret History*), Graham, Green (*History of the FA*), Harvey, Jackson (*Association Football*), JCA (1963), Routledge, Sparling, Tod, Tyler, Warsop, Young (*History of British Football, Football in Sheffield*); BL (24/2/1866, 7/4/1866, 23/3/1872), *F* (21/11/1863, 26/1/1867, 2+9/2/1867, 2/3/1867, 4/1/1868, 1+29/2/1868), *LMerc* (20/6/1865), *RN* (17/3/1872), *S* (19/3/1872), *T* (18/3/1872)

Chapter 4

Alcock (*Association Game, Annual 1876–1882*), Blythe Smart, Bone, *Book of Football*, Booth, Bristow, Catton (*Real Football, Story of Association Football*), *Football Calendar*, Harvey, Hutchison, Jackson (*Association Football*), JCA (275), Kerrigan, Knight, Lubbock, Edith Lyttelton, Edward Lyttelton, Magoun, Pickford and Gibson vol. 4, Robinson, *Scotland – The Birthplace, Silver Wedding*, Sparling, Spence, Trudgill, Wall, Warsop, Winner, Young (*History of British Football, Football in Sheffield*); *F* (9/3/1872), *GH* (5/3/1872, 2/12/1872, 11/10/1875, 7/2/1876, 6/11/1876), *G* (14/12/1872), *PMG* (30+31/10/1867, 1+2/11/1867), *SDT* (6/4/1903), *S* (19/3/1872)

Chapter 5

Alcock (*Annual 1879, 1880*), Bienefeld, Booth, Catton (*Real*

Football), Jackson (*Association Football, Sporting Days*), Mason, Pickford and Gibson vols 1+4, Phythian, Shearman, Sparling, Twydell, Tyler, Wall, Warsop, Wood, Young (*Bolton*); *AN* (5/3/1879, 1/12/1880, 31/3/1880), *BL* (7/4/1883), *BS* (17+24/3/1883, 7/4/1883), *ECC* (3+17/5/1883), *F* (7/4/1883), *IJ* (4/1/1845), *SRI* (22+25+26/1/1881)

Chapter 6

Blythe Smart, Booth, Carter, Catton (*Real Football, Story of Association Football*), Crampsey, Curry, Delaney, Farnsworth, Golesworthy, Green (*History of the FA*), Holt ('Football'), Hunt, Jackson (*Association Football*), JCA (422, 1142, 1350, 1379), Lewis, Mason, Pickford, Pickford and Gibson vols. 1+2, Russell (*Football and the English*), Sutcliffe and Hargreaves, Tischler, Vamplew, Wall; *AN* (23/1/1884, 1/11/1884), *FF* (18+25/10/1884, 24/1/1885), *GH* (20/1/1885), *G* (4/2/1882), *HP* (12/9/1884), *PC* (12/10/1872)

Chapter 7

Alcock (*Annual 1889*), Carter, Catton (*Real Football, Story of Association Football*), Green (*History of the FA, History of the FA Cup*), HO 140/161, Hunt, Inglis (*League Football*), Jackson (*Association Football*), JCA (455, 456, 461, 597, 599, 1379), Mason, Phythian, Pickford, Pickford and Gibson vols. 1+4, Robinson, Tabner, *Book of Football*, Tischler, Tyler, Vasili; *AN* (1/4/1889), *BDP* (15/10/1886, 5/1/1888), *FF* (28/8/1886, 22/6/1893), *LMerc* (1/11/1886), *LivM* (18/1/1886, 11/4/1895), *PMG* (1/4/1889), *PC* (6/4/1889)

Chapter 8

Booth, Cavallini, Corbett, Creek, Fry (*Life Worth Living*, 'Story'), Fry and Budd et al, Green (*History of the FA, History of the FA Cup*), Greenland, Hughes-Onslow, Jackson (*Association Football, Sporting Days*), Jacobs, JCA (279, 850, 951, 1350, 1768, 1878), Mason, Pickford, Seddon, *Book of Football*, Tod, Wall; *AN* (17/12/1884, 2/3/1903, 5/2/1906, 24/9/1906), *FF* (13/12/1884), *LivM* (28/11/1890), *PMG* (17/11/1890, 1/12/1890), *S* (26/3/1914), *T* (19/11/1889, 6/2/1914)

Chapter 9

Alcock (*Annual 1886, 1889*), Arnold, Catton (*Real Football*), Cavallini, Collins, Dunning and Sheard, Huggins, Mangan, Marshall, Marples, Mason, Owen, Pickford, Russell (*Football and the English*, 'Sporadic and Curious'), Tabner, G. Williams, N. Williams; *BDT* (16+17+23/4/1907, 7+11+25+31/5/1907), *GH* (30/11/1876), *LMerc* (9/2/1876), *T* (12/11/1880), *YS* (20/4/1907)

Chapter 10

Brennan, Jackson (*Sporting Days*), Lee, Rubinstein, J. Williams; *AWJ* (14/5/1881), *BN* (20/6/1895), *BL* (14+21/5/1881), *BDP* (1/2/1895), *LivM* (26/4/1900), *PMG* (8/2/1895), *Sk* (6/2/1895, 27/3/1895), *Sc* (9/5/1881), *T* (8/11/1905)

Chapter 11

Bevan et al, Carter, Catton (*Story of Association Football*), *Crystal Palace History*, Garland, Harding (*Football Wizard, Living to Play*), James, JCA (367, 1162), Mason, Needham, Pickford, Pickford and Gibson vols. 2+4, Tabner, *Book of*

Football, Thorne, Vamplew, Wall, Young (*Manchester United*); *AN* (18/4/1904), *FF* (23+30/4/1904), *TWN* (14/8/1909), *TT* (18/10/1919)

Chapter 12

Catton (*Story of Association Football*), Dabscheck, Harding (*Football Wizard, For the Good, Living to Play*), Inglis (*Soccer in the Dock*), James, Mason, M. Taylor; *AN* (7/8/1905, 26/2/1906, 19/3/1906, 16/4/1906, 4/6/1906, 11/1/1909, 17/5/1909, 14/6/1909, 30/8/1909, 6/9/1909, 4/10/1909), *FF* (30/4/1904), *TWN* (7/8/1909, 13/11/1909)

Chapter 13

Booth, Brown and Seaton, Cannadine, Cavallini, Fry (*Life Worth Living*), Fussell, Goldblatt, Green (*History of the FA*), Greenland, Harding (*Football Wizard, For the Good, Living to Play*), Mason, Needham, Priestley, Russell (*Football and the English*), D. Taylor, Vamplew, Weintraub, G. Williams, Wilton

Picture Acknowledgements

Section 1

Section 2

Index